American Slavery on Film

Recent Titles in Hollywood History

The Vietnam War on Film
David Luhrssen

The American West on Film
Johnny D. Boggs

The Civil War on Film
Peg A. Lamphier and Rosanne Welch

World War II on Film
David Luhrssen

The Cold War on Film
Paul Frazier

Sports on Film
Johnny D. Boggs

The 1960s on Film
Jim Willis and Mark Miller

The Great Depression on Film
David Luhrssen

American Women's History on Film
Rosanne Welch and Peg A. Lamphier

American Slavery on Film

Caron Knauer

Hollywood History

BLOOMSBURY ACADEMIC
NEW YORK • LONDON • OXFORD • NEW DELHI • SYDNEY

BLOOMSBURY ACADEMIC
Bloomsbury Publishing Inc
1385 Broadway, New York, NY 10018, USA
50 Bedford Square, London, WC1B 3DP, UK
29 Earlsfort Terrace, Dublin 2, Ireland

BLOOMSBURY, BLOOMSBURY ACADEMIC and the Diana logo
are trademarks of Bloomsbury Publishing Plc

First published in the United States of America by ABC-CLIO 2023
Paperback edition published by Bloomsbury Academic 2025

Copyright © Bloomsbury Publishing Inc, 2025

For legal purposes the Acknowledgments on p. xiii constitute
an extension of this copyright page.

Cover Photo: Nate Parker as "Nat Turner" in Birth of a Nation.
(PictureLux/The Hollywood Archive/Alamy Stock Photo)

All rights reserved. No part of this publication may be reproduced or
transmitted in any form or by any means, electronic or mechanical, including
photocopying, recording, or any information storage or retrieval system,
without prior permission in writing from the publishers.

Bloomsbury Publishing Inc does not have any control over, or responsibility for,
any third-party websites referred to or in this book. All internet addresses given
in this book were correct at the time of going to press. The author and publisher
regret any inconvenience caused if addresses have changed or sites have
ceased to exist, but can accept no responsibility for any such changes.

Library of Congress Cataloging-in-Publication Data
Names: Knauer, Caron, author.
Title: American slavery on film / Caron Knauer.
Description: Santa Barbara, California : ABC-CLIO, [2023] | Series:
Hollywood history | Includes bibliographical references and index.
Identifiers: LCCN 2022037029 | ISBN 9781440877513 (hardcover ;
acid-free paper) | ISBN 9781440877520 (ebook)
Subjects: LCSH: Slavery in motion pictures. | African Americans in motion
pictures. | Motion pictures—Social aspects—United States.
Classification: LCC PN1995.9.S557 K53 2023 |
DDC 791.43/655—dc23/eng/20221014
LC record available at https://lccn.loc.gov/2022037029

ISBN: HB: 978-1-4408-7751-3
PB: 979-8-7651-6700-7
ePDF: 978-1-4408-7752-0
eBook: 979-8-2161-8434-8

Series: Hollywood History

To find out more about our authors and books visit www.bloomsbury.com
and sign up for our newsletters.

Contents

Series Foreword	vii
Preface	ix
Acknowledgments	xiii
Introduction	xv
Chronology of European and American Race-Based Chattel Slavery	xxvii
1. *Uncle Tom's Cabin* (1914)	1
2. *Mandingo* (1975)	19
3. *Roots* (1977)	29
4. *Sankofa* (1993)	47
5. *Nightjohn* (1996)	65
6. *Amistad* (1997)	85
7. *Django Unchained* (2012)	103
8. *12 Years a Slave* (2013)	119
9. *The Birth of a Nation* (2016)	143
10. *Harriet* (2019)	161
Bibliography	187
Index	189

Series Foreword

Just exactly how accurate are Hollywood's film and television portrayals of American history? What do these portrayals of history tell us, not only about the events they depict but also the time in which they were made? Each volume in this unique reference series is devoted to a single topic or key theme in American history, examining 10–12 major motion pictures or television productions. Substantial essays summarize each film, provide historical background of the event or period it depicts, and explain how accurate the film's depiction is, while also analyzing the cultural context in which the film was made. A final resources section provides a comprehensive annotated bibliography of print and electronic sources to aid students and teachers in further research.

The subjects of these Hollywood History volumes were chosen based on both curriculum relevance and inherent interest. Readers will find a wide array of subject choices, including American Slavery on Film, the Civil War on Film, the American West on Film, Vietnam on Film, and the 1960s on Film. Ideal for school assignments and student research, the length, format, and subject areas are designed to meet educators' needs and students' interests.

Preface

The earliest films made in America often included Black characters and stories. And while early films about slavery romanticized it, in part, they also revealed the African American's resistance and rebellion. The first adaptation of Harriet Beecher Stowe's epochal antislavery novel, *Uncle Tom's Cabin* (1852), was directed by Edwin S. Porter and produced by Thomas Edison in 1903; later that year, Porter directed *The Great Train Robbery*, considered the first American feature film. The first of nine film adaptations of *Uncle Tom's Cabin*, which in 1899 was still the New York Public Library's most borrowed book, the 1903 film was the first ever to have subtitles. It portrays in its tableaux, or series of scenes, enslaved African Americans dancing happily, but it also shows Eliza taking her young son to escape to the North on an ice floe after learning he would be sold away from her and Uncle Tom defying a master's orders to whip a fellow enslaved man. Eliza and Tom rebel against the horrors of slavery.

The 1914 adaptation of *Uncle Tom's Cabin* was the first film to star a Black actor, Sam Lucas, in the role as Uncle Tom. This film also radically rewrites Stowe and depicts a young enslaved man shooting the vicious Simon Legree in retaliation for abusing Tom.

Arranged chronologically, the ten films discussed in this book depict the resistance and rebellion of the enslaved as their response to and part of the quotidian aspects of slavery in the South. African American characters are seen getting into good trouble, as the civil rights leader John Lewis (1940–2020) advocated, by speaking out and defying unjust policies, laws, discrimination, and the entire institution of slavery; they are also seen taking violent action.

There are biopics and fictional films, high-budget studio and low-budget independent films, a miniseries and TV movie, a revisionist ahistorical film, and release dates that span more than one hundred years.

Five were directed by Black directors; many were written by Black writers. Each chapter reveals how accurate and truthful or distorted or exploitative the depictions of slavery are, and historical background, privileging Black primary sources and scholarship when possible, is provided. The slavery scholar Eric Foner recently noted that "A host of new sources, many of them making available the perspective of African Americans, has appeared" (2022).

The rags-to-riches legacy of Richard Fleischer's controversial, subversive *Mandingo* (1975) is delineated. It's a sensational movie whose reassessment by critics ranges from being "scandalous racist trash" to a "masterpiece" of race issues in America, and its brutally honest depiction of the evils of slavery shows the militancy of the enslaved as well as a sexually explicit, tender interracial love story. The enduring revelatory power of *Roots*, the phenomenal miniseries that riveted and moved the nation in 1977 and was rebooted in 2016, is probed. *Roots* enabled a mass audience to watch and learn about day-to-day family and work life during slavery.

Nightjohn (1996) is a television movie about the lengths the enslaved went to, despite the harsh punishment, in order to achieve literacy. It's based on Gary Paulsen's eponymous young adult novel and directed by Charles Burnett, an alumnus of the L.A. Rebellion, a group of visionary Black filmmakers who met as UCLA students starting in the 1960s. Haile Gerima is also an alumnus, and his independently made, mystical time-traveling film *Sankofa* (1993)—which had been hard to find—is, thanks to filmmaker Ava DuVernay, available on Netflix. Two biopics—Nate Parker's *The Birth of a Nation* (2016), about the traveling preacher Nat Turner's Insurrection, and Kasi Lemmons's *Harriet* (2019), about Harriet Tubman, the fearless and indefatigable Underground Railroad conductor—profile deeply religious, prophetic resistance leaders and visionaries who fearlessly fought the status quo to abolish slavery, the law of the Southern land.

Steve McQueen's bracing *12 Years a Slave* (2013), based on Solomon Northup's 1853 best-selling memoir, won the Academy Award for Best Picture and made history for being the first film directed by a Black director to win the coveted award.

Quentin Tarantino's ahistorical and ultraviolent *Django Unchained* (2012)—about a formerly enslaved man turned bounty hunter—was inspired by *Mandingo* (1975). And Steven Spielberg's *Amistad* (1997)—about the 1839 mutiny led by Joseph Cinque, a captured African, whose triumphant trial went up to the Supreme Court—presents a riveting and inspiring chapter in American history, a chapter in which despite the odds against them, captured Africans were able to return home. Cinque asked Americans to "give us free," and they did.

FURTHER READING

Foner, Eric. 2022. "The Complicity of the Textbooks." Review of *Teaching White Supremacy: America's Democratic Ordeal and the Forging of Our National Identity*, by Donald Yacovone. *New York Review of Books*, September 22, 2022.

Acknowledgments

Coalescing my passions for film, literature, African American history, and slavery in particular, has been gratifying. The format of ABC-CLIO's Hollywood History series reveals essential and captivating aspects of historical films. I would like to thank Kevin Downing at ABC-CLIO for his editorial guidance and unwavering support.

I couldn't have written this book without the Queens Public Library and New York Public Library and their extensive collections of relevant books and films. Thank you to the librarians at La Guardia Community College for their help and support.

I acknowledge the memory of my loving and erudite father, Edward Knauer, who encouraged my ambitions and instilled in me the love of film, history, and politics. I'd like to thank my wonderful family for being the most devoted support system: my mother, Arleen Knauer; my Aunt Phyllis; my sisters, Debra Hagen, Tammy Rubel, and Benée Knauer; my brother, Ben Knauer; my son, Lonn Knauer Stengel; my daughter, Ariel Jade Garay and son-in-law Lou Garay; and my beautiful, bright, and exuberant granddaughters, Zuri Jade and Yara Eleanor, the sunshine of my life and the apples of my eye. It's been a joy watching all my nieces and nephews grow and develop into loving, joyful people. A special shout out to my nieces, Liz Rubel and Sammie Sachs, who showed up at a critical moment to hold my hand and merge my chapters.

I have gratitude for my extraordinary life coach and friend, Vito Abate, for believing in me and keeping me on point; for my dear friends for opening their generous hearts and sharing their spunky wit and appreciable advice: Betsy Lerner, Paula Litzky, Bob Levine, Vicky Choy, Todd Siegal, Rosalie Muskatt, Mary Roma, Kathy Mills, Ann Dedman, Ginger Anklin, and Kathleen Gasienica; and for the memory of my much-missed friends: Iara Rodrigues, Jeanne Wilde, and Lynn C. Franklin.

Introduction

The capturing, transporting, and enslaving of Africans on "slave ships" across the Atlantic, to the West Indies and South and North America, began in the sixteenth century. However, it was in 1619 that twenty captured Africans—first classified as indentured servants—from the Portuguese-owned colony of Luanda arrived in the English colony of Jamestown, Virginia, and became the first enslaved people in America.

Of the approximately 12.5 million Africans forced to experience the harrowing Middle Passage, "10.7 million survived and only 388,000 came directly to North America" (Gates 2014). The others were sent to the Caribbean and South America.

Racial chattel slavery expanded through all the English colonies on the cusp of becoming the United States and "grew like a cancer, at first slowly almost imperceptibly, then inexorably, as colonists eager for material gain imported hundreds of thousands of Africans to toil in their fields. During the eighteenth century, slavery became entrenched as a pervasive—and in many colonies central—component of the social order, the dark underside of the American dream" (Kolchin 2003, 4). The American dream, built on the foundational promise embedded in the Declaration of Independence, grants "each man" or person the right to life, liberty, and the pursuit of happiness. Although Virginian Thomas Jefferson expressed an antislavery stance, blaming Britain's policies, in the first draft of the declaration, it was deleted. Jefferson owned more than six hundred enslaved people, more than any other president. Sally Hemings, an enslaved woman, was his mistress and partner of thirty years and the mother of at least six of his children.

The social order and the economy of the South became increasingly dependent on racial chattel slavery. By 1837, there were thirteen slave states enriching enslavers and forcing the enslaved to labor under backbreaking conditions while being brutally oppressed, discriminated against, and sexually exploited. There was rice, tobacco, indigo, and cotton, but it was King Cotton that became big business after the War of 1812; there were more millionaires in Mississippi by 1860 than anywhere else in the United States.

The fomenting abolitionist movement to end slavery comprised Black and white Americans. It began in New England and the North in 1830 and rose up with a fury and urgency. It intersected with religion; come-outers were Christians who left churches that supported slavery and wouldn't run for office as the government supported it. The Quakers, also known as the Society of Friends, were among the first to speak out against the injustice and immorality of slavery and the importance of treating all people with basic human rights. Enslaved African Americans express their Africanized Christianity in films depicting slavery and sing "Negro spirituals." The decoded lyrics speak out against oppression. The songs were the soundtrack for a slow-burning revolution.

As the losing Illinois senate candidate, Abraham Lincoln, said in 1858, "A house divided against itself cannot stand." The South wanted to keep slavery intact; however, the North wanted to abolish it like other countries—like England did in 1833 and France in 1848. It led to the Civil War, the war between the North and the South, which began in 1861, a month after President Lincoln was inaugurated. Lincoln abolished slavery in his Emancipation Proclamation after the Union won in 1865, and four million African Americans were finally given their freedom.

The earliest films about enslaved African Americans depicted the myth of a happy plantation worker who sang and danced while working. But the films also showed the reality of a segregated America in which Jim Crow laws were enforced in the South. The more graphic depiction of enslaved African Americans in the later films reflects how society was influenced by the convulsive civil rights movement, whose tremors began in the 1950s before finally erupting full force in the 1960s and 1970s. Legislation was finally passed granting Blacks full equality, nearly one hundred years after slavery was abolished, and a fuller picture of the horrors of slavery began to emerge on screen.

African Americans resisted and rebelled against slavery in daily acts of defiance as well as through revolutionary insurrections—from a mutiny during the Middle Passage, as shown in Steven Spielberg's film *Amistad* (1997), to Nat Turner's Insurrection, shown in Nate Parker's potent *The Birth of a Nation* (2016), and Harriet Tubman's work as a conductor on the Underground Railroad and spy during the Civil War, vividly chronicled in Kasi Lemmons's compelling biopic *Harriet* (2019). Parker and Lemmons, African American filmmakers, suffused their films about rebels with a cause with arcs that show Turner's and Tubman's compulsion to audaciously act on their visions for equality.

Proslavery, white-supremacist beliefs perpetrated the myth that Blacks were inferior to whites and also the idea that they weren't even fully human. In 1852, Harriet Beecher Stowe's influential abolitionist novel *Uncle Tom's Cabin: Life among the Lowly* was published; its original subtitle was *The Man Who Was a Thing*. It exposed Northern readers to the horrors of slavery and was adapted into plays called the Tom plays, which appeared throughout America. Numerous film adaptations, including the 1914 adaptation, were made. Readers learned about the risks the enslaved took to run away to the North to keep their families intact.

Characters like Eliza and Tom, in the earlier Tom films, have a certain dignity and rebelliousness that mitigate the brutal reality of slavery. Some mitigating elements remain in Géza von Radvanyi's 1965 adaptation of *Uncle Tom's Cabin*, but these elements are significantly reduced in a few of the 1970s films and begin to lose ground to sensational sex and violence, which take on a darker and more subversive tone in the 1977 American reedit of this film.

And with films like *Goodbye Uncle Tom* (1971), *Mandingo* (1975), and its sequel *Drum* (1976), a sensational nadir of darkness and cynicism, with little relief in sight, and little hope for reconciliation between the races is reached. This kind of reconciliation comes with *Roots* (1977), which has the redemptive element of family loyalty running through it, and as it develops, it makes room for some bonding between Blacks and whites.

Even though *Uncle Tom's Cabin* perpetrated some unfortunate stereotypes and misinterpretation of its martyred main character, Stowe's novel was a catalyst for the Civil War, as was the 1841 Supreme Court win—despite that seven of the nine justices were Southern enslavers—for the *Amistad* Africans who were able to return to their homeland.

Post–Civil War Jim Crow segregation laws, ubiquitous lynchings of Blacks, white-supremacist terrorist groups like the Ku Klux Klan torturing Blacks and stoking fear, and an epidemic of Black incarceration and police brutality against Blacks remained prevalent but not limited to the South legally until 1968.

The civil rights movement crescendoed in the 1970s, and simultaneously, not since the Harlem Renaissance of the 1920s and 1930s had Black artists the opportunity to voice and express their talents in literature, music, art, and theater. The Black Arts Movement (1965–75) fused the artistic with political expression. Filmmakers including Charles Burnett and Haile Gerima—whose *Nightjohn* (1997) and *Sankofa* (1993) are among the most eloquent and moving films about slavery—were part of the L.A. Film Rebellion, a group of visionary Black filmmakers who met as University of California Los Angeles (UCLA) students starting in the 1960s. They forged a pioneering collective dedicated to making films that veered away from stereotypical characterizations and showed all facets of the African American experience in all genres, from neorealism to the mystical and previously shadowed aspects of slavery. *Sankofa* is the only film discussed that shows Maroon or outlier communities that runaways established.

In 2013, the #Black Lives Matter organization was created to bring awareness of police brutality and systemic racism. Social media and citizen journalism have been game changers. Thanks to Darnella Frazier, a witness who filmed and posted on social media the former Minneapolis police officer, Derek Chauvin, not taking his knee off George Floyd's neck for more than nine minutes in 2020, Chauvin was found guilty of murder and manslaughter and sentenced in 2022 to twenty-one years in prison. It's hard to watch the brutality of Frazier's footage, but it's hard to turn away from it. The power of filmic images endures and convicts.

Robert Rosenstone said, "Historical films trouble and disturb (most) professional historians. Historians will say films are inaccurate. They distort the past, they fictionalize, they trivialize, and romanticize" (5). Additionally, as Winston Churchill, who may or may not have been the first to claim it, said, history itself is "written by the victors." Historical narratives stick until they're challenged—for example, Christopher Columbus's "discovery" of America. In some places, the federal holiday Columbus Day is now called Indigenous Peoples' Day, honoring Native Americans who suffered oppression and marginalization after the Europeans arrived. The representation of American slavery on film legacy was limited for a long time to the dominant—the white—point of view.

The two films about life during slavery in the South that proved, unfortunately, the most influential and enduring, up until the airing of the phenomenal miniseries *Roots*, were Victor Fleming's romantic melodrama *Gone with the Wind* (1939), set from 1861 until 1873, and D. W. Griffith's silent epic *The Birth of a Nation* (1915), set during Reconstruction, 1865–77, the years after Emancipation. Griffith's nearly three-hour racist, but cinematically worthy, film was based on the novel *The Clansman*, by Thomas Dixon (Doubleday, Page & Co., 1905). The film stars Lillian Gish and white actors in blackface playing free Black men as malicious predators, rapists, and murderers. The Ku Klux Klan in the film are saviors, and attacks on Black communities spiked after the film's release. The Black filmmaker and novelist Oscar Micheaux (1884–1951), considered the first Black movie mogul, wrote and directed a silent film, titled *Within Our Gates* (1920)—the oldest extant film directed by a Black filmmaker. An attack against lynching, it was also an attack on the racism of *The Birth of a Nation*, which was controversial. Black and white groups unsuccessfully tried to block the film's opening.

White supremacy and a normalization of slavery embedded in other Hollywood epics that background one-dimensional enslaved characterizations include William Wyler's *Jezebel* (1938), starring Bette Davis as a Southern belle. The South may have lost the war, but it won the battle over its history. Spike Lee starts his incandescent film *BlacKkKlansman* (2018) with the *Gone with the Wind* scene showing footage of scores of wounded and dead Confederate soldiers after the Battle of Atlanta followed by a white man lamenting school integration. In another scene, Lee portrays marauding Ku Klux Klan members in the 1970s watching Griffith's film *The Birth of a Nation* while falling off a bench and howling with laughter.

The late Southern novelist Pat Conroy (1945–2016) says that the novel *Gone with the Wind* "shaped the South" he grew up in. Published in 1936, it expounded the Lost Cause ideology, "created by Southern writers in the decades after the ending of the Civil War to justify why they had fought" who also claimed that slavery was not the root cause of the Civil War and that the enslaved were untroubled by their standing in society (Stokes 2018).

WarnerMedia was pressured in June 2020 upon the launch of its streaming channel, HBO Max, to respond to screenwriter John Ridley's *LA Times* op-ed on June 8, 2020, in which he claimed that *Gone with the Wind* "when it is not ignoring the horrors of slavery, pauses only to perpetuate some of the most painful stereotypes of people of color." The oppression of child labor is shown in the film; however, the Black characters don't have inner lives or identities not associated with the whites for whom they work. "It's not censorship," TCM cohost Dave Karger said, "Instead of canceling, it's contextualizing, it's conversation " about the film that privileged the Southern white Lost Cause point of view (quoted in Hammond 2021).

The film scholar Jacqueline Stewart—in a five-minute video on HBO Max, posted in tandem with the film—contextualizes *Gone with the Wind*. She acknowledges its positive attributes but says that it hasn't been "universally praised" and that Black audiences have protested the film since when it was first released. They were concerned that it perpetuates negative Black stereotypes—devoted servants and characters defined by their "ineptitude," like Prissy (Butterfly McQueen), even though producer David O. Selznick assured the National Association for the Advancement of Colored People (NAACP) that the film would be sensitive to race issues. It portrays the Old South before the war in a "romantic, idyllic setting that's tragically been lost to the past" (Stewart 2020). It doesn't, however, show the brutality of slavery, yet it's shaped how so many people view slavery and Reconstruction. Also available to stream is an hour-long panel of film scholars led by Donald Bogle, titled "The Complicated Legacy of *Gone with the Wind*."

The enduring Lost Cause racist characterizations and images of enslaved African Americans, especially the Mammy caricature, in *Gone with the Wind* (1939) are pervasive and iconic, although it's important to remember what Hattie McDaniel, who played Mammy, famously said: "I'd rather play a maid than be one." She was the first African American actor to win an Academy Award; she won for the Best Supporting Actress. But in 1940 she had to sit apart from her fellow white actors at the awards ceremony. Her role was a pivotal one as, according to Margaret Mitchell's racist words, "It had always been a struggle to teach Scarlett that most of her natural impulses were unladylike. Mammy's victories over Scarlett were hard won and represented guile unknown to the white mind" (1936, 19). Mammy is an enslaved house servant, but she has agency. What she doesn't have is a life apart from her servitude to whites.

Another myth perpetrated by *Gone with the Wind* was that the plantation house was a place of gentility. The plantation house in Richard Fleischer's *Mandingo* (1975)—which Dave Kehr refers to as the "anti–*Gone with the Wind*"—is derelict, its white inhabitants disabled, disgruntled, abusive drunks and its Black inhabitants militant, disgruntled, and empowered. The abuse and brutality portrayed in all the movies discussed is unsettling and ugly; however, the South was a violent society compared to the North. Quentin Tarantino's ultraviolent uneasy blend of history and alternative history make *Django Unchained* (2012) exploitative, yet "DiCaprio does capture the unchecked and capricious use of power that was at the heart of the plantation system" (Bunch 2013).

The enslaved were beaten for being disobedient and attempting to run away, often to catch up with a family member who was sold away or to run back to one's family. Enslaved families were separated without warning—a field laborer might return home from a backbreaking day in the sun to find a family member had been raped, beaten, or sold. According to the Equal Justice Initiative (EJI), "more than half of all enslaved people in the Upper South were separated from a parent or child, and a third of their marriages were destroyed by forced migration" ("Families Torn Apart" 2017).

The announcement in 2017 of a projected HBO speculative series *Confederate*, created by *Game of Thrones*' showrunners, David Benioff and D. B. Weiss, sparked a media controversy. The revelation of the series' conceit—a modern America in which slavery remains a viable institution after the Southern states have successfully seceded from the Union—incited April Reign, the activist/creator of the potent #OscarsSoWhite campaign, to urge viewers to get behind #NoConfederate. An HBO executive promised that "the narrative is not a defense of slavery" and that there "should be no whips and no plantations," but the project was canceled. Toni Morrison, when she was contemplating writing about slavery and fictionalizing the story of the formerly enslaved woman Margaret Garner for her novel *Beloved* (Knopf, 1987), set in 1873, made into a poignant film in 1998 by Jonathan Demme, said, "The need to reexamine and imagine it was repellent." Morrison didn't want to examine victimhood and pity; for a novelist, she said, the "real excitement . . . is not what there is, but what there is not" (1998).

It was the miniseries *Roots*, based on Alex Haley's best-selling novel that showed to an audience of more than a hundred million viewers how enslaved Black Americans experienced and endured slavery and what it was like day to day, from the African's capture in Africa to Emancipation. The CBS show

60 Minutes, in May 2022, aired a riveting story about Frederick Miller, a fifty-six-year-old Black air force veteran, who bought Sharswood, a plantation house in his hometown of Pittsylvania County, Virginia, not knowing until his sister revealed through painstaking research that his ancestors had been enslaved in it. When asked about what he knew about slavery, he told Lesley Stahl that he wasn't taught about it in school nor was it talked about. "For a lot of us," he said, "*Roots* was our first experience with what really happened during slavery. It just wasn't discussed" (quoted in Heim 2022). *Roots* "had forced Americans—the world even—to look anew at slavery and what it had done to the country" (Haygood 2021, 276).

Not all Blacks were enslaved. Some were born free; some were able to buy their own freedom and get freedom papers. Tom Molineaux (1784–1818), America's first celebrity boxer, was a formerly enslaved man who bought his own freedom and fled for England. Solomon Northup was born a free man of color in Washington County, upstate New York, in 1807 or 1808. An abolitionist, a gifted professional violinist, and a farmer, Northup was kidnapped and drugged when he was about thirty-three years old and forced into enslavement in Louisiana where he experienced and witnessed among other dehumanizing practices the horrible treatment some white women perpetrated on the enslaved: *12 Years a Slave* shows Mistress Epps (Sarah Paulson), the vicious, abusive wife of slave owner Epps (Michael Fassbender), torturing Patsey (Lupito Nyong'o), as she's so jealous of her husband's obsession with and lust for her.

A cadre of communicators pleads Northup's case all the way up to the governor of New York, who ultimately secures Northup's freedom. Steve McQueen's Academy Award–winning *12 Years a Slave* (2013) tells Northup's riveting story; however, Gordon Parks told it first in his affecting 1984 PBS television movie *Solomon Northup's Odyssey*, reissued as *Half Slave, Half Free*, part of a National Endowment for the Humanities–funded American Playhouse's three-film series. Some claim that Northup's story is ultimately a "white savior" story, as Samuel Bass helps get Northup's message to the white New York governor, Washington Hunt, enabling Northup to reclaim his freedom. White people held political power exclusively in 1853. These are the facts of Northup's liberation.

A House Divided: Denmark Vesey's Rebellion (1982) was part of the series. Directed by Stan Lathan and starring Yaphet Kotto (1939–2021), it tells the true story of a formerly enslaved literate man who after buying his own freedom planned a rebellion to kill white enslavers liberate the enslaved in Charleston in 1822, and take them to Haiti. After authorities learned of the plot, Vesey and thirty-four other men were hanged. "Broader recognition of Vesey has been a long time coming," the *New York Times* reported in July 2022, noting that many institutions were honoring the bicentenary of Vesey's planned revolt. A statute was erected in Charleston in 2014 after years of pushback (Richardson 2022).

The Trinidadian scholar C. L. R. James in his *Black Jacobins* (1938) linked revolutionary general Toussaint Louverture's Haitian triumph to resistance in the United States. Herbert Aptheker's 1936 doctoral thesis *American Negro Slave Revolts* was one of the earliest texts to state that the enslaved's response to slavery was not "one of passivity and docility." In fact, "discontent and rebelliousness were characteristic" (quoted in Zemon Davis 2000, 18). But stories about revolts and insurrections were not widely taught or portrayed in films, and in some places in America, these events are still omitted from curriculums. Critical Race Theory (CRT), a controversial topic, "states that U.S. social institutions (e.g., the criminal justice system, education system, labor market, housing market, and healthcare system) are laced with racism embedded in laws, regulations, rules, and procedures that lead to differential outcomes by race" (Ray and Gibbons 2021). The state of Texas has suggested the way to teach slavery is that it was the "involuntary relocation" of captured Africans.

Haile Gerima says, "Slavery was a scientific adventure, an attempt by an industrialized society to create a robotic society of mindless human beings, pure labor" (Gerima, quoted in Woolford 1994, 98). The idea was for the enslaved to be happy, and although they were not happy in the real world, they were portrayed as happy in what he calls "the plantation school of literature and cinema" (Gerima, quoted in Woolford 1994, 99). Ulrich Bonnell Phillips (1877–1934) wrote an unfortunately foundational book about Southern slavery, suggesting that enslavers on plantations provided "schools" to "civilize" the enslaved ("Ulrich Phillips Historian," n.d.). Gerima turns that portrayal topsy-turvy in *Sankofa*.

How do African American storytellers and filmmakers depict the defiance of the oppressed? What do film representations reveal about the enslaved's family, religious, and cultural values? How did Maroon community dwellers, runaways, freedom fighters, and abolitionist leaders manage to survive, sometimes thrive, and get written into history? To what effect does the supernatural element in *Sankofa* convey how slavery, as Toni Morrison said, "haunts us all"?

The portrayal of the enslaved, in some ways, parallels and also contrasts with Holocaust film stories. A. O. Scott has described "the moral imperatives imposed by the slaughter of European Jews" as "Never Again and Never Forget." Monica White Ndounou noted that "most films about slavery are told from the point of the view of white owners, not the enslaved, while most Holocaust films privilege the perspective of victims and survivors, not the Nazi perpetrators" (2019, 73). The films discussed portray victims, but they also show the enslaved's daily acts of resistance, defiant survivors, rebellious leaders, reconciliation, and redemption. Ruth Franklin claims that films about the Holocaust are relevant insofar as they reveal their "own kind of truth; it illuminates the complexity of the victim's experience," and the same is true about films about the enslaved. As the late

African American museum architect Philip Frelon (1953–2019) told the *Baltimore Sun* in 2005, "It's not all about being a victim. The important part is that we persevered."

Ever since Twentieth Century Fox paid "a record sum of $600,000" for the rights to William Styron's controversial, Pulitzer Prize–winning novel, *The Confessions of Nat Turner* (1967), in 1968, a film about the literate leader of the most well-known slave insurrection has been percolating in the collective consciousness (Ryfle 2016, 31). It took until 2016, however, for the film to get made. A labor of love for actor/director, Nate Parker, who cannily titled it *The Birth of a Nation*; it's a powerful, if flawed, film about a man some call a hero and some call a pariah. It's a film suffused with religion, prophetic vision, revolution, family, and moral suasion.

Frederick Douglass, in his slave narrative, talks about the risks he took to learn to read. Literacy for Blacks was against the law. Race pseudoscience, like phrenology, shown in *Django Unchained*, unsuccessfully tried to prove that Blacks were intellectually inferior to whites. But whites knew that Blacks could learn and had intellectual capability. If Blacks could read, however, it would be impossible to keep them enslaved. Charles Burnett's coruscating masterpiece *Nightjohn* (1996) about a free man of color going back into slavery to teach young people to read is about a freedom fighter. Literacy laws, as discussed in the book, were made harsher over time. One reason was the fear of Blacks being able to forge their own freedom papers.

Films not discussed in the book but important to note include Herbert Biberman's *Slaves* (1965)—a loose adaptation of *Uncle Tom's Cabin*—starring Ossie Davis and debuting a young Dionne Warwick, which highlights resistance and rebellion. The screenplay was cowritten by John Oliver Killens, a well-known Black writer, educator, and leader of the Black Arts Movement in the 1960s. Biberman was one of the blacklisted Hollywood Ten; his classic, visionary film *Salt of the Earth* (1954) is now considered a feminist and unionist classic.

The lauded television series *Underground* (2016–17) uses thriller tropes to depict slavery and operators on the Underground Railroad. Barry Jenkins's *The Underground Railroad* (2020), based on Colson Whitehead's Pulitzer Prize–winning eponymous novel, is a metaphysical atmospheric story that takes place, for the most part, outside the confines of society. And the adaptation of James McBride's National Book Award–winning novel *The Good Lord Bird* (Showtime, 2020) has as its lead character John Brown (Ethan Hawke)—the radical abolitionist who led a slave rebellion and attack on Harpers Ferry. Barack and Michelle Obama's film company, Higher Ground Productions, is developing a film based on *Frederick Douglass: Prophet of Freedom*, Pulitzer Prize–winning David W. Blight's 2018 biography; this will be the first feature film about Douglass, arguably the most famous man in nineteenth-century America.

Four years before *Gone with the Wind*, there was King Vidor's *So Red the Rose* (1935), based on the 1934 best-selling novel by Southerner Stark Young. Based on true people and events and set in Natchez, Mississippi, in the early1860s, the film adaptation of Young's Civil War romance is unique for its scenes depicting defiant enslaved African Americans at the moment of liberation. Led by the enslaved Cato (Clarence Muse), who wrests control of the livestock, the plantation owner, Valette Bedford (Margaret Sullavan), suppresses a slave insurrection. Union soldiers pillage the plantation. The Civil War's impact on the enslaved in this film offers a stark contrast to its portrayal in *Gone with the Wind*.

Frank Yerby's best-selling novel, *The Foxes of Harrow* (1946), was the first book written by an African American to sell (for $150,000) to a major Hollywood studio, Twentieth Century Fox. The 1947 film was directed by John A. Stahl. The rebellious enslaved woman, Belle, is played by an uncredited Suzette Harbin, a former beauty queen. She defiantly and tragically refuses to obey her "maître," the New Orleans term for "master" who comes to her cabin to recruit her newborn child to be his newborn son's caretaker. She tells him her child is a warrior, not a slave. She grabs her son and runs to the river, threatening to jump in. Her husband and maître run after her; her husband grabs the child and pleads with her to come with him. But Belle jumps in, drowning herself. Her man is devastated, but he says, "She's free now." It's a riveting scene, even though the story told in the novel was severely truncated in the film.

Belle resists white exploitation. Another character, Caleen, performs voodoo rituals to African drumming. The story focuses on Stephen Fox (Rex Harrison), an Irish immigrant gambler, and his love for Odalie (Maureen O'Hara). He buys Belle after winning at cards, and she's defiant. An enslaved man tries to grab her; she bites him and runs away, and he goes running after her. Stephen says she's the beautiful savage, Belle Savage. The woman runs, the man pursues, paralleling his relationship with Odalie who says to Stephen, "You make me uneasy, the way you look at me like I'm a slave as if you own me." Yerby, who was biracial, in a later novel A *Darkness at Ingraham's Crest* (Doubleday, 1979), the sequel to *The Man from Dahomey* (1971), featured a militant slave hero (Van Deburg 1984, 146).

Tamango (1958) is a fascinating film about a mutiny captured Africans stage on a slave ship to Cuba. Directed by John Berry and starring Dorothy Dandridge, it also features an interracial relationship. Raoul Walsh's *Band of Angels* (1957), based on Robert Penn Warren's best-selling novel, inspired by a true story, is, at heart, a "tragic mulatto" story. It explores the complications of an interracial romantic relationship between Amantha Starr (Yvonne de Carlo), and Hamish Bond (Clark Gable) set against the backdrop of the beginning of the Civil War. When her wealthy plantation owner father dies, Amantha finds out she's biracial; her late mother was Black and enslaved. Rau-Ru, played by thirty-year-old Sidney Poitier

(1927–2022), Bond's majordomo and surrogate son is an "agitator," a free and educated African American. Bond "rescued" him in Africa when he was grabbing people with the help of African tribesmen. Rau-Ru's first action is defending Amantha from being raped by a white man. Rau-Ru is resentful of his master for everything he stands for. He implores Amantha to accept her Blackness. He becomes the leader of Black insurgents as a Union lieutenant and plots his mentor's demise. Rau-Ru says to Amantha: "Freedom's a white word. And the fact is, you and I, aside from being male and female are exactly alike: No identity beyond the confines of Masser Hamish's protection."

The characterizations discussed in the films chosen do have identities beyond the white people they are forced to serve and obey. They refuse to give in, give up, or shut up.

The Uruguayan writer Eduardo Galeano claimed, "There is no silent history. However much they burn it, however much they smash it, however much they lie about it, human history refuses to shut up." Slavery from the point of view of the resistant, rebellious, and resilient enslaved refuses to shut up. Generals and prophets Nat Turner and Harriet Tubman sounded the call and militated against slavery by any means necessary. They were Americans who demanded life, liberty, and the pursuit of happiness.

FURTHER READING

Bunch, Lonnie, III. 2013. "What *Django Unchained* Got Wrong: A Review from National Museum of African American History and Culture Director Lonnie Bunch." *Smithsonian*, January 14, 2013.

Conroy, Pat. 1996. Preface to *Gone with the Wind*, by Margaret Mitchell. New York: Scribner.

"Families Torn Apart by Slavery Sought Reunion After Emancipation." 2017. *Equal Justice Initiative*, February 24, 2017. https://eji.org/news/families-torn-apart-by-slavery-sought-reunion/.

Gates, Henry Louis, Jr. 2014. "How Many Slaves Landed in the U.S." *The Root*, January 6, 2014.

Haygood, Wil. 2021. *Colorization: One Hundred Years of Black Films in a White World*. New York: Alfred A. Knopf.

Heim, Joe. 2022. "An Old Virginia Plantation, a New Owner and a Family Legacy Unveiled." *Philadelphia Tribune*, January 24, 2022.

Kolchin, Peter. 2003. *American Slavery 1619–1877*. New York: Hill and Wang.

Mitchell, Margaret. 1936. *Gone with the Wind*. New York: Macmillan.

Morrison, Toni. 1998. "The Site of Memory." In *Inventing the Truth: The Art and Craft of Memoir*, edited by William Zinsser. Boston: Houghton Mifflin.

Ray, Rashawn, and Alexandra Gibbons. 2021. "Why Are States Banning Critical Race Theory?" Fixgov, November 2021. https://www.brookings.edu/blog/fixgov/2021/07/02/why-are-states-banning-critical-race-theory/.

Richardson, Kalia. 2022. "200 Years Later, Charleston Honors Denmark Vesey's Attempted Uprising." *New York Times*, July 15, 2022.

Rosenstone, Robert. 1995. "The Historical Film as Real History." *FilmHistoria Online* 5 (1): 5–23.

Scott, A. O. 2008. "Never Forget. You're Reminded." *New York Times*, November 21, 2008.

Stewart, Jacqueline. 2020. "Why We Can't Turn Away from *Gone with the Wind*." CNN, June 25, 2020.

Stokes, Melvyn. 2018. "From Uncle Tom to Nat Turner: An Overview of Slavery in American Film, 1903–2016." *Transatlantic American Studies Journal* 1. https://doi.org/10.4000/transatlantica.12814.

"Ulrich Phillips, Historian Born." n.d. *African American Registry*. Accessed September 24, 2022. https://aaregistry.org/story/ulrich-phillips-born/.

Van Deburg, William L.1984. *Slavery & Race in American Popular Culture*. Madison: University of Wisconsin Press.

Woolford, Pamela. 1994. "Filming Slavery. A Conversation with Halie Gerima." *Transition* 64:90–99.

Chronology of European and American Race-Based Chattel Slavery

1441	The European slave trade begins in Africa when two Portuguese captains capture, transport, and enslave twelve Africans from Cabo Branco (modern Mauritania).
1452	Sugar is planted for the first time on the Portuguese island of Madeira, creating the first sugar-slave complex. For the first time, enslaved Africans are put to work on sugar plantations.
September 1526	Approximately one hundred enslaved African laborers brought by Lucas Vázquez de Ayllón in a Spanish expedition arrive in *La Florida* to form and support the new Spanish settlement San Miguel de Gualdape, close to present-day Sapelo Island, Georgia. The short-lived colony is intact for less than two months; many of the enslaved rebel. The settlement is abandoned by November 1526.
1560–65	Enslaved and free Africans are brought by the Spanish admiral and explorer Pedro Menendez de

	Aviles and perform labor to establish St. Augustine, America's oldest city, in what is now Florida. In 1565, De Aviles becomes the first governor of *La Florida*.
1562	Triangular Trade is initiated by the British; they capture and bring approximately three hundred Africans from Sierra Leone to the Spanish colony of Santo Domingo and to sell in the West Indies.
1619	The *White Lion*, an English vessel operating under a Dutch letter of marque, arrives in Point Comfort, today Fort Comfort in Hampton, Virginia, at the English colony of Jamestown, with twenty captured African men and women from the Portuguese-owned colony of Luanda, now Angola. These Africans, first classified as indentured servants, are about to become the first enslaved people in America.
July 9, 1640	John Punch, an indentured Black Virginian who runs away, becomes the first man to be enslaved for life after being captured.
1641	Massachusetts is the first state to recognize slavery as legal.
1662	A law in Virginia stipulates that if a mother is enslaved, any child born to her will also be enslaved.
1676	Bacon's Rebellion is the first uprising of colonists against Britain and the Virginia colonial governor William Berkley. Nathaniel Bacon, a Virginia planter, leads enslaved Blacks and white indentured servants contesting control of Powhattan Indian land. The aftermath intensifies race slavery and the segregation of Blacks and whites in Virginia.
1705	The Virginia Code, also known as the Casual Killing Act, decriminalizes consequences for murdering an enslaved person when in the act of correcting them.

April 6, 1712	The New York slave rebellion of 1712 begins when a group of enslaved Africans set fire to Peter Van Tilburgh's outhouse on Maiden Lane in New York City, initializing a slave revolt in which nine whites are killed and culminating in a trial after which twenty-seven enslaved people are convicted and twenty-one are executed.
September 9, 1739	The Stono Rebellion, also known as Cato's Conspiracy or Cato's Rebellion, is the largest slave revolt in the South. It takes place on the banks of the Stono River in the British colony of South Carolina, which has more Blacks than whites; it is led by the Angolan Jemmy who with twenty enslaved men rebel on Sunday when white men are in church. A recent law requires white men to carry firearms to church. More than sixty people, twenty-five colonists, and thirty-five to fifty Africans are killed.
1741	New York Slave Conspiracy, also known as the Slave Insurrection of 1841, occurs but is never proven. Enslaved people and poor whites are accused of a plan to burn myriad sites and take over New York City during spring and summer 1741. The first fire cited is at Fort George. Thirty Blacks and four whites are executed.
December 30, 1775	General George Washington, revising an earlier edict, orders recruiting officers to accept free Blacks in the American Army. More than 5,000 Blacks, mostly Northerners, fight against the British.
July 4, 1776	The United States of America declares its independence from Great Britain on July 2, 1776; the Second Continental Congress on July 4 adopts the final text of the Declaration of Independence, stating that in America "all men are created equal, that they are endowed by their Creator with certain unalienable Rights, that among these are Life, Liberty and the pursuit of Happiness."

March 1, 1780	The Gradual Abolition Act of 1780 passes in Pennsylvania. It is America's and the world's first gradual abolition law. Enslaved people born into slavery are gradually emancipated before slavery is rendered illegal. Other Northern states follow suit, enabling a free African American population to flourish and possess basic human and American rights according to the Declaration of Independence.
1787	The Three Fifths Compromise states that three fifths of a state's enslaved population count toward its total population—a number used for determining representation in Congress and the tax obligations of each state. The result of the compromise, Article 1, Section 2, Clause 3. Section 2 of the Fourteenth Amendment (1868) later supersedes this clause and explicitly repeals the compromise.
1791–1804	The once-enslaved Haitian general, Toussaint Louverture, leads a successful revolt against France, the colonizer. On January 1, 1804, the entire island formerly known as Saint-Domingue is declared independent under the Arawak name of Haiti. It is the world's first Black republic and the first independent country in the Caribbean.
February 12, 1793	Congress passes the first Fugitive Slave Act, authorizing local governments to capture and return runaway enslaved people and also inflict penalties and make it a crime for anyone to intervene in the arrest of or to harbor a runaway enslaved person.
1793	Eli Whitney invents the cotton gin, which reduces the labor of removing seeds. However, it does not reduce the need for enslaved labor to grow and pick the cotton; in fact, it increases demand for the production of cotton.
1793	John Graves Simcoe, the first lieutenant governor of Upper Canada, initiates the first abolition act to end slavery in Canada.

Spring and Summer 1800	Gabriel's Rebellion: Gabriel Prosser, a literate enslaved blacksmith and skilled artisan, and twenty-six other Black artisans are publicly hanged for planning to overtake Richmond, Virginia, and convince Governor James Monroe that Blacks deserved equality with whites. No whites perish.
1807	Britain abolishes slave trading with an Act of Parliament.
January 1, 1808	The Act Prohibiting Importation of Slaves of 1807 is a U.S. federal law that stipulates that no new slaves are permitted to be imported into the United States. It takes effect on January 1, 1808.
January 8–10, 1811	The German Coast Uprising, the largest rebellion of enslaved people in American history, takes place in New Orleans. Nearly five hundred enslaved armed men, led by Charles Deslondes after killing two white men, walk for two days burning five sugar plantations. More than ninety-five Blacks are killed by militias and executions after a trial.
1816	The American Colonization Society (ACS), originally known as the American Society for Colonizing the Free People of Color, is formed. It founds the colony of Liberia in West Africa in 1847.
April 9, 1816	The American Methodist Episcopal Church (AME Church) is founded. It is the first church established by African Americans. Its mission statement focuses on racial rather than theological issues. It grows out of the Free African Society (FAS) that Richard Allen and others founded in Philadelphia in 1787.
March 3, 1820	The Missouri Compromise admits Missouri as a slave state and Maine as a free state to the Union and bans slavery in states north of the Louisiana Purchase.
July 2, 1822	Denmark Vesey, a free carpenter, is hanged after being captured for allegedly planning an insurrection in Charleston, South Carolina.

1825	The first fugitive slave narrative is published in the United States. *The Life of William Grimes, the Runaway Slave, Written by Himself* reveals for the first time to readers in the North the horrors of chattel slavery in the American South as well as the pervasiveness of racial injustice in New England.
March 16, 1827	*Freedom's Journal*, the first newspaper founded by African Americans, Reverend Samuel Cornish and John Russwurm, both born free, publishes its first four-column weekly in New York City. There are more than forty Black-owned newspapers by the beginning of the Civil War.
August 14, 1829	The Greenup Slave Revolt occurs. While a slave driver named Gordon is transporting sixty enslaved people to a market to be sold in Mississippi, a few break free in Greenup, Kentucky, and beat Gordon. Sixteen escaped. Four enslaved men are hanged in November 1829.
September 1829	*David Walker's Appeal to the Coloured Citizens of the World*, a radical antislavery pamphlet published in Boston advocates for slaves to unite and revolt against their masters. Walker was born free as his mother was free. He was an abolitionist who also advocated literacy for African Americans. Walker discusses the Greenup Slave Revolt.
January 1, 1831	William Lloyd Garrison publishes the first issue of the abolitionist weekly newspaper, *The Liberator*, in Boston and continues publishing it until December 29, 1865.
August 1–3, 1831	Nat Turner's Insurrection in Southampton County, Virginia, is the largest successful revolt of the enslaved in American history. Turner feels ordained by God to end slavery. Turner and at first a small band and then a growing number of other enslaved Virginian rebels who join him kill close to sixty white men, women, and children. White militias massacre more than two hundred Blacks in retribution. Turner hides in the woods for six weeks but is found and tried in October.

November 11, 1831	Nat Turner is hanged. While imprisoned, the lawyer Thomas R. Gray interviews Turner and publishes the pamphlet *The Confessions of Nat Turner, the leader of the late insurrection in Southampton, Va., as fully and voluntarily made to Thomas R. Gray* shortly after the trial and execution of Nat Turner in November 1831.
1833	The Slavery Abolition Act of 1833 stipulates that Britain end slavery in most of its colonies, including Canada. In 1834 and 1838, slavery is abolished in the West Indies.
1834	Abolitionist and free Black David Ruggles, a New Yorker, opens the first African American bookstore on Lispenard Street in what is today the Tribeca area in New York City. Ruggles founds the antislavery newspaper *Mirror of Liberty* and is one of the early organizers of a network that becomes the Underground Railroad.
August 24, 1839	The *Amistad*, a Spanish slave ship traveling from Cuba to the United States, is seized by the USS *Washington* off the coast of Long Island and escorted to New London, Connecticut. The Spanish captains are freed, and the Africans are imprisoned in New Haven pending an investigation of the *Amistad* revolt.
March 9, 1841	The Supreme Court case the *United States v. Schooner Amistad* rules that the *Amistad* Africans are enslaved illegally and under American law are now free.
November 1841	The mutiny of the *Creole*, after which 128 enslaved people achieve freedom. It is the largest successful slave revolt in American history.
1842	The Webster-Ashburton Treaty, stipulating that by establishing a joint naval system off the African coast, the United States, and Great Britain will collaborate on suppressing the slave trade. The United States deploys the African Squadron, a permanent antislavery patrol, which stays on the prowl until the start of the Civil War in 1861.

May 1, 1845	*Narrative of the Life of Frederick Douglass, an American Slave, Written by Himself* is published by the Anti-Slavery Office, with a preface by William Lloyd Garrison.
March 23, 1849	Henry "Box" Brown (1815–97) flees slavery by having Samuel Smith ship him in a wooden box via the Adams Express Company to abolitionists in Philadelphia.
September 1849	Brown and Stearns publishes Henry "Box" Brown's *Narrative of the Life of Henry Box Brown, Written by Himself*, which Brown develops into an antislavery stage show. Eight thousand copies are sold within two months after publication.
September 18, 1850	The Fugitive Slave Law, also known as the Compromise of 1850, is passed. This is a pair of federal laws that allows for the capture and return of runaway enslaved people within the territory of the United States.
March 20, 1852	John P. Jewett and Company publishes Harriet Beecher Stowe's antislavery novel *Uncle Tom's Cabin* after its serialization in the abolitionist weekly newspaper, the *Washington Era* beginning June 5, 1851. It sells three hundred thousand copies in America within its first year of publication and more than a million copies in England. Play adaptations called "Tom shows" pop up all over the country spurring racial stereotypes.
1853	*Twelve Years a Slave: Narrative of Solomon Northup, Citizen of New York, Kidnapped in Washington City in 1841, and Rescued in 1853, from a Cotton Plantation Near the Red River in Louisiana* as told to and written by David Wilson is published by Derby & Miller, Auburn, New York.
May 30, 1854	The Kansas Nebraska Act, drafted by Senator Stephen Douglas of Illinois, allows slavery to exist in new federal territories and extend into territories where it had once been banned.

March 6, 1857	Dred Scott loses his fight for freedom in the Supreme Court's *Dred Scott v. Sanford* case. Scott sues for his freedom when his master takes him into free territory. Roger B. Taney writes the final majority opinion stating that Blacks are not citizens of the United States, and Congress does not have the power to prohibit slavery in any federal territory.
August–October 1858	Abraham Lincoln, the Republican candidate for president, debates Democrat presidential candidate Stephen A. Douglas seven times. The Republican party at this time is antislavery; the Democratic party is proslavery. The parties subsequently switch positions.
October 16–18, 1859	John Brown's Raid on the American arsenal Harpers Ferry, Virginia—since 1863, West Virginia. A fervent abolitionist, Brown's goal is to trigger a slave revolt by Southern states by leading twenty-one men; fourteen people die, and nine others are wounded during the raid. Brown is executed on December 2, 1859, for insurrection, murder, and treason.
1860	*The Clotilda*, the last known slave ship to arrive in the United States, arrives in Mobile, Alabama, with Africans captured from the Kingdom of Dahomey, now Benin.
1860–61	Abraham Lincoln is elected president of the United States. Eleven Southern states secede from the Union and form the Confederate States. The Black population as revealed by America's 1860 census is approximately 4.5 million; close to 500,000 are free; approximately 47 percent (226,000) live in free states (http://nationalhumanitiescenter.org/pds/maai/identity/text3/text3read.htm).
1861	*Incidents in the Life of a Slave Girl* by Harriet Ann Jacobs, edited by Lydia Maria Child, is published by Thayer and Eldridge.
March 1861	The Corwin Amendment is ratified in some but not enough states to become law; it uses the term

	"domestic institution," and it protects slavery. It would have become the Thirteenth Amendment if passed.
April 12, 1861	Confederate troops fire on Fort Sumter in South Carolina's Charleston Harbor. Union forces surrender more than a day later. This incident begins the Civil War.
February 21, 1862	President Abraham Lincoln orders the hanging of Nathaniel Gordon, a slave trader, the first man to be hanged for this crime.
September 22, 1862	President Abraham Lincoln's executive order of the Emancipation Proclamation, freeing the Southern enslaved population, is issued.
January 1, 1863	Emancipation Proclamation takes effect. Slavery is abolished in states that seceded from the United States, and approximately three million people are freed. Black men are able to fight for the Union Army and Navy.
March 3, 1863	The U.S. Congress passes the Civil War Conscription Act, the first wartime draft of U.S. citizens in American history.
April 2, 1863	The photo of Whipped Peter revealing the horrific brutality of slavery is published. It spurs many Northerners to advocate for the abolition of slavery.
June 1 and 2, 1863	Harriet Tubman leads the Civil War raid at Combahee Ferry, freeing more than seven hundred formerly enslaved people.
July 31, 1863	In his General Order No. 252, President Abraham Lincoln orders that any indignities visited upon Black troops will be revenged on an equal number of Confederate POWs.
July 18, 1863	The first all-Black regiment, the Fifty-Fourth Massachusetts Volunteer Infantry, leads a valorous attack on Fort Wagner in South Carolina. Most of the nearly two hundred thousand Black soldiers fighting for the Union in the Civil War are free men; however, some are formerly enslaved men who escaped slavery.

January 9, 1864	William Walker, a Black Civil Rights Union soldier, is executed for organizing a strike for Black soldiers to secure pay equal to that of whites.
April 12, 1864	The Civil War's Battle at Fort Pillow takes place in Henning, Tennessee. Confederate soldiers, led by General Nathan Bedford Forrest, massacre more than three hundred Black soldiers and their white officers after they surrender.
June 15, 1864	Congress passes a bill to equalize pay for Black Union soldiers. In September 1864, the men of the Fifty-Fourth Massachusetts are retroactively paid in full for their eighteen months of service.
1865–66	A series of laws known as the "Black codes" and exclusionary acts are passed in Southern states. They are designed to restrict the activities of freed Black people and ensure their availability as a labor force; it spurs the beginning of Jim Crow laws.
1865	The white supremacist, racist, and domestic terrorist organization Ku Klux Klan (KKK) is created. Vigilante group members intimidate, threaten, beat up, and kill Blacks.
March 3, 1865	The Freedmen's Bureau is created by the War Department. Its mission is to provide relief and help formerly enslaved people become self-sufficient. It is abolished in 1872.
April 9, 1865	General Robert E. Lee surrenders the Southern troops to General Ulysses S. Grant's Union Army at Virginia's Appomattox Court House. This officially marks the end of the Civil War.
April 14, 1865	President Abraham Lincoln is assassinated by John Wilkes Booth at Ford's Theater while watching the comedy *Our American Cousin*. Lincoln dies on April 15. Andrew Johnson becomes president.
December 18, 1865	Slavery is abolished. The Thirteenth Amendment is ratified and added to the U.S. Constitution. Approximately four million formerly enslaved people are freed.

December 1865	Reconstruction begins. Congress assembles in December 1865. Radical Republicans such as Republican Thaddeus Stevens of Pennsylvania and Senator Charles Sumner from Massachusetts call for the establishment of new Southern governments based on equality before the law and universal male suffrage.
March 1866	The Civil Rights Act is passed despite President Andrew Johnson's veto.
1867	The 1867 Military Reconstruction Act offers new opportunities for African Americans. It is designed to manage the transition from enslaved to free and to forge a new path to deal with the disorder in the South.
July 9, 1868	Passed by Congress on June 13, 1866, and ratified July 9, 1868, the Fourteenth Amendment extends liberties and rights granted by the Bill of Rights to formerly enslaved people.
February 3, 1870	The Fifteenth Amendment to the U.S. Constitution, granting African American men the right to vote, is ratified. It reads, "The right of citizens of the United States to vote shall not be denied or abridged by the United States or by any State on account of race, color, or previous condition of servitude."
April 20, 1871	President Ulysses Grant signs the Ku Klux Klan Act, also known as the Civil Rights Act of 1871; it includes Section 1983 of the U.S. Code and remains the foundation for federal civil rights lawsuits.
1872	William Still self-publishes *The Underground Railroad*, his documentary account of formerly enslaved people who achieved freedom and escaped bondage.
1877	The Compromise of 1877 marks the end of the Reconstruction era and the beginning of the Jim Crow era. To settle the hotly contested 1876 presidential election between Republican Rutherford B. Hayes and Democrat Samuel Tilden, Democrats agree that Hayes becomes president when federal troops are withdrawn from the South.

1896	The *Plessy v. Ferguson* Supreme Court case upholds racial segregation and the separate but equal doctrine. Homer Plessy, an African American man, in 1892 refused to sit in a train car for Black people. It leads to harsh Jim Crow segregation laws.
1903	The first silent short film adaptation of Harriet Beecher Stowe's novel *Uncle Tom's Cabin*, directed by Edwin S. Porter, is released by the Edison Manufacturing Company.
1909	The National Association for the Advancement of Colored People (NAACP) is established.
August 10, 1914	*Uncle Tom's Cabin*, directed by William Robert Daly, debuts. It's the first film in which a Black actor appears. White actors in blackface previously appeared as Black characters.
1918	The Dyer Bill, the first anti-lynching bill, is introduced to Congress.
April 1919	Red Summer of 1919 begins. Mob violence and racist attacks in 1919 are widespread. They are in many places initiated by white servicemen and centered upon the 380,000 Black veterans just returned from the war. Black veterans are perceived "a threat to Jim Crow and racial subordination," notes a report by the Equal Justice Initiative.
1930	The Production Code of 1930 is established for films; however, it's not strictly enforced until 1934. The Motion Picture Producers and Distributors Association (MPPA) agreement stipulates that regarding interracial romance, it is forbidden to depict miscegenation, sexual, marital, or cohabitation relationships between the white and Black race on film.
April 1, 1937	The collection of interviews of formerly enslaved people's narratives, directed by the Work Projects Administration's Federal Writers Project (FWP) and under the guidance of folklorist John A. Lomax, begins.
May 17, 1954	The landmark Supreme Court judgment *Brown v. Board of Education of Topeka* rules that the desegregation of public school is the law of the

	land: all states' laws establishing school segregation are unlawful.
July 2, 1964	Passage of the Civil Rights Act, signed into law by President Lyndon Johnson. It is the most sweeping civil rights legislation since Reconstruction.
August 6, 1965	The Voting Rights Act, signed into law by President Lyndon Johnson, outlaws discriminatory voting practices, including the difficult literacy tests African Americans had to take before they could vote. Many Southern states endorsed these practices after the Civil War.
1966–67	Stokely Carmichael, who will change his name to Kwame Ture, succeeds John Lewis as the chairman of Student Nonviolent Coordinating Committee (SNCC). Under his guidance, SNCC advocates Black Power, becoming a more militant and less nonviolent organization, alienating some of its white members.
May 7, 1975	*Mandingo*, directed by Richard Fleischer, a brutally honest depiction of race slavery based on Kyle Onstott's eponymous best-selling novel, opens. Its sequel *Drum*, directed by Steve Carver, is released in 1976.
January 23, 1977	The premiere of *Roots*, based on Alex Haley's best-selling novel, on ABC television is a cultural phenomenon. This twelve-hour miniseries airs on eight consecutive winter nights shattering ratings and capturing close to 130 viewers by its final episode. A reboot consisting of four two-hour episodes starts airing on Memorial Day in 2016.
February 17, 1982	*A House Divided: Denmark Vesey's Rebellion*, a TV movie directed by Stan Lathan about Denmark Vesey's planning of the insurrection that would have been the largest slave uprising, airs on PBS.
December 10, 1984	*Solomon Northup's Odyssey*, the first film/TV movie adaptation of Solomon Northup's 1853 best-selling memoir, airs on PBS. It is released on video in 1985 under the title *Half Slave, Half Free*.

January 20, 1986	Martin Luther King Jr. Day honors the birthday of the Civil Rights leader and is celebrated on the third Monday of January. It's the first holiday to honor an African American.
December 15, 1989	*Glory*, the Civil War drama directed by Ed Zwick, opens. It tells the story of the African American regiment, the Fifty-Fourth Massachusetts Infantry during the Civil War. Denzel Washington wins the Oscar for Best Supporting Actor.
February 22, 1993	*Sankofa*, a time-travel story written and directed by Haile Gerima, about a contemporary Black model who is transported back into slavery to learn about her ancestors, debuts at the Berlin Film Festival. It is screened in many cities, including New York, Philadelphia, Atlanta, Baltimore, Chicago, Detroit, Boston, and Washington, DC, where it has long runs and grosses more than $3 million. It's widely released and streams for the first time on Netflix in September 2021.
June 1, 1996	*Nightjohn*, directed by Charles Burnett and based on Gary Paulsen's eponymous young adult novel about the punishment and pain the enslaved endure to become literate, airs on the Disney Channel.
December 25, 1997	*Amistad*, about how the captured Africans who stage an insurrection on the slave ship *Amistad* are tried and freed, directed by Steven Spielberg, opens and is released theatrically.
December 25, 2012	*Django Unchained*, written and directed by Quentin Tarantino, about an enslaved man who rescues his wife from slavery and is mentored by a German American bounty hunter, opens and is released theatrically.
November 8, 2013	*12 Years a Slave*, directed by Steve McQueen, based on Solomon Northup's memoir about being a free man of color who was illegally forced into slavery, is released theatrically.
March 9, 2016	*Underground*, an American television period drama series about the Underground Railroad set in antebellum Georgia, debuts on WGN America; it airs until May 2017.

October 17, 2016	*The Birth of a Nation*, a biopic about Nat Turner's Insurrection directed by and starring Nate Parker, opens after premiering at the Sundance Film Festival.
April 9, 2018	A piece of the *Clotilda*, the last slave ship to arrive in America, is found in Mobile Bay, Alabama. The ship sailed in 1860 from present day Benin carrying one hundred and ten people. Thirty-two of the ship's survivors establish Africatown in 1872 in Mobile.
November 1, 2019	*Harriet*, directed by Kasi Lemmons, a biopic about Underground Railroad conductor Harriet Tubman, opens theatrically after premiering at the Toronto Film Festival.
October–November 2020	*The Good Lord Bird*, based on James McBride's award-winning novel about John Brown's Raid on Harpers Ferry, streams its limited event series of seven episodes on Showtime.
May 14, 2021	*The Underground Railroad,* the limited ten-episode series directed by Barry Jenkins and based on Colson Whitehead's eponymous novel, starts streaming on Amazon Prime.
June 17, 2021	President Joseph R. Biden declares June 19 the U.S. federal holiday Juneteenth National Independence Day, which commemorates the end of slavery in America. It's the second national holiday honoring African Americans.
September 8, 2021	The twelve-ton statue of Confederate general Robert E. Lee, more than 130 years after it was installed in Richmond, Virginia, is removed by the state of Virginia.
March 29, 2022	President Joseph R. Biden signs the Emmett Till Anti-Lynching Act into law, making lynching a federal hate crime.
April 26, 2022	Harvard University commits $100 million to "redress its ties to slavery" by creating and endowing the Legacy of Slavery Fund for scholars

	and students to examine and document Harvard's connections to slavery.
July 13, 2022	Dr. Mary McLeod Bethune, civil rights activist and educator, becomes the first Black American to be honored by a statue in the National Statuary Hall in the U.S. Capitol. It replaces a statue of the Confederate general Edmund Kirby Smith.

Chapter 1

Uncle Tom's Cabin (1914)

The 1914 film adaptation of Harriet Beecher Stowe's mega-best-selling antislavery novel of social reform, *Uncle Tom's Cabin; or, Life among the Lowly* (1852), was directed by William Robert Daly (born in 1872). The fifty-four-minute, silent, black-and-white film with intertitles—title cards that explain the scene rather than transcribe dialogue—was the first film to star an African American actor in a leading role. Sam Lucas (1848–1916), an actor, songwriter, musician, composer, and according to James Weldon Johnson, "The Grand Old Man of the Negro Stage," played Uncle Tom in the film as he did in numerous stage adaptations (Reynolds 2011, 230–32). Thirty-six years after he last played Tom on the stage, "Lucas was lured out of retirement . . . to recreate his historic role on film and, in the process, set an important milestone in American movie history" (Dunne 2012). Although many African American actors also appear in the film in non-speaking roles and as extras, supporting biracial (called "Mulatto" in the film) roles, including Eliza and George Harris, enslaved house servants, are played by white actors.

The 1914 film relies for the most part on George L. Aikens's popular theatrical adaptation, which captures the melodrama of the novel while also depicting the dehumanization of enslaved African Americans, especially the horror of family separation. It also shows the abolitionist mission to end slavery and the escape routes and stops, known as the Underground Railroad, to Canada, where slavery was abolished in 1834. The film opens with a foreword that reads: "This is the story of an exotic race whose ancestors born beneath a tropic sun were brought to the New World by heartless traders and sold into slavery." The first shot shows a man walking with a cane toward cabins in front of which several enslaved people are dancing. Another title card states: "Many slaves ran away to escape unjust treatment by their masters." This is followed by several men on horses and a reward sign, signed by John Vance, offering one hundred dollars for a runaway slave named Jim Vance. An enslaved man, Jim Vance, hides in a tree as the camera pans down on a handful of men and horses, referred to as a posse, getting ready for the chase. The posse leaves, and Vance comes down from the tree.

On the porch of the house, sit the "kindly" plantation owner Shelby, his wife, and young son and Uncle Tom, the "obedient servant." George Harris, a literate "Mulatto" played by the popular white Broadway actor and film director Irving Cummings (1888–1959), is portrayed on the Shelby Plantation writing to his wife, Eliza Harris, played by Teresa Michelena (1881–1963), that he is escaping to freedom in Canada and that she and the couple's young son, Harry, should join him as soon as they can. She should, of course, also rip up the letter. Eliza learns that her master, who with his mother are introduced as "great favorites on the plantation," and the religious Uncle Tom will be sold away, as Shelby is in dire financial straits. She decides to run away.

She waits until night when she and her son run to the river and after being chased by Marks the lawyer and Tom Loper (the actors' names are now unavailable) and other slave catchers and a slew of bloodhounds, they manage to get to the river. In one of Stowe's most iconic images, preserved in theatrical, cinematic, and commercial iterations, Eliza jumps from ice floe to ice floe while clutching her son; notably, for the first time on film, the river and the ice floes were real. Eliza meets up with George, who's been helped in hiding on the Underground Railroad by Phineas Fletcher, a Quaker, and the couple escapes to safety.

Uncle Tom's fate, however, is tragic. Young Shelby, who cries when Uncle Tom is taken away, promises to buy him when he gets older. Tom is taken on a boat to New Orleans, and on the boat he befriends Little Eva, played by Marie Eline (1902–81), traveling with her aunt Ophelia. When Eva falls off the boat, Uncle Tom dives into the water to save her from a "watery grave." Tom and Eva become friends. He is loving, nurturing, and protective; he is her savior. Eva subsequently asks her father, Augustine St. Clare, to buy Tom, and he does.

While on the St. Clare Plantation, Tom reads to Eva from the Bible and meets Topsy, the young, enslaved girl played in blackface by the white actress Boots Wall. Topsy, depicted with myriad pigtails signifying the racist caricature of a "picaninny," gesticulates wildly and jumps around while Aunt Ophelia accuses and chides her for stealing a scarf. Eva befriends her and teaches her not to steal.

When Eva gets sick, Topsy is inconsolable, having known her first friend. On her deathbed, before she rises to heaven, Eva asks her father to free Tom. He promises to do so, but when St. Clare is stabbed to death, Tom is taken to the slave market and sold down the river to Simon Legree, a stumblingly drunk and racist who owns a Louisiana plantation and many slaves. When

Tom is asked to lash his fellow slave, he doesn't do it, defying Legree for the first time. Tom is beaten for it. And when Legree wants Tom to tell where Cassy, the "Mulatto" woman who's doubly enslaved as his concubine, has gone, Tom refuses and is beaten to death. Then, a young, enslaved man, the man Tom refused to beat, fills the right side of the screen; his gun is the center of the action. Simon Legree is riding home on his horse, and he is shot dead by the enslaved man. The enslaved man's expression is righteously triumphant: justice has finally been served.

As Tom passes away, he sees a spectral, special effects image, of Eva; he will join her in heaven. Young Shelby, now a man, is on his way to buy back Tom, as he promised. Tom's on the ground, arms outstretched like Christ on the cross. Shelby holds him up. Before he dies, Tom says to Shelby, "Young Massah George has come! The Lawd has given me the victory. Glory be to his Name. I die content knowin' you all did not forget old Uncle Tom." Tom is, ultimately, a martyr and Christ figure.

Most moviegoers in 1914 had more exposure to the stage adaptations known as Tom Shows than they had to the novel. Daly's adaptation goes back to the novel in some key ways, though he also relies on some of the Tom Show tropes as well as characters audiences recognized, such as Marks the lawyer, Tom Loper the slave catcher, as well as recognizable actors, like Marie Eline, playing Eva in the movies for the second time, and Irving Cummings as George Harris. But if this film "focused little on the issues central to Stowe—the moral and social implications of slavery for blacks as well as whites" (Lupack 1999, 219), it still exposed the rampant injustice of chattel slavery based on racial subjugation as well as the South's Big Cotton slavocracy consciousness that made so many millionaires in states like Mississippi, where in 1850 half of all American millionaires lived.

The film is framed by an actor playing Abraham Lincoln. It opens with an image of America's sixteenth president (1861–65) looking at Union soldiers scurrying off to battle while he sits down to read *Uncle Tom's Cabin*. The title card reads: "With malice towards none with charity for all"—extrapolated from Lincoln's second inaugural address, given a little more than a month before he was assassinated on April 15, 1865. The film ends with Lincoln delivering words from his Emancipation Proclamation, delivered on January 1, 1863. The title card states: "And upon this act, sincerely believed to be an act of justice, warranted by the Constitution upon military necessity, I invoke the considerate judgment of mankind and the gracious favor of Almighty God."

HISTORICAL BACKGROUND

Harriet Beecher Stowe (1811–96) was born in Hartford, Connecticut, and came from a large, intellectual family. Her father, Lyman Beecher, was a

Calvinist preacher, as was her brother, Henry Ward Beecher, who preached abolitionism at Plymouth Church, a stop on the Underground Railroad in Brooklyn, and was at one time "the most famous man in America" (Applegate 2006, 6). Stowe published her novel *Uncle Tom's Cabin; or, Life among the Lowly* (the original subtitle was *The Man That Was a Thing*) in 1852. It was her first novel, but second work of fiction. *The National Era*, the antislavery national newspaper in Washington, DC, serialized *Uncle Tom's Cabin* in forty-one weekly installments, between June 5, 1852, and April 1, 1853.

Uncle Tom's Cabin, published by John P. Jewett and Company in 1852, was Stowe's impassioned response to personal and political events: to the anguish she experienced after the passing of her young eighteen-month-old son, Charley, the sixth of her seven children, feeling so deeply and personally the horror of family separation of the enslaved. *Uncle Tom's Cabin* foregrounds enslaved characters escaping from the South to Canada from the injustice of chattel slavery, the kind of slavery known to Americans. Enslaved people were bought, sold, and owned until resold, the equivalent of legal property. As a deeply religious Calvinist and an abolitionist, Stowe felt compelled to speak out about the injustice of enslaving people and re-enslaving people who were either born free or had bought their freedom.

Fifteen Southern states were slave states before the Civil War (1861–65). Stowe taught in Cincinnati, Ohio, a free state, and in 1833, she traveled across the Ohio River to Kentucky, a slave state, in the same year that William Lloyd Garrison organized the American Anti-Slavery Society in Philadelphia. There she saw firsthand the horrors of slavery. While teaching in Ohio, Stowe visited abolitionist John Rankin in Ripley, Ohio, and she interviewed several former slaves who had escaped to freedom along the Underground Railroad.

Concurrent with the South's continued threats to secede from the Union and the abolitionist (mostly the North's) antislavery fervor fomenting, Congress passed the second fugitive slave act—the first was passed in 1793. The Fugitive Slave Act of 1850 was part of the Compromise of 1850, approved on September 18, to appease both the Southern slaveholding states and the Northern Free-Soilers, a short-lived political party opposed to slavery. After winning the Mexican American War (1846–48) and achieving its expansionist goal of manifest destiny, the United States acquired new territories from Mexico, including California, Utah, Arizona, New Mexico, western Colorado, and Texas. The five bills of the Compromise were conceived by Whig senator Henry Clay and Democrat senator Stephen Douglas to prosecute and regulate slavery in these states. The law made it mandatory for whites in all states, including those in which slavery was outlawed, to track down, catch, and return any enslaved people who were free or who had escaped.

Considered by some to be one of the most critically misguided pieces of legislation in U.S. history, it proved strikingly cruel, even for a proslavery measure. The law was endorsed by "the long-revered Whig senators Daniel Webster of Massachusetts and Henry Clay of Kentucky. By imposing harsh penalties on Northerners who abetted Blacks attempting to escape from slavery, the law helped preserve the Union by confirming the clause in the Constitution that mandated the return of any 'Person held to Service or Labour in One State' who escaped 'into another'" (Reynolds 2011, 118). Anyone who defied the law and did not assist in capturing a fugitive they encountered or "interfered with the arrest of a slave, or tried to free a slave already in custody was subject to a heavy fine and imprisonment." This law made catching slaves a profitable business.

The act also permitted enslavers to kidnap people and force them into federal court. After a short hearing, a commissioner would determine the status of the person in custody. Commissioners were paid ten dollars upon ruling that a person was enslaved, but only five dollars if they determined that he or she was free. Anyone interfering with the recapture of a fugitive faced prison time and thousands of dollars in fines.

Six years later, in 1857, the Supreme Court went one step further than Congress. In the *Dred Scott v. John F. A. Sandford* decision, the court ruled that, enslaved or free, members of the "unhappy black race separated from the white by indelible marks" were not citizens of the United States. Chief justice Roger Taney delivered the ruling, which many scholars agree was one of the worst in the court's history. Although the words of the Declaration of Independence claim that "all men are created equal," the enslaved African race were not intended to be included. After this ruling, slave catchers and their posses ran roughshod over the South. Approximately fifteen thousand free Blacks immigrated to Canada, Haiti, the British Caribbean, and Africa after the adoption of the 1850 federal law (Reynolds 2011, 163).

As abolitionist activism was growing, the federal government was prevailed upon by those in power to transcend its rightful jurisdiction to defend slavery by any means necessary. This incited such intense resistance in the North that Southerners, with good reason, feared that slavery was at risk of being safeguarded in the Union. And "yet if the Fugitive Slave Act of 1850 was expected to bolster slavery in any concrete fashion, there is little evidence it actually did. In fact, though the Fugitive Slave Act itself marked a low point in American legislative history, its very egregiousness ultimately helped to bring down the barbaric institution it was crafted to defend" (Cobb 2015).

The Fugitive Slave Law, also known as the Bloodhound Law, produced widespread outrage in the North and convinced thousands of Northerners that slavery should be barred from the western territories. Free Blacks formed more vigilance committees throughout the North to be on the lookout for slave catchers and alert the Black community. Concurrent to such regressive, punitive policies like the Fugitive Slave Act, the abolitionist movement continued to gain momentum as progressive forces militated against slavery, helping to clandestinely create escape routes—the Underground Railroad, which operated mostly at night so runaways wouldn't be noticed by the myriad slave catchers who made their living capturing and returning them.

Although the Underground Railroad was not a physical pathway, the existence of it was, in fact, known to many. While the theory that coded quilts with secret messages enabled the enslaved to find routes of escape has been debunked, the 2011 Pulitzer Prize–winning historian Eric Foner's latest book, *Gateway to Freedom: The Hidden History of the Underground Railroad* (2015), revealed substantive evidence brought to light by a small notebook discovered in Columbia University's archives by Madeline Lewis, an undergraduate student there, in 2007. Titled *Record of Fugitives*, by Sydney Howard Gay, the New York–based editor of the *National Anti-Slavery Standard* from 1843 to 1857, it is filled with interviews he conducted with fugitives he helped from 1855 to 1856, including Harriet Tubman, the most prominent "conductor" of the Underground Railroad.

Like the Black abolitionist William Still—the Philadelphia-based Black abolitionist who authored the foundational 1872 book *The Underground Railroad*—Gay interviewed more than two hundred runaways, men, women, and children on their way to Canada, to many of whom he offered refuge in his office. He and Louis Napoleon, "a black porter who worked in Gay's office and was the key operative in meeting fugitives who arrived in New York" took part in "practical abolitionism" in the years leading up to the Civil War and the Emancipation Proclamation (Foner 2015, 130).

Although Josiah Henson, whose autobiography inspired Stowe to write *Uncle Tom's Cabin*, escaped to Canada in 1830 before the stops on the Underground Railroad were in place, he subsequently came back to the United States to aid 118 enslaved people on their journey to freedom in Canada. Journals of the day published information about getaway routes. There were donation parties and bake sales to fund it. There were Come-Outers, abolitionists who left their churches in the 1830s because of the hypocrisy of religious leaders advocating slavery. There were politicians unafraid to advocate for emancipation and help the enslaved to freedom, from Pennsylvania to New England to Canada, by finding safe spaces and "stations" like homes, schools, and church basements. People called "stationmasters" helped protect the enslaved on their journey.

Of the total of four million enslaved people, five thousand fugitives escaped yearly to freedom between 1835 and 1860; 76 percent were younger than age 35, and 89 percent were male (Foner 2015, 136). Slave catchers captured children as well. While Canada offered the formerly enslaved the chance to be involved in civic life and to become jurors, sadly, many of the enslaved would come to realize that their lives in the Northern cities in the United States often weren't much improved. Racism and segregation were rampant, and by and large, they didn't possess the necessary skills to find work. Most enslaved people were illiterate, as teaching them to read and write was against the law, though some whites did so, in hiding, defying the law.

The Quakers, more formally known as the Religious Society of Friends, whose founder George Fox spoke out against slavery as early as 1657, is a pacifist Christian religious group that sheltered the enslaved overnight in their homes, churches, and basements, like the Plymouth Church in Brooklyn Heights, New York, until the enslaved could get to boats and freedom. The eighteenth-century Quakers was the first white American group to publicly reject slavery and aid and abet abolitionism to help the enslaved escape to Canada via the water and land routes of the Underground Railroad. Quakers sometimes "provided cover for fleeing slaves by posing as white slave traders, for example, or offered hiding places on their farms or in townhouses during the daytime. George Washington, shortly before he became president, complained that one of his slaves had disappeared; Washington wrote that he suspected 'a society of Quakers formed for such purposes' had helped the runaway" (Foner 2015, 128).

Stowe claimed that *Uncle Tom's Cabin*, her first novel was "written by God." It is the book that many, including Abraham Lincoln, believed had helped ignite the Civil War. President Lincoln when meeting Stowe in 1862 is said to have said to her, "So this is the little lady who made this big war." Whether true or apocryphal, there's no parallel in American history to suggest that any work of fiction before or since was such a catalytic force.

Stowe's novel sold more than three hundred thousand copies in its first year after publication, one million copies in Great Britain during the same period, and was published in nearly every major language worldwide. It was the best-selling novel of the nineteenth century, and the century's second best-selling book after the Bible. It was the biggest American best seller until Margaret Mitchell's pro-South, in some ways anti-Tom, *Gone with the Wind* (Leslie Fiedler claims that Mitchell's Mammy *is* Uncle Tom) was published in 1936; it sold 1 million copies the year it was published. Stowe also published a "collection of documents and testimony," *A Key to Uncle Tom's Cabin* (1853), which she used to prove the truth of her novel's representation of slavery. Although the novel has had its detractors, including James Baldwin who attacked its sentimentality and racism in his 1949 essay "Everybody's Protest Novel," that it vividly showed the evils of slavery cannot and has never been argued.

DEPICTION AND CULTURAL CONTEXT

The 1914 adaptation of *Uncle Tom's Cabin* was the sixth film adaptation. Sam Lucas was between 68 and 72 when he played Tom, who in the novel is a somewhat younger man (Reynolds 2011, 231). He was the first African

American actor to portray Tom on stage and had been doing so since 1878. Tom in the novel is a strong, powerful, and noble presence, but he is more reactive than proactive, except when he twice defies Simon Legree. When he defies Legree's order to flog his fellow slave, Legree beats him, as he does in the novel. Although the narrative is cohesive and can be followed by a viewer not familiar with the novel, the film's shocking and subversive denouement isn't in the novel and is unique to this adaptation. When the enslaved man Tom refused to beat kills Simon Legree, the character is empowered in ways that revealed screenwriter Edward McWade and William Daly's more progressive racial stance than seen in previous adaptations.

The scene is a radical rewriting of Stowe's novel. The Black-on-white justified violence, and the close-up of the man's anger, would have astounded the viewer in 1914. In no other adaptation does this occur. Linda Williams notes that "the spectacle of black revenge is deeply incendiary—so incendiary, in fact, that some prints of Daly's film (British National Film Archive) omit the scene" (Williams 2001, 234). The contemporary reviews do not mention Legree's murder. In addition to three well-known slave rebellions—those planned by Nat Turner, Gabriel Prosser, and Denmark Vesey—some enslaved people did rebel, resist, and commit violent acts against their oppressors; however, these kinds of stories were rarely reported, represented, or seen in any media.

There is a scene taken from the novel in which Legree catches his enslaved mistress Cassy consoling Tom after Tom refuses to lash an enslaved man. Legree punishes her and sends her to the field, but she is determined to get her freedom even if it means her death. When Legree is brought into the house drunk, she laughs, takes out a gun, and contemplates killing him but, ultimately, has a change of heart. Cassy's "starkly heroic" action is one of the first portrayals on screen of an empowered, enslaved Black woman rebelling against the status quo (Wallace 2000, 12). This film is quite daring and compelling in its depiction of Black and female anger; however, a true American story of an enslaved female's insurrection or resistance is nonexistent. George Siegmann's monstrous Legree provokes hate and fearlessness in his victims and in other whites as well—he is as hideous a caricature as Stowe wrote him.

The film preserves Stowe's antislavery message; a good deal of the time, it portrays slavery from the point of view of the enslaved. Early in the film, there's a close-up shot: a portrait of three Black boys fishing in a boat on a river. The boys are expressive and exuberant; they're happy-go-lucky, innocent children. But a title card instantly reveals that "[m]any slaves ran away to escape unjust treatment by their masters." One horrific example of unjust treatment endemic to slavery was the selling of children away from their parents and separating family members. However, enslavers were aware that doing this caused more enslaved people to run away, in order to reunite with their families; therefore, enslavers had an incentive to keep families together.

Research has shown that the pressure of government foreclosures more than any other reason forced enslavers to break up families (Thornton et al. 2009). In the film, Shelby is forced to sell young Harry, George and Eliza Harris's son, and Tom, who has a family, when Haley, a slave trader, takes over Shelby's mortgage to prevent it from going into foreclosure. Portrayed as a kind owner whose young son is attached to Harry and Tom, Shelby is unhappy and reluctant to sell two of the most beloved and popular enslaved people on his plantation. Shelby's dilemma, therefore, is historically accurate and at the same time melodramatic and faithful to the sentimentality of its source material.

All slaves were not treated equally. Lighter-skinned enslaved people were sometimes treated better than their darker-skinned brethren, in some cases, because they were the offspring of masters. They were more often house servants rather than field slaves. George Harris is referred to as a "mulatto," and although Eliza is a mulatto as well, she is not labeled as such. The device of letters is used to separate the slaves on the plantation—George writes a letter to Eliza to let her know he is running away—and this shows that Stowe's house-enslaved people were able to become literate, unlike most plantation field slaves in general, who were denied literacy, in large part, because it was believed literacy would enable the enslaved to write freedom passes and organize rebellions. Stowe's enslaved do not plan rebellions; however, they do plan their escapes. And Uncle Tom, an enslaved man working in the field, is clearly able to read, as he in the novel and film reads and quotes the Bible.

Reading was sometimes taught as part of religious instruction, which may have been practiced more on plantations run by more lenient enslavers, although writing was not for the most part taught so that the enslaved could not write their pass to freedom. However, there are exceptions, and the poet Phillis Wheatley, the first African American writer to publish a work of poetry, was six years old when her Boston enslavers taught her to write. Overall, fewer than 5 percent of African American children and adults were literate in the 1850s (Carter et al. 2006).

Some enslaved children lived with their biological parents; many, however, were separated from their families. Topsy in the novel and film provides vivid comic relief. Played by an adult white actress in blackface, she is frenetic and irrepressible as the enslaved girl who never knew her parents, who was never nurtured. Michele Wallace notes that Topsy's "characterization seems the most resistant to any kind of evolutionary change, from century to century and medium to medium" (Wallace 2000). The image of an enslaved child is frozen in the character of Topsy. She is the stereotypical wild child who has no sense of morals. She steals and covets pretty sashes and ribbons that she has been denied; she wears a formless sack dress, as many of the enslaved did.

But Topsy has guile and gumption; she rebels against the constraints of the obedient child/slave. She and Eva bond immediately, and Eva tells Topsy that if she loves her back, Topsy will stop stealing; a comedic spin-off film, titled *Topsy and Eva*, starring the Duncan Sisters, a vaudeville act, directed by Del Lord was produced in 1927; the Steven Spielberg of his day, D. W. Griffith directed some scenes. Uptight Ophelia's frustration with Topsy was also fun for viewers to watch as she upbraids and attempts to tame Topsy who appears very much the same in the novel as she does in all the film adaptations. She is incorrigible; slavery has victimized and corrupted her childhood. It isn't her fault that she needs to be tamed; she was created by the "peculiar institution." And she was created by vaudevillian representations of exaggerated comedic blackness.

From its early silent days, Hollywood was responsible for erroneously presenting stories of the Wild West as a domain ruled by white men; in fact, some key players like the frontiersman Jim Beckwourth, featured as a white man in the film *Tomahawk* (1951) were Black. But the western was the most popular genre in silent films, and the audience knew its tropes. Stephen Railton says *Uncle Tom's Cabin* was influenced by westerns: "Like the film's repeated use of the word 'posse' in its titles, what this shoot-out," the one in the mountains pitting George Harris and the other fugitives against the slave catchers "reveals is the influence of Western movies like *The Great Train Robbery* on Daly's script. The popularity of the Tom Shows pulled Stowe's story in the direction of their conventions, and the movie-watching public's appetite for westerns reshaped *Uncle Tom's Cabin*. It is at points like this, where the history of American film and the history of American culture intersect, that show how much *Uncle Tom's Cabin* reveals about both" (Railton 2009).

As Michele Wallace has noted about the earliest days of the film business, "You had some of the most racially progressive people in entertainment." Many knew the value of Stowe's novel. The novel "probably still holds the record as the most frequently filmed American book. By the time the movies came along, American audiences knew *Uncle Tom's Cabin* as well as any primitive tribe knows its ancestral myths" (Railton 2009). Daly's adaptation and the early films may have portrayed some frolicking, but they also accurately depicted slave auction markets and prospective buyers opening the mouths of the enslaved to see their teeth and scrutinizing their limbs to assess their strength. The slave markets are seen as dehumanizing conduits for the separating of families.

The early cinematic adaptations of *Uncle Tom's Cabin* for the most part relied on the Aikens adaptation. The theatrical Tom Shows were ubiquitous in the years after the novel was published. The shows were "part of the common culture at the end of the 19th century and in the early

20th century" (Frick 2012, 31). They were a theatrical phenomenon that "bridged culture, commerce and ideology—they preserved Stowe's abolitionist message" (Ford 2012). The shows and films also revealed Stowe's temperance message—Legree, the brutal slave owner, is an angry drunk who can barely stand up; his exaggerated villainous physicality is synonymous with alcoholism.

On the other hand, the Quakers, the virtuously abstaining good guys wearing the wide-brimmed hats with the small buckle in the front, endeavor to protect the enslaved from slave catchers and their bloodhounds giving them chase. The Quakers are the heroes. They're self-possessed and confident as contrasted with the frenetic, wild-eyed posse of Marks and the other slave catchers. The Quakers' courageous acts of resistance provided refuge for the enslaved, enabling them to safely escape to freedom, and this is historically accurate as shown in the film.

While the film allows its underdog characters to defy unjust laws and express their rage by taking action, its portrayal of slavery is still mitigated by cakewalk dancing, Topsy's wickedness, and the entertainment value that Blacks had been providing for whites since the mid-nineteenth century, when the popular and ubiquitous blackface minstrel shows perpetrated racist stereotypes. These representations aren't faithful to the novel and didn't depict the brutal realities of the arduous labor the enslaved were forced to do. The shows also portrayed a Tom who was older and more acquiescent to his masters' demands than Stowe's Tom, who never sold out any of his race. In fact, he gets whipped for not revealing information he knows. Many contemporary scholars like David S. Reynolds and writers and journalists of color, including Patricia Turner, Gary Younge, and the eminent African American Harvard scholar Henry Louis Gates Jr. have written about how wrongly Tom is construed. Gates, who states that Frederick Douglass was a great fan of Stowe's novel and protagonist, said, "[T]he transformation of Uncle Tom from an almost mythical hero to black people to becoming the ultimate term of race betrayal is one of the great mysteries and ironies in African-American history" (Gates 2007).

The Jamaican-born Black nationalist leader Marcus Garvey (1887–1940) was anti-Tom, as were and are many progressive African American leaders, like Malcolm X who in 1964 famously called Martin Luther King Jr. an Uncle Tom. In 1914, Garvey established the Universal Negro Improvement Association (UNIA), whose motto was "One God, One Aim, One Destiny." The UNIA set up the Negro Factories Corporation (NFC) to help promote economic self-reliance among Blacks. He spearheaded the return to Africa movement and had at least two million followers. The United States entered World War I in 1917, and in 1920, Garvey said, "Negroes fought in Europe for a thing foreign to themselves: Democracy. Now they must fight for themselves. The time for cowardice is past. The old-time Negro has gone, buried with Uncle Tom" (quoted in Van Leeuwen 2000). This is the first time "a public figure used Uncle Tom as a pejorative term" (Railton 2009). Sadly, it stuck, though many are trying to turn the tide and restore Tom's reputation.

Though Hollywood had been making race movies since its inception, *Uncle Tom's Cabin* is the only notable film about African Americans released in 1914. There were ten silent films based on Stowe's *Uncle Tom's Cabin*, three of which—the 1903, 1914, and 1927—are extant. These films provide a baseline representation of enslaved African Americans in films. Also, "It was released two months before Edison's *Great Train Robbery*, making it arguably the first American dramatic film" (Railton 2009). Although these early adaptations preserved the core of Stowe's abolitionist message, it was sometimes watered down. Yet, in a scene not in the novel, but added to Imp-Universal's 1913 adaptation, George Harris is "branded with the 'sizzling initial' of his owner"—something that was actually done to slaves (Frick 2012, 202). Still, enslaved characters had some self-determination in these adaptations.

The brutal and dehumanizing reality and accurate depictions of slavery endeavored to enlighten and inspire audiences—for example, seeing an enslaved person tear up a hundred-dollar-reward poster for returning the fugitive he's running away with—while entertaining them with melodrama, exciting chases, and the comedic caricatures found within the myriad plays, iterations, and commercial products and tie-ins based on her novel. Commercial merchandise, known as Tomitudes, "generated more tie-ins than any other book till the 20th century" (Stevenson 2007).

While the thirteen-minute film released in 1903 does portray in its tableaux a couple of minutes of enslaved African Americans happily dancing, it also shows Eliza escaping on the ice floes after learning her son would be sold away from her and Uncle Tom defying a master's orders to whip a fellow enslaved man. Eliza and Tom have a certain dignity and rebelliousness that mitigate the horrors of slavery. Vitagraph's 1910 adaptation, the first three-reeler, differs not only from Stowe's novel but from the previous film version in a few ways: Little Harry is given to Tom when they're both sold, and most significantly, Tom helps Eliza escape, revealing agency as well as "a Tom more subversive than his predecessors." As a consequence, LeGree (his name is spelled differently in this adaptation) beat him and compelled him to "join the search with bloodhounds" to find and return Eliza (Railton 2009).

Slaves escaping to freedom happened most often at night; escaping during the day was fraught with the ferocious bloodhounds slave catchers utilized. There are many violent scenes in the novel of bloodhounds—an advertisement of a theatrical version in 1880 shows Eliza being stalked by bloodhounds attacking and punishing enslaved Blacks attempting to run away. There are myriad references to and images of the dogs in the film. When the slave catcher in the film is prevailed upon to chase Eliza, he says, "I'll put the bloodhounds on her track: I'll catch her."

Cuban bloodhounds, in particular, were "bred and celebrated for their ferocity and tenacity in subduing black rebellions. They were tools of surveillance and fear, helping to annihilate indigenous populations and solidify the expansion of American capitalism through slavery. These dogs' superhuman biological systems were bred to sense race" (Yingling and Parry 2016). Some police guides even promoted the discriminatory popular theory that African Americans had a unique smell and produced a stronger scent than whites.

The U.S. government also used bloodhounds to fight Native Americans, in particular, in 1835–42, when "the US government brought them to what is now Florida to fight the Seminole Nation, which comprised a collection of runaway slaves and indigenous peoples who united to contest the US government's imperial expansion" (Yingling and Parry 2016). By the 1840s, the practice of keeping "slave dogs" was widespread. "Newspaper advertisements—like one in the *West Tennessee Democrat* describing the 'Finest dogs for catching negroes'—document the rise of professional slave hunting. Trackers interbred Cuban hounds with local dogs as slave hunting became a profitable venture for white men throughout the South" (Yingling and Parry 2016).

Ex-slave narratives and the oral tradition mention the ubiquity of dogs as weapons. But the dogs also trailed and attacked white Union soldiers escaping from Confederate prisons. These experiences gave Northerners a new paradigm for understanding the horrors of Southern slavery. In 1894, the Tennessee-based newspaper *Rideau Record* lauded bloodhounds as "indispensable to the complete equipment of a good police department"—particularly, the "practice of using canines to terrorize black Americans" (Doddington 2012). Bloodhounds were used even after slavery was abolished. Police dogs were used during the civil rights movement—that is, the "dogs of Birmingham."

Trainers agreed that "hounds work better when trained to one particular scent" and advocated racialized dog training in which only Black subjects were used to train bloodhound puppies to trail human subjects. The South had a virulent obsession with bloodhounds, and they troll through *Uncle Tom's Cabin*. As late as 1905, Mississippi allocated state funds to train police dogs to hunt fugitives; a concerned citizen named Edward Day warned society would revert to "barbarism" if such policies went unchecked (Doddington 2012).

Interviews with former slaves documented in the 1930s reiterate the fact that, despite the numerous threats from wild animals, it was the use of trained dogs that most frightened them. A barking bloodhound was sometimes the last sound an enslaved person would hear. That people were forced to face death by vicious dogs trained to kill "aroused sympathies against slavery more than philosophical or legal arguments could do. By violently enforcing slavery's regimes of racism and profit, revealing the depravity of the enslavers and the humanity of the enslaved, and enraging abolitionists internationally, hounds were central to the rise and fall of slavery in the Americas" (Yingling and Parry 2016). They're accurately depicted as weaponized accomplices to the slave catchers in the film.

The 1927 adaptation, directed by Harry A. Pollard and starring James B. Lowe (1879–1963), allocated in its budget $20,000, a record price, for a team of English Ledburn bloodhounds whose ancestry could be traced back to the slave days in Virginia. The film, one of the most expensive films of the silent era, was ambitious, though quite flawed, and its antislavery message more watered down than before. It conveyed sentimental images of the Old South like riverboats on the Mississippi as well as depicting the political/historical context of American soldiers righting a terrible wrong. Sixty years had passed since the Civil War ended, but the story of the end of slavery was one that remained inflammatory to the South, and the studio executives and Pollard, who had played Uncle Tom in blackface in a 1913 adaptation, had no idea about the South's lingering resentment over losing the Civil War.

This inability to recognize that bitterness would haunt the film and doom its chance of finding widespread success (Williams 2001, 463). As production dragged on, one of the main concerns of Universal studio head Carl Laemmle had been to not offend the white South. Southern papers protested that any remake of Stowe's novel was "a direct insult to the old true South" (http://utc.iath.virginia.edu). A few controversial scenes, including one at a slave auction showing an infant being sold away from her mother, were deleted after studio screenings (Frick 2012, 212). But in the North, the movie was the sixth most popular film of the year.

Although the 1914 film set the precedent for casting Tom with an African American actor, Eliza, George, Cassy, and even Topsy are played by white actors with dark eyes. Eliza was played by Marguerite Fischer (1886–1975), Pollard's wife. Hollywood's rule was casting whites in mulatto roles. The concept of a biracial person was problematic in terms of representation because miscegenation was at this time a very great and palpable fear on the part of many Americans. George Siegmann (1882–1928), who played the power-mad mulatto, Silas Lynch, in *The Birth of a Nation*, appears as Simon Legree. Paul Robeson was considered for Tom, but the Black actor Charles Gilpin, who had created the part of Emperor Jones, was hired and then fired because of creative differences with Pollard. Pollard and other studio executives found Gilpin's portrayal too aggressive and reportedly ordered Gilpin to be meek and submissive in his interpretation (Williams 2001, 383). Pollard claimed a submissive Tom would be palatable for audiences and that an edgier one would alienate the audience. James B. Lowe got the role. He was forty years old and robust, more like Stowe's Tom than any other film Tom had been. His performance was measured and unshowy.

The 1927 film focuses more on Eliza's escape than it does on Uncle Tom's troubles. It ends with a scene showing Union general William T. Sherman's soldiers arriving (Birdoff 1947, 119). On horseback, they flood the streets, bringing the word of freedom. Nearly a hundred Black extras rejoice in the streets, and the divided house of America is coming back together. The title card says, "And the song they sang was a new song of bondage broken and chains forever lifted." This scene appears to be a direct response to the Ku Klux Klan gallop to the rescue of the whites in D. W. Griffith's *The Birth of a Nation* (1915).

And then there were anti-Tom tomes and shows, most horrifically notable, Thomas Dixon's *The Clansman: A Historical Romance of the Ku Klux Klan* (1905) set during Reconstruction, and its film adaptation, *The Birth of a Nation*, Griffith's virulently racist, controversial, though artistically innovative film valorizing the Lost Cause of the Confederacy. It pits a Union family against a Confederate one, portraying free Blacks as criminals. Its African American antagonist (played by a white actor in blackface) is a sexual predator who kills a white woman. Its release generated protests by Black advocacy groups, and it spurred a resurgence of the KKK. The *Clansman* was Dixon's second volume in his *Clan Trilogy*. It "began growing in his imagination while he was watching a theatrical performance of *Uncle Tom's Cabin*. *The Leopard's Spots*, the first novel he wrote, even contains several characters from Stowe's novel" (Railton 2009).

Stowe's novel was inspired in part by a former enslaved man, Josiah Henson, who mentions his wife's fear of escaping, risking being "hunted down by bloodhounds" in his best-selling autobiography, *The Life of Josiah Henson, Formerly a Slave, Now an Inhabitant of Canada, as Narrated by Himself*, published in 1849. Henson (1789–1883), born in Maryland, "experienced a religious conversion at eighteen" and like Stowe's Tom preached to other slaves (Reynolds 2011, 105). Also, like Tom, he was treated kindly by his master, Isaac Riley, until due to financial hardship, Riley was forced to sell him. Henson was taken by boat toward New Orleans and then sold to a plantation in the Deep South. There he faced and served the master he referred to as R., about whom Henson said, "Coarse and vulgar in his habits, unprincipled and cruel in his general deportment, and especially addicted to the vice of licentiousness" (quoted in Reynolds 2011, 104).

Like George Harris, Henson escaped to Canada and freedom in 1830. And like Tom, he remained firmly rooted in and abided by his Christian honor and refusal to beat a fellow slave, which "presented a sign of strength, not weakness" (Reynolds 2011, 106). To defend her novel's accurate portrayal of slavery and her enslaved characters, Stowe wrote and published her *Key to Uncle Tom's Cabin: Presenting the Original Facts and Documents upon Which the Story Is Founded, Together with Corroborative Statements*

Verifying the Truth of the Work in 1853. In it, she claimed that Uncle Tom was a composite character, in part, inspired by Henson.

One historian suggests that the intensely religious protagonist Thomas, an enslaved man who preaches to his peers, of Richard Hildreth's novel *Memoirs of Archy Moore* is Uncle Tom's prototype (Reynolds 2011, 106); however, this Thomas kills the master who killed his wife and leaves the plantation and Christianity, unlike Tom. Another possible inspiration is Thomas Magruder whose obituary in the *Saturday Evening Post* was headlined "DEATH OF THE ORIGINAL UNCLE TOM." Magruder was a deeply religious Methodist, for whom a future governor of Indiana, Noah Noble, built a cabin known as Uncle Tom's Cabin.

And Stowe in her *Key to Uncle Tom's Cabin* also reveals that her novel draws inspiration for the character of the enslaved "mulatto" runaway, George Harris, from *Narratives of the Sufferings of Lewis and Milton Clarke* (1846), brothers, and in particular, Harris's euphoria when he gets to Canada safely echoes Lewis Clarke's. Other elements from this book that she mines are stories of mothers murdering their children to spare them from slavery and her depiction of Legree's drunkenness (Reynolds 2011, 111). Tom is a fiercely moral believer. He is not an acquiescent sellout, as the Tom Shows signified, and he is not a traitor to his race. Stowe's and Daly's Uncle Tom is a defiant hero.

CONCLUSION

The 1914 film adaptation is radical and subversive insofar as it portrays Black-on-white violence, something not out of Stowe's novel but invented for the adaptation. The film charts an American consciousness confessing its racist past and doesn't spare in its brutality. Lucas as Uncle Tom is a noble presence. He's tall, and his posture is never less than perfectly erect; his beautiful hands display long, elegant fingers. This Tom is not a yes man. Sam Lucas's Tom defies Legree in two explicit ways: he refuses to flog a fellow slave, and he refuses to give Legree information about Cassy's whereabouts. He is a devoutly Christian man who famously in the novel tells his "owner" that he may own his body, but only God owns his soul. He is a Christ figure who dies for the sins of the American people who perpetrated chattel slavery, which led to harshly unfair Jim Crow laws, brutal policing policies, and rampant racism against African Americans.

The film was chosen in 2012 to be included in the National Film Registry of the Library of Congress and cited, according to Susan King, as being "culturally, historically, or aesthetically significant." In addition to that, it is a captivating and subversive story of a martyred enslaved African American man who, in fact, defied his master by being true to and prioritizing his righteousness and religious beliefs.

FURTHER READING

Applegate, Debby. 2006. *The Most Famous Man in America: The Biography of Henry Ward Beecher*. New York: Doubleday.
Birdoff, Harry. 1947. *The World's Greatest Hit: Uncle Tom's Cabin*. New York: S.F. Vanni.
Blaisdell, George. 1914. "Uncle Tom's Cabin Review." *The Moving Picture World*, August 22, 1914.
Carter, Susan B., Scott Sigmund Gartner, Michael R. Haines, Alan L. Olmstead, Richard Sutch, and Gavin Wright. 2006. *Historical Statistics of the United States*. New York: Cambridge University Press.
Cobb, James. 2015. "One of American History's Worst Laws Was Passed 165 Years Ago." *Time*, September 18, 2015.
DeCanio, Stephen J. 1990. "'Uncle Tom's Cabin': A Reappraisal." *Centennial Review* 34, no. 4: 587–93. www.jstor.org/stable/23738772.
Dennison, Stephanie, and Song Hwee Li, eds. 2012. *Remapping World Cinema: Identity, Culture and Politics in Film*. New York: Wallflower Press.
Doddington, David. 2012. "Slavery and Dogs in the Antebellum South." *Sniffing the Past: Dogs and History*, February 23, 2012.
Dunne, Susan. 2012. "1914 '*Uncle Tom's Cabin*' among Movies Added to National Film Registry." *Hartford Courant*, December 19, 2012.
Fieldler, Leslie A. 1979. *The Inadvertent Epic: From Uncle Tom's Cabin to Roots*. New York: Simon and Schuster.
Foner, Eric. 2015. *Gateway to Freedom: The Hidden History of the Underground Railroad*. New York: Norton.
Ford, Jane. 2012. "The Story of *Uncle Tom's Cabin* Spread from Novel to Theater and Screen." *UVA Today*, November 12, 2012.
Frick, John W. 2012. *Uncle Tom's Cabin on the American Stage and Screen*. New York: Palgrave Macmillan.
Gates, Henry Louis, Jr. 2007. "Gates Takes a New Look at Uncle Tom." Interview by Neal Conan. *Talk of the Nation*, NPR/WNYC, February 19, 2007.
Goble, Alan, ed. 1999. *The Complete Index to Literary Sources in Film*. London: Bowker-Saur.
Goodheart, Adam. 2015. "The Secret History of the Underground Railroad." *The Atlantic*. Review of Eric Foner's 2015 *Gateway to Freedom: The Hidden History of the Underground Railroad*.
Gordon-Reed, Annette. 2011. "'Uncle Tom's Cabin' and the Art of Persuasion." *New Yorker*, June 6, 2011.
"Harriet Beecher Stowe House." n.d. Accessed July 26, 2022. https://www.nps.gov/people/harriet-beecher-stowe.htm.
Henson, Josiah. 2017. *The Life of Josiah Henson, Formerly a Slave, Now an Inhabitant of Canada, as Narrated by Himself*. Reseda: Enhanced Media.
King, Susan. 2012. "National Film Registry Selects 25 Films for Preservation." *Los Angeles Times*, December 19, 2012.
Lupack, Barbara. 1999. *Nineteenth Century Women at the Movies: Adapting Classic Women's Fiction to Film*. Madison: Popular Press.
Newby-Alexander, Cassandra L. 2017. *Virginia Waterways and the Underground Railroad*. American Heritage Series. Charleston, SC: Arcadia Publishing.

Ohlheiser, Abby. 2013. "Most of America's Silent Films Are Lost Forever." *The Atlantic*, December 4, 2013.

Parry, Tyler D., and Charlton W. Yingling. 2020. "Slave Hounds and Abolition in the Americas." *Past & Present* 246, no. 1 (February): 69–108.

Railton, Stephen. 2009. "Uncle Tom's Cabin & American Culture: A Multi-Media Archive." http://utc.iath.virginia.edu/.

Reynolds, David S. 2011. *Mightier Than the Sword: Uncle Tom's Cabin and the Battle for America*. New York: W. W. Norton.

Schermerhorn, Calvin. 2009. "The Everyday Life of Enslaved People in the Antebellum South." *OAH Magazine of History* 23, no. 2(April): 31–36. Antebellum Slavery. Oxford University Press on behalf of Organization of American Historians.

Schuessler, Jennifer. 2016. "Words from the Past Illuminate a Station on the Path to Freedom." *New York Times*, January 15, 2016.

Scott, Emmett J. *2018. Scott's Official History of the American Negro in the World War*. London: Forgotten Books.

Simeo Starkey, Brando. 2013. "Jim Crow, Social Norms, and the Birth of *Uncle Tom*." *Alabama Civil Rights & Civil Liberties Law Review* 3, no. 2 (March): 69–99.

Stevenson, Louise. 2007. "Virtue Displayed: The Tie-Ins of *Uncle Tom's Cabin*." Paper presented at the Harriet Beecher Stowe Center, Hartford, CT, August 2007.

Talbot, Paul. 2009. *Mondo Mandingo: The Falconhurst Books and Films*. New York: iUniverse.

Thornton, Mark, Mark A. Yanochik, and Bradley T. Ewing. 2009. "Selling Slave Families down the River: Property Rights and the Public Auction." *Independent Review* 14, no. 1 (Summer): 71–79.

Turner, Patricia A. 1994. *Ceramic Uncles & Celluloid Mammies: Black Images & Their Influences on Culture*. Charlottesville: University of Virginia Press.

Van Leeuwen, David. 2000. "Marcus Garvey and the Universal Negro Improvement Association." htttp://nationalhumanitiescenter.org/tserve/twenty/tkeyinfo/garvey.htm.

Wallace, Michele. 2000. "Uncle Tom's Cabin: Before and after the Jim Crow Era." *TDR* 44, no. 1 (Spring): 136–56. MIT Press. https://www.jstor.org/stable/1146824.

Williams, Linda. 2001. *Playing the Race Card: Melodramas of Black and White from Uncle Tom to O.J. Simpson*. Princeton: Princeton University Press.

Yingling, Charlton, and Tyler Parry. 2016. "The Canine Terror." *Jacobin*, May 19, 2016.

Younge, Gary. "Don't Blame Uncle Tom." *The Guardian*, March 29, 2002.

Chapter 2

Mandingo (1975)

The lurid and sensational hit film *Mandingo* (1975), based on the best-selling Falconhurst series of books by Kyle Onstott, reveals a damning look at slavery. It is one of the first films to depict slavery from the enslaved's point of view and to feature explicit interracial sex. Its reputation has a fascinating arc. It was considered when first released an exploitative film; now, it's considered to be an audacious film that shows Black resistance and rebellion against slavery.

The film is set in the 1840s, but it is very much a product of its time, as it encodes Black empowerment. In 1975, the Black Panthers and the slogan of Black Power were ubiquitous media images.

Mandingo, set on a decrepit plantation, tells the story of Hammond, called Ham (Perry King), an enslaver's son who is in love with an enslaved woman, Ellen (Brenda Sykes) and angry at and won't sleep with his wife, Blanche (Susan George) when he finds out she isn't a virgin. It's revealed that she has had sex with her brother, Charles. Blanche forces Mede (Ken Norton), Ham's Mandingo prizefighter, to be her lover. She threatens the fighter by saying she'll claim he raped her if he doesn't sleep with her. After Blanche gives birth to a Black baby, Ham in a vicious rage poisons her, beats Mede, throws him in a vat of boiling water, and sticks a pitchfork through him.

Dino De Laurentiis (1919–2010), the prolific Italian American producer of two Federico Fellini films in Italy in the 1950s, moved to the United States in 1976 and produced megahits like *Serpico* (1973) and *Death Wish* (1974). He bought the film rights to Kyle Onstott's *Mandingo* (the Falconhurst book series, the first of which was published in 1958 and taken more seriously in Italy than in the United States). De Laurentiis sought the heavyweight champion Muhammed Ali to play Mede; Ali turned down the role, as it was at cross purposes with his belief in Islam (Talbot 2009, 97).

Films in the Blaxploitation genre, generally referencing films made by Black filmmakers exploring Black lifestyles and appealing to a Black audience, had been performing well at the box office since the early 1970s. *Mandingo* was targeted for a Black audience, and Paramount committed to distributing the film. De Laurentiis claimed that *Mandingo* was intended to "reach beyond the sentimentalized South of other films with uncompromising honesty and realism to show the true brutalizing nature of slavery" (quoted in DeVos, 2013, 9).

The film was ridiculed and disparaged by some as immoral, indecent, campy, and melodramatic. It was criticized for showing sexually explicit interracial sex. The critic Roger Egbert called it "racist trash" (1975). The *New York Times* critic, Vincent Canby, called it "hardcore pornography" (1975). Charles Shere of the *Oakland Tribune* claimed the film showed the "racialized sexual exploitation" of slavery (1975); it was, in fact, "the first film to affirm the constituent nature of sexual exploitation in American slavery" (DeVos 2013, 14). Campbell Jr. juxtaposes the film with D. W. Griffith's *The Birth of a Nation* (1915), claiming that "Griffith's concept of white nobility and black bestiality had simply been reversed." But audiences flocked to it, making it "the eighteenth highest grossing film of the year" (DeVos 2013, 6).

The poster for the film was designed by the artist who designed the poster for *Gone with the Wind*, although it portrays an interracial couple. It's ironic that *Gone with the Wind* is referenced, as some have noted, it's "the anti–*Gone with the Wind*" take on the antebellum South. Whereas *Gone with the Wind* romanticizes the South and portrays Tara as a plantation in all its splendor, Falconhurst is rundown and seedy. The enslaved in *Gone with the Wind* are content with their lot, and they have no inner life or life outside those they serve. Cicero and Mem in *Mandingo* are militant men who militate against their forced oppression.

The screenplay by Norman Wexler, who among other works wrote the highly regarded social justice–themed films *Joe* (1970), *Serpico* (1973), and *Saturday Night Fever* (1977), reveals substantive character development and a boundary-crossing interracial love story. Wexler claimed he improved the source material, Onstott's novel, in several ways. He removed the child that Blanche gives birth to as a result of her brother, Charles's impregnating her, and he provided more dimension to Onstott's characters. Mem was weak and submissive in the book, but Wexler rewrote the character as an enlightened, proud Black man who secretly learns to read and ultimately rebels violently against his enslavement. In the film, Mem is beaten for reading; in the book, he's idle and steals and drinks alcohol (Talbot 2009, 101). Wexler wanted to show the brutal reality of slavery, not romanticize it.

The adroit direction was done by Richard Fleischer (1915–2006), whose eclectic oeuvre includes *The Vikings* (1958), *Fantastic Voyage* (1966), *Doctor Doolittle* (1967), *The Boston Strangler* (1968), *Barabbas* (1971), and *Soylent Green* (1973). Fleischer researched slavery; he fiercely prepared for his previous historical films, *The Vikings* and *Barabbas* (Talbot 2009, 103). He said, "The whole slave story has been lied about, covered up and romanticized so much that I thought it really had to stop. The only way to stop was to be as brutal as I could possibly be, to show how these people suffered. I'm not going to show you them suffering backstage—I want you to look at them" (1976).

Ken Norton (1943–2013), the 1978 World Boxing Council (WBC) heavyweight champion boxer, made his film debut playing the enslaved Mandingo fighter Mede (short for Ganymede). The film was a box office success and made Norton an "instant sex symbol, an instant hero" (Norton 1977). It was one of the biggest hits of 1975. The May 19, 1975 *Box* reported that "the film grossed $20,717.00 opening day at the Criterion and RKO 86th Street theaters in New York City, setting house records" (AFI 1975).

Dave Kehr reevaluated the film for the *New York Times* in 2008 and called it a "thinly veiled Holocaust film," and "Fleischer's 1975 slavery epic as the director's last great crime film, in which the role of the faceless killer is played by an entire social system" (2008).

The film critic Keser calls *Mandingo* Fleischer's best film and one in which he "confronts all three hot wires of American history—race, class and gender." He calls it,

> [a] remarkable and deeply political film, long championed by Robin Wood as "the greatest film about race ever made in Hollywood." Without sentimentality or official pieties ... to appropriate a phrase by John Berger from another context, *Mandingo* uniquely serves as "the eye we cannot shut," the persistent vision of competing powers—the slave's physical strength (and by extension sexual potency) against the master's sovereign power to define reality and decide life or death. (2015)

The film was shot at the Houmas House Plantation in Darrow, Louisiana, and the Ashland Plantation, which is also known as the Ashland-Belle Helene Plantation, also in Darrow. Falconhurst, a decrepit plantation in a state of disrepair, is owned by the elderly and ailing slave owner Warren Maxwell (James Mason). The film opens with a long shot of a distressed plantation house. Muddy Waters's blues song is played—"Born in this time to never be free. Happiness is one thing I have never known"—while enslaved people walk toward the plantation house led by a man in a white shirt. Waters "played a key role in the development of electric blues and rock-and-roll and was the greatest contemporary exponent of the influential Mississippi Delta blues style" (Palmer 1983).

A slave trader, Brownlee (Paul Benedict) is inspecting a Black man's fingers, mouth, and backside and asks, "How much for this wench and sucker? Can't get more than $700 in New Orleans." His backside is checked for hemorrhoids. There's a close-up view of the enslaved's faces showing their horror. Maxwell asks Brownlee whether he has altered any of the enslaved; Brownlee says he hasn't. Cicero (Ji-Tu Cumbuka) has an R branded on his arm for having attempted to run away. Maxwell offers $1,500 for three; they're sold for $2,500. Referring to Cicero, Brownlee says, "This one might last seven years." Maxwell tells him to chain "the three bucks" in the barn.

Maxwell has rheumatism, and he's told that his pain will be relieved if he keeps his feet on a young Black boy lying at his feet—an image that is seen throughout the film. The boy is forced to stay in one place. Young boys also wave large leaves fanning the white family while they are dining.

Warren and his son, Hammond, known as Ham, live on the plantation without significant others; the elder urges his son to marry and have a son. Ham enjoys sex with enslaved women and has an intimate relationship with one of them. He marries his cousin, Blanche (Susan George) and is furious when he realizes she is not a virgin. In Falconhurst, the enslaved women are called "wenches," babies are referred to as "suckers," and all desires are called "cravins." In one moving scene, Ellen tells Ham she is having his baby, and she asks him if he will let it be free. He resists at first, and she implores him, saying it's especially important that a son has freedom and is able to learn to read. After thinking it over, he agrees to her request. Unfortunately, after Ellen is brutally beaten by Blanche—her rage fueled by jealousy and alcohol—she is pushed downstairs by her and, thus, loses the baby.

This depiction of the aggressive, violent Southern white woman is surprising for films up to this point but foreshadows the cruel and sadistic Mistress Epps (Sarah Paulson) in *12 Years a Slave* (2013) whose jealousy of her husband's lust for the enslaved woman, Patsey, drives her to abuse. The promise of the white man, father of a biracial love child, granting his child freedom is foiled by his vicious wife. Ham has an opportunity to right the wrongs of his father and his society but is denied the young Black woman with whom he has a love affair.

Cicero, the Mandingo fighter, is inspired by Maxwell's personal servant, Agamemnon, or Mem (Richard Ward) who has taught him about freedom—a subject the enslaved were forbidden to discuss. Cicero leads an aborted uprising against white enslavers. He is captured, and at Cicero's hanging, Mede, who took part in the revolt, begins to question slavery, having until then benefited from and appreciated Ham's preferential treatment. Although the revolt is thwarted, the scenes of the enslaved fighting back, fighting for the human rights denied them, land powerfully. Explosive Black rage is expressed.

Ji-Tu Cumbuka said that it was "really hard for him filming at the plantation that had actually been used as a breeding plantation for slaves and that had a hanging tree" (used in the film for his character's hanging) (quoted by Talbot 2009, 125).

Blanche's explicit sex scene with Mede shows a side of slavery not portrayed on film before. A white woman having sex with a Black man was considered miscegenation, or interracial sexual relations, which was outlawed by the Motion Picture Production Code of 1930, now known as the Hays Production Code, named for Will H. Hays. This code was a set of moral guidelines designed for the industry to censor sexual and graphic content in films and images of films released by major film studios from 1930 to 1968. In 1968, the Motion Picture Association of America (MPAA) established a new ratings system for parents to know what content was appropriate for children and teenagers. *Mandingo* was rated R, restricted to viewers aged seventeen and older; however, in another time, it would have been rated X for its pornographic and sexually explicit content.

The fight scenes of Mede against his opponent are brutal and show that the enslaved fighter was used profitably as entertainment and sport for the white man's pleasure.

Ham, whose limp renders him handicapped, marvels at Mede's strength when he cuts down a giant tree. The Black man is objectified in other ways too.

Mandingo looks at racial hatred and Black rage squarely in the eye. The darkness and cynicism of the depiction of slavery in *Mandingo* leaves little room for reconciliation between whites and Blacks. Urban Black audiences loved it; the critics when the film was first released not so much.

Ham has a limp due to a pony accident when he was six, after his mother died. Lucrezia Borgia (Lillian Hayman), the house servant and cook, has had twenty-four children. Mason's enslaved don't have religion, he says. He believes they'll think they're as good as white folks once they become religious. "Abolitionists believe slaves are as good as whites," Mason says, but he claims that, "God has ordained slavery."

Cicero, after his rebellion is thwarted, says that in Africa, "[w]e're born free, masters of our own selves and of the forests and rivers. . . . Don't you think deep down that peckerwood don't know we're as human as he is? Why does he keep us from reading and learning and religion?" Cicero goes on to say, "You know what's done with enslaved people who can read—put out an eye, one not two, a slave is hung up on rope by his feet as punishment for reading."

Price & Birch Exchange is where slaves and mules are for sale: a woman and her three children; the women are topless, and men are roped together at the neck. A woman with a German accent puts her hand on Mede's crotch. She's a widow looking for pleasure; she's willing to pay up $4,000 for him, but Ham outbids her. He wants the Mandingo to fight and to breed.

Maxwell says Cicero is trouble and needs to be tamed and that there have been too many slavery uprisings, especially in Georgia and South Carolina. He says that people are still talking about Nat Turner, and abolitionist newspapers give people ideas.

Ham puts Mede in a hot bath; Warren says, "Them Romans always salted their slaves." Then Mede is fighting.

Cicero steals a gun and shoots and wounds four white people. Mede catches Cicero but lets him go when Cicero calls him a dog, "When they say fetch, you fetch." Cicero is captured and before being lynched, he says, "I'd rather die than be a slave—you were oppressed in your own land. This is just as much my land as it is your'n—and after you hang me, kiss my ass." The drum beats. The white men listen intently, their expressions guilty with complicity.

The fight in New Orleans is an epic battle between Mede and Topaz (Duane Allen)—champion of the island of Jamaica. It's a fight to the finish, no-holds-barred. Ham says, "I yield the fight, stop it," Mede wins—looks like he killed Topaz; he gets offered $10,000 for Mede, but Ham won't sell. It's a heartbreaking scene of enslaved men saying good-bye to each other, as some are about to be sold. In a vicious rage after Blanche gives birth to a Black baby, and in the most horrific scene, Hammond beats Mede, throws him in a vat of boiling water, and sticks a pitchfork through him.

DRUM (1976)

Also based on a Falconhurst novel by Kyle Onstott, the sequel to *Mandingo* again stars Ken Norton; he's a biracial enslaved man named Drum. Warren Oates plays Hammond Maxwell, who's in charge of the plantation. Also adapted by Norman Wexler and directed by Steve Carver (1945–2021)—an action film director of films, including Pam Grier's female gladiator film *The Arena* (1974). Grier plays an enslaved woman named Regine. The poster claimed that "*Mandingo* lit the fuse—*Drum* is the Explosion," and the tagline claimed that "The White Men Wanted a Stud to Breed Slaves. The White Women Wanted Much More." It features interracial lesbian as well as interracial incestual sex. A white woman practically rapes Drum.

The incoherent story follows a pampered mistress in Cuba who, after a lesbian relationship with Tamboura, becomes a New Orleans whorehouse madam. The film is filled with nudity, sex, and vulgar language. A homosexual enslaver talks obsessively about the enslaved fornicating. He also talks about castrating them if they do not behave.

The film opens with a haunting blues song that includes the lyrics, "They want me to cry and moan, they say they want me to tell my story one time before I die." Beautifully illustrated black and red woodcuttings, African images of a slave ship, African warriors, and various other slavery images flash across the screen. A "Slave Wanted" poster appears, and the voice-over narrator explains that the Port of Savanna in Cuba was once a place for free men and women but that now it is a slave market. Yaphet Kotto plays Blaise, an enslaved man who plans a revolt, but as in *Mandingo*, after many gunshots, it is thwarted.

Drum received an R rating; it's explicit. And Lillian Hayman appears, as she did in *Mandingo*, as the cook Lucrezia Borgia. Similar to *Mandingo*, the main theme here is white lust for Black bodies. Its humor is raunchy, and ironically, the film "celebrates what it ostensibly condemns (slavery and decadence in the antebellum South)" (*After Dark*, quoted by Talbot 2009, 210). Slavery is sexualized, and the picture of humanity, Black and white, is quite depraved.

HISTORICAL BACKGROUND

Kyle Onstott and the Falconhurst Novels

In 1957, the seventy-year-old Southern dog breeder Kyle Onstott, wrote his first novel, *Mandingo*. It was published by Denlinger's, a small Virginia-based publisher. Inspired by his adopted son, Philip, an anthropologist whose focus was on West African tribes, Onstott constructed the world of "Falconhurst"—an Alabama plantation specializing in "breeding physically superior slaves chosen exclusively from descendants of the Mandingo people (or more properly, Mandinka), a historic ethnic group inhabiting large portions of West Africa" (DeVos 2013, 4).

The novel, a "publishing phenomenon . . . created a whole subgenre of pulp known as 'slave fiction.' Five million copies were sold in the soft cover edition." Thirteen follow-up novels set in Falconhurst were published over the next thirty years (Talbot 2009, xi). The book was adapted by Jack Kirkland as an eponymous Broadway play in 1961 and starred Franchot Tone as Maxwell, who bred enslaved people, and Dennis Hopper as his son. It opened on May 22, 1961, and closed on May 27. after eight performances and a negative *New York Times* review by Howard Taubman, who wrote, "At a time when insight and wisdom are desperately wanted, *Mandingo* offers only a shabby, coarse, surface treatment of slavery." It's one of the few Broadway shows depicting slavery besides *Amazing Grace* (2015) about John Newton, the British ex–slave trader who wrote the beloved protest hymn "Amazing Grace." Jeremy O'Harris's 2019 play, *Slave Play*, is not, in fact, about slavery. It's a contemporary story about interracial role-playing couples attending "Antebellum Sexual Performance Therapy."

Black Power

The Black Power Movement (BPM) was an "all-encompassing movement that called for political, economic, and cultural changes" in the Black community (Freeland 2009, 6). The revolutionary movement expressing racial pride, aligned with the Black Arts Movements, gained momentum in the 1960s and 1970s due to several key factors, including Malcolm X's Black nationalism in the 1950s and 1960s; the independence achieved by many African countries; and Patrice Lumumba's rise in the Congo. The struggle for self-determination and economic self-reliance and to finally overcome white domination by mobilizing, demonstrating, and planning collective action was more urgent than ever (Freeland 2009, 6). The Godfather of Soul James Brown's expression of Black Power was his 1968 anthemic song, "Say It Loud, I'm Black and I'm Proud" cowritten by Alfred "Pee Wee" Ellis. "Black Is Beautiful" was a popular slogan.

Brutally graphic films about slavery released at the time include the Italian-made film *Passion Plantation* a.k.a. *Black Emmanuelle, White Emmanuelle* (1976), about a sadistic enslaver's daughter, written and directed by Mario Pinzauti, and *Goodbye Uncle Tom* (1971), the disturbing and graphic shockumentary directed by Gualtiero Jacopetti and Franco Prosperi. Filmed in Haiti with the cooperation of the Haitian dictator, "Baby Doc" Duvalier, the filmmakers claim their intent was to show the no-holds-barred dehumanizing practices of slavery and to "do *Mandingo* as a documentary" (Prosperi, quoted by Talbot 2009, 242). The atrocities depicted are unsavory and pornographic (an X-rated version was released by Cannon Pictures); however, some images, like cages, hangings, and the enslaved being force-fed molasses, are historically accurate. The last scene of the film reimagines Nat Turner's insurrection. Film critic Pauline Kael cited *Goodbye Uncle Tom* as "the most specific and rabid incitement of the race war," claiming the filmmakers were "irresponsible" (1972).

A landmark Supreme Court case, *Loving v. Virginia*, was decided in 1967, three weeks after the release of the iconic film, *Guess Who's Coming to Dinner*, featuring the actors Sidney Poitier (1927–2022) and Katharine Houghton (born 1945) as an interracial couple who get married. The Supreme Court declared the prohibition of state laws against interracial marriage unconstitutional. It claimed that the Fourteenth Amendment protected individuals from any government discrimination due to race. A white man, Richard Loving, wanted to marry a Black woman, Mildred Jeter, but it was illegal to do so in Washington, DC, where they lived. Although it was impossible to enforce the law, twelve states still had laws against interracial marriage until the 1970s.

DEPICTION AND CULTURAL CONTEXT: A BLACK WOMAN AND A WHITE MAN

Brenda Sykes said that when she first read the script, she did not want to do the film due to its violence and graphic sex. But after rereading it, she realized that "it could be educational for all Americans. It is about a terrible period of history. The point of the film is that Blacks would still be what they were in the antebellum South if they hadn't been fighters." And although her great-grandmother who had been born enslaved and was alive when Sykes was a child, she "really didn't know anything about that part of American history" other than what she was "told" in school (quoted by Talbot 2009, 111).

Mandingo looks at the Southern power and economic structure that supported slavery. The realistic portrayal of slavery in *Mandingo* is contrasted with the "romantic sentimentalism" of previous films about slavery: "In historical fact, behind every Tara [the O'Hara's *Gone with the Wind* plantation house in Georgia] there was a Falconhurst where human degradation was permitted, not because the people involved in slavery were necessarily evil, but the system was and it destroyed not only good people but ultimately a whole civilization on which it was based" (Fleischer quoted by Talbot 2009, 106). Fleischer says that he did extensive research, that he "found every book [he] could get his hands on about the South." The defiance of an enslaved person is depicted in Cicero's revolt. A genuinely loving interracial relationship between Ham and Ellen transcends Ham's position of power.

FURTHER READING

AFI. 1975. "Box Office." May 19, 1975, 4782. Accessed September 24, 2022. https://catalog.afi.com/Catalog/moviedetails/55588.

Canby, Vincent. 1975. "What Makes a Movie Immoral?" *New York Times*, May 18, 1975.

DeVos, Andrew. 2013. "Expect the Truth. Exploiting History with *Mandingo*." *American Studies* 52 (2): 5–21.

Ebert, Roger. 1975. "*Mandingo* review." Rogerebert.com, July 25, 1975.

Fleischer, Richard. 1976. "Richard Fleischer on *Mandingo*." Interview by Ian Cameron and Douglas Pye. Movie 22, February 1976, 24.

Freeland, Gregory K. 2009. "'We're a Winner': Popular Music and the Black Power Movement." *Social Movement Studies*, July 23, 2009.

Guerrero, Ed. 1993. *Framing Blackness: The African American Image in Film*. Philadelphia: Temple University Press.

Horton, Dana Renee. 2018. "'You Will Sell the Negress!': Using the Post-Neo-Slave Narrative to Revise Representations of Women in *Django Unchained* and *12 Years a Slave*." *Americana: The Journal of American Popular Culture (1900–present)* 17 (Fall). https://americanpopularculture.com/journal/articles/fall_2018/horton.htm.

Kael, Pauline. 1972. "The Current Cinema: Notes on Black Movies." *New Yorker*, December 2, 1972, 163.

Kehr, Dave. 2008. "In a Corrupt World Where the Violent Bear It Away." *New York Times*, February 17, 2008.

Keser, Robert. 2015. "The Greatest Film about Race Ever Filmed in Hollywood: Richard Fleischer's *Mandingo*." *Bright Lights Film Journal*, October 12, 2015.

Norton, Ken. 1977. "Ken Norton Interview by Lawrence Linderman." *Penthouse*, October 1977, 28.

Palmer, Robert. 1983. "Muddy Water, Blues Performer, Dies." *New York Times*, May 1, 1983.

Shere, Charles. 1975. "*Mandingo*—Portrayal of Slavery's Corruption." *Oakland Tribune*, May 13, 1975.

Talbot, Paul. 2009. *Mondo Mandingo: The Falconhurst Books and Films*. New York: iUniverse.

White Ndounou, Monica. 2019. "Slavery Now: 1970s Influence Post-20th Century Films on American Slavery." In *Black Cultural Production after Civil Rights*, edited by Robert J. Patterson, 79. Urbana: University of Illinois Press.

Williams, Linda. 2004. "Skin Flicks on the Racial Border: Pornography, Exploitation, and Interracial Lust." In *Porn Studies*, 1–26. Durham: Duke University Press.

Wood, Robin. 1998. "*Mandingo*: The Vindication of an Abused Masterpiece." In *Sexual Politics and Narrative Film*, 265–82. New York: Columbia University Press.

Chapter 3

Roots (1977)

The groundbreaking and addictive eight-episode, twelve-hour ABC miniseries took up residence in millions of American living rooms on eight consecutive very cold winter nights in 1977 starting on January 23, reaching more than half of the American population and 85 percent of the American television audience, 36 million viewers, more than any television series in history. It was also broadcast in more than fifty territories on five continents, including Australia, Japan, Canada, South Korea, and Spain. The final episode was viewed by more than 100 million American viewers; by some accounts, it was close to 130 million (Delmont 2016, 30). It sparked a pervasive and penetrating national discussion about slavery and its legacy. There were two spin-offs: *Roots the Next Generation* (1979), the sequel set from the 1880s to World War II, and *Roots, The Gift* (1988), a Christmas story set in 1775, featuring a failed slave revolt and Kunta Kinte's and Fiddler's attempt to escape slavery via a proto–Underground Railroad. A reboot, discussed below, streamed and aired in 2016.

The budget was $6 million. It had the largest Black cast in the history of commercial television. It was filmed in Savannah. Award-winning composer, musician, and producer Quincy Jones did the music.

Based on the Pulitzer Prize–winning *Roots: The Saga of an American Family* (Doubleday, 1976); 1976 was also the year of the bicentennial. The publisher's first printing of two hundred thousand was the largest ever for a hardcover book. Alexander Palmer Haley's best-selling (more than two million copies sold) historical novel—what he eventually called faction, a combination of fact and fiction—took him twelve years fraught with financial struggles to research and write. Alex Haley, as he was known, was inspired by his maternal grandmother, Cynthia Palmer, whose stories of their ancestor known as "The African" made a deep impression on Haley, setting him on a quest to dig up material in the National Archives. His compelling narrative spans more than a hundred years and seven generations of an African American family, focusing on the few generations of whom were enslaved in the South. The book was a cause célèbre and sold more than fifteen million hardcover copies. By the time the first episode aired, the book had sold more than one million copies.

The documentary filmmaker and television producer David L. Wolper optioned the book while Haley was still completing it, and the main screenwriter, William Blinn, and Ernest Kinoy were writing the adaptation simultaneously. Haley was on the set the whole time the miniseries was being filmed. He consulted, nurtured, and told stories; he instructed the costume designer for authenticity that the enslaved's clothes should be cleaned by being washed in the river, and he apparently enriched the film as well as the actors and filmmakers (Page 1993).

Haley, whose working title for the book was *Before the Anger*, researched his family's genealogy and relying on his family's oral tradition, traced his line back to a Mandinkan ancestor, Kunta Kinte, who in 1767, as the story goes, was going down to the river for material to make a drum when he was captured and put on a slave ship to America. Haley researched the slave trade and met with a griot, an African storyteller, in the village of Juffure in the Gambia in West Africa.

A gifted storyteller, Haley was born in 1921. His first best seller was *Autobiography of Malcolm X as told to Alex Haley* (Grove Press, 1965), the memoir of the civil rights icon, whose time in prison for robbery was spent reading about law, American history, and politics catalyzed him into a leader famous for advocating African Americans to fight for racial equality "by any means necessary," even if that meant violence. Haley had a gift for storytelling; as a Coast Guard journalist, he ghostwrote letters for his shipmates, then sold stories to the *Coast Guard Magazine*, and decided to become a journalist. He published interviews with Malcolm X in *Reader's Digest* in 1950 and in *Playboy Magazine* in May 1963; in January 1965, *Playboy* published Haley's interview with the reverend Martin Luther King Jr.

Haley created the television series *Palmerstown USA* in 1980–81 and *Queen*, starring Halle Berry, based on his novel *Queen: The Story of an American Family* (William Morrow), cowritten by David Stevens and published posthumously in 1993, about his paternal grandmother. Haley died of a heart attack in 1992. He was seventy years old.

LeVar Burton, the African American actor who played the young Kunta Kinte, says, "This was the first time the story of an African landing on these shores was being told from our point of view. The story was not being told from the point of view of the white, slave-bearing plantation owner," and this was a revelation.

Kamau Bell notes that part of David Wolper's genius was that he cast many of America's well-known TV dads, including Chuck Connors, Lorne Greene, Robert Reed, and Lloyd Bridges, as villains (2016). Ed Asner (1929–2021), known to television audiences as Lou Grant, Mary Richards's boss on the popular Emmy Award–winning sitcom, *The Mary Tyler Moore Show* (1970–77), played an invented character, "the morally conflicted white slave ship captain Thomas Davies whose conscience was meant to make white audiences feel better about their ancestors' role in slavery" (Keishin Armstrong 2016).

The quotidian details of racial slavery had rarely been examined from the enslaved's point of view so closely on film before. The enslaved showed resilience and resistance and even joy despite the subjugation and inhumane treatment foisted on them by the people who controlled and brutally punished them when they refused to abide by tyrannical rules. *Roots* reveals stories of the heartbreak individuals and families endured: arduous labor, poor living conditions, being forced to belong to other people, the separation of families, and the devastating loss of loved ones being sold away. Until the law of the land abolished slavery, crimes were systematically committed against Black humanity.

Popular, melodramatic, and mega best-selling American novels about race, including Harriet Beecher Stowe's *Uncle Tom's Cabin* (1852) and Margaret Mitchell's *Gone with the Wind* (1936), have historically been sweeping influencers providing indelible images of race relations during slavery in the antebellum South. About Haley's novel, James Baldwin claimed:

> "*Roots*" is a study of continuities, of consequences, of how a people perpetuate themselves, how each generation helps to doom, or helps to liberate, the coming one—the action of love, or the effect of the absence of love, in time. It suggests, with great power, how each of us, however unconsciously, can't but be the vehicle of the history which has produced us.
>
> Well, we can perish in this vehicle, children, or we can move on up the road. (1976)

More than a hundred years after slavery was abolished, *Roots* enabled viewers to experience it, through stories of people who suffered through, survived, and ultimately triumphed over it. The civil rights and Black Power movements that erupted in the 1950s and 1960s brought attention to racist inequities; policies and laws granting equality were put in place. African Americans and human rights activists continue to fight against the racism that undergirded slavery and pervaded, leading to systemic and unfair police and prison policies.

Roots is a family saga—it's about familial and romantic love, bondage and freedom, a country divided against itself, and identity and culture. The generational, universal aspect of the story is a large part of its appeal. *Roots'* final scene takes place right after the emancipation of the slaves has been proclaimed. Haley's great-great-grandfather, Chicken George, and his family declare freedom on a hill, reaching their arms to the future and to the past, acknowledging Kunta Kinte, and reconciling their people's status now as free African Americans. The struggle for equality looms large.

Reviews were mixed. The *Hollywood Reporter* claimed the miniseries was a "magnificent vehicle" and that "there is no doubt that this searingly honest look at a part of our American history that has been suppressed and distorted for 200 years will have a strong social impact" (Murphy 1977). *Variety* acknowledged its depiction of "the struggles of the blacks to preserve their own freedom and dignity. It's a remarkable presentation" (1977). However, John J. O'Connor of the *New York Times* noted that it was a "distortion or, at the very least, oversimplification of the source material" (1977), and Richard Schickel of *Time* magazine faulted no less than the subject matter, claiming that slavery was "a crime so monstrous that, like the Holocaust, it is beyond anyone's ability to re-create in intelligent dramatic terms" (1977).

Stan Margulies, a producer of *Roots*, said "We wanted the viewer to feel what a whipping was like. The issue of slavery has been difficult to reconcile, it's hard to handle like the Holocaust. The treatment of African Americans makes a mockery of freedom, independence, democracy, etc." (Dubin et al. 2007). It took more than one hundred years after slavery was abolished for a book and film to show to a mass audience how the individual and family experienced it. *Roots* provoked a cathartic response and resonated with a multiracial audience. America was two hundred years old, Black Power was ubiquitous, and its collective consciousness acknowledged and confronted the "peculiar institution" of racial chattel slavery.

Wolper was proud of being part of a team that "showed slavery from the Black point of view and came out cleansed, healing the sins of two hundred years ago; we put the truth out there" (Dubin et al. 2007).

A voice-over announces, "We are proud to present the triumph of an American family." The series opens in the Gambia, West Africa, in 1750 with an African song playing. Kunta Kinte is born to a Muslim family. He is the son of Omora (Thalmus Rosella) and Binta (Cicely Tyson). Kunta is fifteen and starting manhood initiation training. Kunta's grandmother, Yaisa is fiercely played by the iconic actress, director, poet, and writer Maya Angelou; the notorious former football player O. J. Simpson plays Kadi Touray, the father of Fanta a young woman Kunta encounters when he's attempting to catch a bird without a weapon, ruffling her feathers after accidently bumping into her. Touray runs after and chases Kunta down, forcing him to apologize to Fanta. When an incredulous Kunta first sees captured men with ropes tied around their hands and necks—they're led by a Black man, and white men are attending—he reports to his tribe that he has seen white men.

It's 1767. Captain Thomas Davies (Ed Asner), manning his first slave slip, the *Lord Ligonier*, looks at the diagram of packed Africans on the ship whose destination is Annapolis, Maryland. Davies enumerates 250 wrist shackles, neck rings, and thumbscrews to punish without damaging or "knocking down the purchase price." There are branding irons marked with the ship's name. Davies learns that approximately 170 people can fit on the ship. "Blacks are slow but strong, suited to be slaves," Slater (Ralph Waite) says. "It's good for them us taking them like that. They're the better off for it. For one thing, there's Christianity which has got to be better than that heathen Allah they have now. And they're cannibals. They have no language, just grunts and groans."

Kunta is taking part in initiation rites in becoming a man; this is juxtaposed with the slave ship's arrival. Kunta sees an African complicit in leading a coffle of people; their necks and hands are tied with ropes, and there are several white men guarding the ship.

Slater talks about the competition for Africans, claiming they're pricier when purchasing them from their chiefs. Four Black men and a white man chase Kunta and capture him with a rope and chain. He runs trying to elude them; he slashes one with his machete. Kunta struggles against the chains, trying to break them, while the men stand around him smiling at his futility. He gets lashed and then gets back in line. Captain Davies discusses how to pack the Africans—can fit two hundred if you pack them tight, but you lose some. Kunta is surprised to see his mentor, Wrestler (Ji-Tu Cumbuka) on the ship.

The Africans are on their backs, chained down on the ship. They're groaning, their heads are going back and forth; they're coughing, crying, sweating, and moving their feet around. At times, they're unchained to get air and exercise and dance. The white men call them monkeys. The Africans are covered with feces and vomit; water is thrown on them. People are screaming and shivering, a few jump overboard, which prompts Slater to say: "There goes a hundred guineas to the sharks." Kunta realizes the people are from different tribes: the Fulani, the Solari, the Wolof, the Serere. He says, "We will learn each other's languages. We will be one village. We will live." A white guy is chasing an African girl around to rape her, but she climbs up on the sail and jumps into the water.

Kunta says a Mandinkan maiden must have strength; the young woman says, "I am no longer a Mandinkan." Kunta's culture is deeply embedded in his soul, and it will never leave him. The fiercely independent and defiant Kunta Kinte was born free; some enslaved people were born into slavery. Kinte had had a life of dignity, free will, and self-determination.

Kunta and other captured Africans stage a failed rebellion against the whites on the boat. Kunta arrives in Annapolis; his wounds are washed. He is imprisoned in a holding jail cell. A white man recalls when indentured bond servants were "stout Cornishmen and Scots, pickpockets from Newgate Prison. And when they ran away you couldn't always find them. But when a Black slave runs away, you can always find them." Kunta is sold at the slave auction to John Reynolds (Lorne Greene) whose plantation is in Spotsylvania, Virginia. Kunta is given the name Toby, which he rejects. Kunta befriends Fiddler (Louis Gossett Jr.) who asks him, "What it like to be free? Must be something special." A touching and loving friendship develops between the Fiddler and Kunta Kinte.

Fiddler is genial; he plays by the rules. Fiddler is charming, charismatic, talented, *and* conciliatory, but he also has a strong sense of self-identity. He instructs Kunta Kinte in the ways of the plantation, teaches him English, and how to load a wagon. Fiddler tells Kunta that his enslaver said his name is Toby. Kunta gets angry and says his name loudly. Fiddler gets angry and frustrated and keeps telling him his name is Toby. Kunta is defiant, and he is ultimately whipped mercilessly until he finally utters Toby. This brutal scene shows how the identity of the enslaved person was determined by his or her enslaver and how this Mandinkan was stripped of his very sense of selfhood. At one point, Kunta hears drumming coming from the forest. He follows it and meets an older man from a nearby African village who tells him they must always remember their culture, that he feels sorry for the young people who have no idea who they are. "They got no remembrance of the old ways," he says.

Kunta, now played by John Amos, wants to run away from the Reynolds' plantation. Fiddler reminds him he'll get twenty lashes if he runs away, ten if he looks a white man in the eye or doesn't have papers. There's no way to beat the law; "white folks live by it and black folks die by it." Kunta encounters his girlfriend from Africa, Fanta, now called Maggie (Beverly Todd). They make love. He runs away again; a slave catcher catches him and cuts his foot off. Kunta begins a flirtation with Bell Reynolds (Madge Sinclair), who is enslaved in the Reynolds' house. She tells him she's not an African, she's American. Bell is a loving nanny to the daughter of the house—the doctor's daughter, Missy-Anne Reynolds (Sandy Duncan). Kunta Kinte laments with a friend from Africa that most of the enslaved have no one to tell them about the old ways. Kunta and Bell fall in love and marry. Kunta hears about abolitionists in the North who set the enslaved free; he plans to run away again. He's told that a drummer will send a message when it's an opportune time to run away. Bell tells Kunta about her man Ben who got caught running away; he was hanged, and her baby girls were sold off. Bell gives birth to Kizzy, which means "stay put" in Mandinkan. Kunta promises Bell she'll never be taken from her. Fiddler dies in Kunta's arms; Kunta cries. Kizzy, now grown up (Leslie Uggams) takes care of Missy-Anne who teaches her to read.

When Bell finds out that Kizzy has learned to read, she slaps her and says if white people find out, she'll be sold. Kunta and his family seem to have control of their lives and the cabin they live in. Kizzy says her grandpa was a "griot." Kizzy's boyfriend Noah (Lawrence Hilton-Jacobs) talks about running away; he stole a knife. Kizzy is reading and gets caught by Missy-Anne's father. Noah tells Kizzy about his plans to run away.

Kizzy questions how and why slavery is justified and Missy Anne tells her that "Whites are smarter than Blacks. Like men are smarter than women." Kizzy responds saying, "Abolitionists want to change things." "They're evil people," says Missy-Anne, "like Quakers, they're against God." In a heartbreaking scene, Kizzy is sold after it's revealed that she helped Noah forge his pass. Her devastated parents cry and beg as Kizzy is forced into a carriage screaming. The family's grief is overwhelming. They will never be a family again.

Kizzy gets raped immediately on her arrival at her new home. She is told that her enslaver, Tom Moore (Chuck Connors), likes Black women and he will continue "studying" her until she has a baby. This painful scene captures the harsh reality of the plight of enslaved young women. Tom is a drunk who has no moral conflict about it. It is challenging for a viewer to relate to the rapist's cavalier attitude and utter lack of ambiguity. It is not portrayed as dark or depraved; raping young Black women was an everyday thing for enslavers like Tom Moore. Kizzy declares, "You can take my body, but you can't touch my spirit or take away my dream to be free."

Kizzy's son was fathered by Moore. Because of his love for cockfighting, his name becomes Chicken George. He's mentored by Mingo (Scatman Crothers). It's 1841, and the now grown-up Chicken George (Ben Vereen) is part of the white men's cockfighting event. An enslaved man talks about buying his freedom papers. He says, "All you need is a willing master and the money. We trainers cost the most—$2,000–$2,500." Chicken George learns that the price for his wife Tildy (Olivia Cole) would be $1,500. It would cost $6,000 for his whole family; he has four children. Chicken George is stopped on the road and asked if he knows Nat Turner.

In 1862, the white character of Ol' George Johnson (Brad Davis) comes into the life of Chicken George's son, Tom Harvey. George is looking for a job in the fields. Johnson is the first white person they have encountered who says he is "plain honest about hisself" (Haley 1976, 819). Johnson tells them he hasn't interacted with Blacks before, but he judges people by "how they act" (Haley 1976, 819). A genuine friendship between the white man and the Black man ensues.

Chicken George is sent to England to work as a cockfighter and is away for fourteen years. He returns to his family and learns they had been sold to Sam Harvey's plantation in North Carolina; he finds and reunites with them. He also learns that his mother, Kizzy, has died. The Emancipation Proclamation frees the enslaved; Chicken George takes his family to Henning, Tennessee, where he buys land. Chicken George relays the story of his family back to Kunta Kinte, and Alex Haley appears, connecting the lineage of his family to Chicken George and Kunta Kinte.

In 2016, *Roots*, the miniseries, was rebooted. It is, like the original, compulsively watchable, entertaining, and emotional in its storytelling. The cinematography, production values, and acting are exemplary. New scholarship about the Gambian life is embedded in the series, and a scene in which Black soldiers fight for the Union at Fort Pillow is added. Approximately 5.3 million viewers watched the premiere episode, broadcast simultaneously on Memorial Day on the History Channel, A & E, and Lifetime (O'Connell 2016).

Kunta Kinte, played by the British actor Malachi Kirby, is an educated young man from a distinguished and prosperous family contrasted with the original in which Kinte lives in a remote village. "He spoke probably four languages," said producer Mark Wolper, David Wolper's son (Beresford et al. 2016). Kunta's ambition is to go to university in Timbuktu. There was "civilization, scholarship, lineage and royalty before the Africans were stolen and brought to these shores," said Anika Noni Rose, the Tony Award–winning actress who plays Kizzy (quoted in Ryzik 2016).

"We wanted to focus thematically more on defiance, resistance, and the ability to overcome the shackles of the body," Rose said (quoted in Ryzik 2016). Kunta Kinte is shown breaking through his chains on the ship. Black people are weary of "seeing themselves enchained and downtrodden." In addition to going back to Haley's novel as source material, the filmmakers listened to slave narratives collected in the Library of Congress.

Background information about the Mandinka enslaving people as the Greeks, Romans, and Hebrews did, is provided, and the Mandinkan language is spoken and subtitled. It is shown that some Mandinka were corrupted by European guns and gold. The Africans wear elaborate costumes; they play instruments.

Ahmir "Questlove" Thompson, the *Roots* drummer and co-front man, scored the soundtrack, which includes the song "Trouble of the World"—a traditional spiritual sung by enslaved African Americans about finding peace in heaven. He won the Academy Award for the electrifying documentary *Summer of Soul* (2021), about a nearly forgotten Black music festival that took place in Harlem in 1969. Two of the writers of *Roots*, Charles Murray and Alison McDonald, who wrote the adaptation are Black. Actor/director Mario Van Peebles directed the second episode. His father was late director Melvin Van Peebles (1932–2021), whose iconic film *Sweet Sweetback Baadasssss Song* (1971) in 2020 was cited by the Library of Congress's National Film Registry for its "historical and cultural significance" (Itzkoff 2020). Mario's son, Mandela Van Peebles, plays Noah.

Chicken George is played by René-Jean Page, and his role is expanded. The cockfighting scenes are much longer and more elaborate than in the original. The Nat Turner reference is more developed and penetrating, and the year his insurrection took place has been corrected to 1831. Enslaved people are claiming that the prophet Nat Turner is coming and that he and his band are killing white people. "Whole families and babies are dead. They beat Margaret Whitehead with a fence post; he's a cannibal," a character says, "cutting up and giving bodies to his men to eat." Black men are hanging from trees.

Chicken George joins the Memphis Battery Line as a Union soldier after learning that if a Black man can get to a fort, he can get a gun and fight. Chicken George befriends Cyrus (T.I.), who begs for a rifle. General Nathan Forrest (Jackson Beals) leads the Confederacy at the battle at Fort Pillow, and the Union Army surrenders. But Confederate soldiers shoot the Black soldiers. The final episode shows Chicken George and his friend Cyrus fighting against the attacks led by General Forest at Fort Pillow, a scene not in the original. Chicken George cuts Cyrus's arm off to save him, and they both survive. Chicken George joins a volunteer army and continues to fight. When he returns home, he tells his family that "Nathan Forrest couldn't kill us fast enough, no more than twenty colored boys made it out."

Laurence Fishburne plays Alex Haley and provides the coda. He says, "The truth can never be known; it can only be told in a story. A boy was taken from his family and carried halfway around the world. He started a new family and became a hero for his family."

HISTORICAL BACKGROUND

Haley's genealogical and Gambian research had inaccuracies. Mark Ottaway, in his short but controversial *Sunday London Times* exposé "Tangled Roots," claimed that "the man who provided Haley with the vital link to [his African ancestor] Kunta Kinte was a man of notorious unreliability who probably knew beforehand what Haley wanted to hear" (1977). On his return trip home, he found out he won a special (neither fiction nor nonfiction) Pulitzer Prize. However, Haley was subsequently accused of plagiarizing several dozen paragraphs, from folklorist Harold Courlander's novel *The African* (Crown, 1967) and in 1978 paid Courlander $650,000 in an out-of-court settlement. Haley at first claimed he hadn't heard of nor read the book; however, he ultimately admitted that sections of descriptions of the Middle Passage in *The African* turned up in *Roots* (Lubasch 1978).

The best-selling writer, poet, and civil rights leader Margaret Walker Alexander also accused Haley of plagiarizing slavery scenes of her novel *Jubilee* (Houghton Mifflin, 1966), based on stories her grandmother told her. Haley chalked Walker's and Courlander's claims up to "the inevitable sniping that any important and successful book has to endure. Facts, information, and general literary ideas cannot be copyrighted. What is in question here is the author's original expression" (Dickey 1977). Walker Alexander's case was thrown out of court.

The Middle Passage

Approximately one-third of the Africans forced onto ships did not survive the Middle Passage due to illness and terrible conditions, but many jumped off the ship as if they were jumping out of a burning building. The poet Robert Haydn referred to the Middle Passage as a "journey through death." Africans were packed so tight on the ship; the voyages generally lasted from two to three months. The enslaved were force-fed. Approximately 20 percent died of disease; women weren't chained, enabling white men to rape them. Approximately 10 percent tried to revolt; most weren't successful.

Of the 12.5 million captured Africans who arrived in the New World from 1525 to 1866, 15 percent died en route, 388,000 came to North America (Gates 2014). The rest were taken to the Caribbean and South America. Once on land, they were washed, examined, poked, and prodded. Slave advertisements in colonial newspapers described the "lusty, fresh cargo." Men were often more valuable until a certain age. Prices for women were based on their age, "breeding prospects," and "sexual attractiveness."

As the enslaved were considered property, the legal process for manumitting or freeing an enslaved person in the states where it was legal was analogous to a property holder abandoning the right to his property. The carve-outs or exceptions to the law prevented "the old and sick enslaved from being a burden or public charge and some ensured the person would leave the colony within a year" (Matison 1948, 149). Laws were passed in states like Georgia in 1801 that required permission from the legislature. Several states, including Louisiana in 1857, Arkansas and New Mexico in 1859, and Maryland in 1860, passed laws that "absolutely prohibited manumissions" (Matison 1948, 150).

Free enslaved people would acquire enslaved people to help them buy their freedom; the practice of "benevolent Negro holding" spread (Matison 1948, 152). However, a law was passed in Virginia in 1882 preventing a Black person from buying an enslaved person excepting their spouse or child. A written agreement was essential to hold up in court. The enslaved who were "skilled artisans" could do extra work for pay toward their freedom and in some places were able to hire themselves out to earn money. In this case, "self-hire led to self-purchase" (Jackson, quoted by Matison 1948, 151).

A Maryland enslaved man named Nathan, thirty-one years old and of good "bodily strength," in 1818 purchased himself from Ann Berry, a widow. The price: $220—"thousands of dollars in today's money" (Ruane 2017). And in 1806, Aaron Jones, thirty-five, manumitted himself. His owner, Ann Sprigg, set his price at $400, which was high at the time, but allowed Jones to "set up an installment plan: For his freedom, Jones would pay Sprigg $100 each year for four years. Sprigg charged no interest" (Ruane 2017).

Denmark Vesey, a.k.a. Telemaque (1767–1822), was a pastor whose plan for a large-scale rebellion in Charleston, South Carolina, in 1822 was thwarted. He bought his freedom with money won in a lottery. Some mined gold, one free woman opened a school to earn money, and one man paid $7,000 for his whole family. Frederick Douglass received money from British supporters who paid his former Maryland enslaver Hugh Auld a payment of $711.66. Upon receipt, Auld drew up Douglass's papers saying he was free, so he could in 1846 return to America from England, where slavery had been abolished in 1833.

George Moses Horton, born enslaved, according to J. Saunders Redding "in North Carolina about the year 1797," endeavored to buy his freedom by selling his poetry "charging twenty-five cents for a poem of moderate warmth and fifty-cents for one of exceptional fervor" (1988). He published his collection of poems, titled *The Hope of Liberty*, in 1829, and was the first Black author in the South to publish a book as well as the only American to publish a book while being enslaved (Beatty-Brown 1942). Horton spoke out against slavery in his work; he also wrote humorous poems. He achieved notoriety in his time; however, he was unsuccessful in buying his freedom, which he achieved in 1865 when slavery was abolished. Don Tate published a children's book, titled *Poet: The Remarkable Story of George Moses Horton* (Peachtree) in 2018.

Some people deceived the enslaved trying to buy their freedom by taking their money and then reselling them. Some enslaved received help from the American Colonization Society—an organization founded in 1817 that supported and advocated the enslaved to go back to Africa and helped build the colony of Liberia, established in 1847. There was usually an intermediary, and that was most likely a free Black. The power that the enslaved had to buy their own freedom, known as the "self-purchase movement," undermined "the moral and practical foundation for the slave system" (Matison 1948, 167). It proved that Blacks were capable of living as free people, contrary to proslavery beliefs, and it also "aroused the envy and discontent" of other enslaved people—emotions that led to resistance, advocacy, and policy change (Matison 1948, 169).

Europeans, like the Spanish and Portuguese, traded with Africans since the 1400s and thought they were different but not inferior. Europeans entered into alliances with local leaders and middlemen whose job it was to procure men. Many were captured as prisoners of war. Guns were used to buy Africans. Myths fabricated by the slave trade were perpetrated, including that gunpowder was crushed African bones, that Africans were cannibals and barbarians, and that whites needed to save their souls.

Fort Pillow

The Civil War Battle of Fort Pillow occurred on April 12, 1864, in Henning, Tennessee, the western part of the state. Confederate soldiers, led by the vicious general Nathan Bedford Forrest, massacred "more than three hundred Black soldiers and their white officers after they had surrendered" (Reynolds 2020, 809). However, this assessment is controversial to this day, and there are contradictory narratives regarding whether the Union soldiers did, in fact, surrender. If they did, they should have been captured as prisoners of war and not killed.

Forrest, a white supremacist, became, after the Civil War (in 1867), the first grand wizard of the Ku Klux Klan. More than two hundred thousand enslaved men fought in the army and navy for the Union; however, the Confederacy didn't recognize Blacks as legitimate soldiers (Levin 2016). What on the surface appeared to be a relatively "minor military engagement at a strategically insignificant site—resulted in a horrific, racially motivated atrocity" (Van Arragon 2012). Union soldiers held the site since 1862, although Confederate soldiers built it. The fort was being protected by Major William Bradford. What is not contested however, is that Black soldiers died at a disproportionate rate to whites. "While 70 percent of white soldiers survived, only 35 percent of African American soldiers survived" (Leaming 1893).

The consequences of the outrage sparked by the racist genocide at Fort Pillow led to better pay for Black soldiers and fewer massacres. Edwin McMasters Stanton (1814–69), President Lincoln's secretary of war, in 1863 created the Bureau of Colored Troops. At first, Blacks weren't paid as much as whites. Frederick Douglass met with Lincoln to advocate for equal pay, and William Walker, with the South Carolina Third Volunteers, led a strike in 1863 for equal pay. The equal pay Blacks were granted in 1865 was retroactive (Van Arragon 2012).

Cockfighting

Cockfighting, which arrived in America from England, involved gambling prizes up to $10,000—"a popular blood sport in the South, especially after 1776," it reached its pinnacle right before the Civil War, particularly in North Carolina, Virginia, and Maryland. From twenty-one to fifty "cockers" would participate in an event (Wyatt-Brown 1986, 133–135). The fighting pits also offered opportunities for interracial and interclass socialization and entertainment (Maunula 2007). Although they likely outnumbered male churchgoers, not much is documented about cockers and those who enjoyed horse racing. Clergymen spoke out against gambling of all kinds, and the general assembly banned cockfighting in South Carolina in 1887, but that didn't stop it. Cockers viewed themselves as "the custodians of an ancient tradition of courage, competition, and masculine aggression" ("Cockfighting," n.d.). Massachusetts passed a law in 1836 and England in 1849 against any sport involving animal cruelty.

Northerners, for the most part, didn't engage in the game, though, politicians like presidents George Washington and Andrew Jackson and the British Whig Horace Wolpole indulged in it. Poorer whites and the enslaved sometimes participated together. Although cockfighting is frowned upon, it still takes place in South Carolina and Mexico, where in March 2022, it was the scene of gun violence and many deaths.

The Complicity of Africans

In his *New York Times* op-ed about the complicated issue of reparations for descendants of enslaved people, Henry Louis Gates Jr. notes, "The historians John Thornton and Linda Heywood of Boston University estimate that 90 percent of those shipped to the New World were enslaved by elite Africans and then sold to European traders" (Gates 2010). This transactional business led to an estimated 12.5 million Africans enchained and forced into slavery in America, South America, and the Caribbean. The African involvement in the slave trade dramatically decreased "after 1807, when abolitionists, first in Britain and then, a year later, in the United States, succeeded in banning the importation of slaves" (Gates 2010).

Schaffer notes the connection between Kunta Kinte and his linguistic skill and Joseph Cinque, the fearless leader of the *Amistad* revolt. They were both Mandinkas from the Mande tribe. "The takeover of the Amistad" by Mende men "must have enhanced the reputation for leadership of this ethnic group in the antebellum United States" (2005, 10). Schaffer traces the origins of the banjo, the kora, "a 21-string calabash instrument," and "griots who rhythmically chant," and discusses how early African musical practices evolved into modern-day rap. He notes the linguistic legacy on Gullah culture and the "Mandification of Southern English" and how it contributed to the creation of the American Southern accent (Schaffer 2005, 45).

DEPICTION AND CULTURAL CONTEXT

Black and white actors talked about being overwhelmed with emotion as they played their roles as enslaved and enslaver characters. Richard Roundtree, who plays Kizzy's boyfriend Sam, and had in 1971 played Shaft had a hard time getting down on his knees to beg his enslaver not to be angry that he was a little late bringing the horse and carriage back. White actors felt apologetic for the racists they had to portray. It was difficult for Lloyd Bridges, who plays Evan Brent, to use a whip. Robert Reed, who plays the overseer, Dr. William Reynolds, is compelled in a heart-wrenching scene to tell Bell that her daughter Kizzy will be sold because she was caught reading. In fact, Kizzy was set up by her hypocritical white enslaver and "friend," the doctor's daughter, Missy-Anne, because she turned down her offer to work in the house. Bell gets on her hands and knees, begging the doctor to beat her daughter, to "tear off her hide," but not to send her away. Even as gifted an actor as Reed cannot bear to be treating a loving human being so pitilessly.

Many of the African American actors were unusually excited about the material they were bringing to life. Though some had been acting on stage and doing television movies for more than twenty years, none had ever had the opportunity to play a role that was so much about their heritage and told from their point of view. But for some, the role of an enslaved character was so disturbing that 80 percent of the extras in the slave-ship scene did not return the second day for shooting because they were too overwhelmed by the experience (Dubin et al. 2007).

Roots was the first widely seen film or television movie about slavery to counter and correct *Gone with the Wind* and D. W. Griffith's *The Birth of a Nation*. Haley found strength in Black families. Although Black characters were featured on popular sitcoms like *The Jeffersons* (1975–85) and *Good Times* (1974–79), Blacks hadn't been portrayed much on dramatic series television. A notable exception was based on Ernest Gaines's novel *The Autobiography of Miss Jane Pitman* (Dial Press, 1971); the eponymous television adaptation, starring Cicely Tyson (1924–2021) as a 110-year-old formerly enslaved civil rights activist, aired on CBS in 1974.

Most of the characterizations in *Roots* were unlike any previously seen on television. Haley's son William claimed, "If they would have had Black writers, this would have been a different movie" (Dubin et al. 2007). Wolper counters that Alex Haley did not want a Black writer because he or she would give his or her point of view, and Haley wanted his point of view (Dubin et al. 2007).

Wolper, in 1977, said it was tough to make a miniseries where the Blacks were heroes and the whites were villains in a country that was 80 percent white and 11.5 percent Black. ABC executives and its sales force were nervous about its prospects. They also worried that the frontal nudity being shown on primetime television for the first time might be problematic.

Roots sparked a huge interest in Black genealogy, focusing on "reaffirming the positive aspects of Black culture." There was *Roots*mania and *Roots* Fever. Gates says he and other scholars had "*Roots* envy." "Afrocentricity," coined in the 1980s by African American activist Molefi Asante, was catalyzed by *Roots*. It's defined as "a cultural and political movement whose mainly African American adherents regard themselves and all other Blacks as syncretic Africans and believe that their worldview should positively reflect traditional African values" (Early 2020). It paved the way for "Afrofuturism," a term invented in 1994 by Mark Dery in his essay "Black to the Future," a genre that centers Black history and culture and incorporates "science-fiction, technology, and futuristic elements into literature, music, and the visual arts" (Washington 2022).

African Americans were inspired in great numbers to trace their genealogy. Henry Louis Gates Jr. credits Haley with inspiring his 2006–8 Public Broadcasting Service's genealogy series *African American Lives*, which focused on the family history of prominent African Americans and *Finding Your Roots*, in which DNA research reveals famous multiracial people's ancestry and history and which debuted in 2012 and is in its eighth season in 2022. One episode provoked the late Georgia congressman John Lewis (1940–80) to tears when Gates surprised him with his great-great-grandfather's Reconstruction-era 1867 Alabama voting registration papers. After Reconstruction ended, Blacks' voting rights were blocked (Ho 2012). Actor Ben Affleck stalled the release date of his episode in 2015 after it was reported that he had asked Gates to not reveal that he had slave-owning ancestors. This caused a "censorship scandal" when Gates disclosed that Affleck had inappropriately challenged Gates's "editorial control" (Gayle 2015). Affleck ultimately apologized for trying to influence the show's content.

David Duke, the former grand wizard of the Knights of the Ku Klux Klan, founded in 1975, to suggest a less bigoted and "kinder, gentler" white-supremacist organization, charged ABC with airing a "vicious malignment of the white majority in America and a serious distortion of the truth" (quoted by Johnson 1977).

Melville J. Herskovits's 1941 groundbreaking and controversial book *The Myth of the Negro Past* (Harper & Brothers) claimed that African Americans carry the rich culture of Africa within themselves, that it wasn't wiped out during the Middle Passage, as some historians had postulated. "Not really a new idea," August Meier states. Herskovits, an anthropologist, built on other writers, including the seminal Black writer, W. E. B. Du Bois, who, though "unable to back it up with depth research had propounded the theory in the 1890s" (1978). Charles S. Johnson and E. Franklin Frazier, Black sociologists, who acknowledged that while African American culture, especially "music, dance, and folk stories" was influenced by African culture, Black cultural practices and lifestyle were a subculture of American life, the result of adapting to oppressive racist slavery. It wasn't until "the surge of black separatism accompanying the black revolt came during the late 1960s, when identity with Africa and pride in the distinctiveness of Afro-American culture gained new strength, that the perspective offered by Du Bois and Herskovits became widely accepted" (Meier 1978).

Herskovits made many trips to Africa and started the first African studies program in the United States in 1948 at Northwestern University. The scholar Vincent Brown affectionately referred to him as the Elvis Presley of African American studies in the documentary *Herskovits at the Heart of Blackness* (2009) as some felt that he appropriated, popularized, and ultimately overshadowed the work of Black scholars.

Ebou Manga, a Hamilton College student from the Gambia who assisted Haley and taught him some Mandinkan words upon which he drew, also educated him about the griots, the oral historians. Jan Vansina (1929–2017), the Belgian anthropologist, Africanist, and author of *Oral Tradition: A Study in Historical Methodology* (Routledge, 1961), militated against the prevailing belief that a culture had no history if it didn't have written texts. While there were written languages in Africa, including Egyptian hieroglyphs, most sub–Saharan African texts didn't survive and were not available to the Europeans. The oral tradition became "a sanctuary of human dignity" (Davis 2006). Haley believed that the oral tradition is equal to any historical source material (Norrell 2015, 101). Norrell said Haley might not have been a historian, but he was a "witness bearer" (2015, 179). Haley listened to the folkloric stories and said, "I was just trying to give my people a myth to live by" (quoted by Page 1993). An example is the baby-naming ceremony when Kunta Kinte holds his newborn daughter, Kizzy, up to the heavens at night and tells her to "behold the only thing greater than yourself."

Nat Turner's insurrection is mentioned in *Roots* as taking place in 1841; however, the rampage he led during which approximately sixty white people and children were killed took place ten years earlier in 1831. When Turner was found hiding six weeks after the insurrection, he was captured and hanged. The year of the event was corrected in the reboot.

References to *Roots* in popular culture are plentiful. Hip-hop artists including Missy Elliott, Lil Wayne, Kanye West, and Kendrick Lamar in his song "King Kunta" mention Kunta Kinte. Ice Cube in his song "No Vaseline" alludes to Kunta Kinte being whipped for not saying his name is Toby. A Tribe Called Quest's song "What" includes the lyric, "What's Alex Haley if it doesn't have roots?" The Black comedian Dave Chappelle in 2003 performed a few hilarious satirical sketches, billed as "*Roots* 25th anniversary outtakes," about Kunta Kinte. There's one in which Kinte is getting lashed for not saying his name is Toby. Chappelle breaks the fourth wall and yells at the actor who's "whipping him," saying he told him not to do it so hard. When the shirtless Chappelle turns his back to the camera, it's revealed that he's wearing thick padding. Spike Lee has Mookie, the character he plays in his 1989 film *Do the Right Thing*, respond to his sister when she urges him to get a job: "Slavery days are over. My name ain't Kunta Kinte."

CONCLUSION

Roots' revelatory depiction of slavery in America prevails. The miniseries captured the zeitgeist of the Black Power movement, and it enabled an unprecedented number of viewers to learn about slavery in ways it wasn't and isn't taught in school. The *New York Times* said the miniseries *Roots* was the "most significant civil rights event since the Selma-to-Montgomery march of 1965" (quoted in Henig 2014).

FURTHER READING

Baldwin, James. 1976. "Review: 'Roots.'" *New York Times Book Review*, September 26, 1976.
Beatty-Brown, Florence. 1942. "George Moses Horton." *Negro Bulletin* 5, no. 5 (February): 103.
"Cockfighting." n.d. South Carolina Encyclopedia. Accessed September 27, 2022. https://www.scencyclopedia.org/sce/entries/cockfighting/.
Beresford, Bruce, Thomas Carter, Phillip Noyce, and Mario Van Peebles, dirs. 2016. *Roots*. The Film Afrika Worldwide, History Channel, and the Wolper Organization.

Davis, David Brion. 2006. *Inhuman Bondage: The Rise and Fall of Slavery in the New World*. New York: Oxford University Press.

Delmont, Matthew F. 2016. *Making Roots: A Nation Captivated*. Oakland: University of California Press.

Dickey, Christopher. 1977. "Roots Author Facing Accusations." *Washington Post*, April 28, 1977.

Dodson, Howard. 2003. "America's Cultural Roots Traced to Enslaved African Ancestors." *National Geographic*, February 5, 2003.

Donington, Katie. 2017. "Roots: A Necessary Portrayal of Transatlantic Slavery." *History Extra*, March 24, 2017. https://www.historyextra.com/period/modern/roots-a-necessary-portrayal-of-transatlantic-slavery/.

Dubin, Charles S., John Erman, Kevin Hooks, and Marvin J. Chomsky, dirs. 2007. *Roots*. Seven-Disc 30th Anniversary Edition, DVD. Warner Brothers.

Dundes, Alan. 1994. *The Cockfight A Casebook*. Madison: University of Wisconsin Press.

Early, Gerald. 2020. "Afrocentrism." *Britanica.com*. https://www.britannica.com/event/Afrocentrism.

Gates, Henry Louis, Jr. 2010. "Ending the Slavery Blame-Game" *New York Times*, April 23, 2010.

Gates, Henry Louis, Jr. 2012. "A Life Spent Tracing Roots." Interview by Neal Conan. NPR, May 8, 2012.

Gates, Henry Louis, Jr. 2014. "How Many Slaves Landed in the U.S." *The Root*, January 6, 2014.

Gayle, Damien. "Ben Affleck admits embarrassment led him to try to hide slave-owning ancestor." *The Guardian*, April 22, 2015.

Haley, Alex. 1976. *Roots*. New York: Doubleday.

Haywood, Wil. 2021. "How the TV Adaptation of *Roots* Sparked a Cultural Awakening." *Lit Hub*, October 20, 2021.

Henig, Adam. 2014. *Alex Haley's Roots*. PB Press Books. https://ahenig031.pressbooks.com/chapter/chapter-1/.

Ho, Rodney. 2012. "John Lewis Digs through His Roots on PBS's 'Finding Your Roots' Sunday." *Atlanta Journal-Constitution*, March 23, 2012.

Itzkoff, Dave. 2020. "*The Dark Knight* and the *Blues Brothers* Join National Film Registry." *New York Times*, December 14, 2020.

Johnson, Thomas A. 1977. "'Roots' Has Widespread and Inspiring Influence." *New York Times*, March 19, 1977.

Kamau Bell, W. 2016. "The Star of the Original *Roots* Explains Why the Remake Is Must-Watch Television." *Mother Jones*, May/June 2016.

Keishin Armstrong, Jennifer. 2016. "*Roots*: The Most Important TV Show Ever?" BBC Culture, June 1, 2016.

Leaming, Mack J. "The Fort Pillow Massacre, 1864." April 15, 1893. https://www.gilderlehrman.org/sites/default/files/inline-pdfs/05080.01_fps.pdf, copyright 2017.

Levin, Kevin M. 2016. "*Roots*, Fort Pillow, and the Legacy of Racial Violence." Civil War Memory, June 3, 2016. https://cwmemory.com/blog/.

Lubasch, Arnold H. 1978. "*Roots* Plagiarism Suit Is Settled." *New York Times*, December 15, 1978.

Matison, Samuel Eliot. 1948. "Manumission by Purchase." *Journal of Negro History* 33, no. 2 (April): 146–67.

Maunula, Marko. 2007. "Of Chickens and Men: Cockfighting and Equality in the South." *Southern Cultures* 13, no. 4 (Winter): 76–85. The Global South. University of North Carolina Press.

Mechanic, Michael. 2016. "We Watched *Roots* with a *Roots* Expert—Part III." Mother Jones, June 2, 2016.

Meier, August. 1978. "The Triumph of Melville J. Herskovits." *Reviews in American History* 6, no. 1 (March): 21–28.

Murphy, Morna. 1977. "*Roots* review." *Hollywood Reporter*, January 21, 1977.

Nobile, Philip. 2018. "The Strange Evolution of Henry Louis Gates's Estimate of Alex Haley and *Roots*." *History News Network*, February 25, 2018.

Norrell, Robert J. 2015. *Alex Haley and the Books That Changed a Nation*. New York: St. Martin's Press.

Norrell, Robert J. 2018. "*Roots*: The Re-making of Africa and Slavery in the American Mind." In *Celluloid Chains: Slavery in the Americas through Film*, edited by Rudyard J. Alcocer, Kristen Block, and Dawn Duke, 24–39. Knoxville: University of Tennessee Press.

O'Connell, Mikey. 2016. "TV Ratings. *Roots* Returns with a Robust 5.3 Million Viewers." *The Hollywood Reporter*, May 31, 2016.

Osagie, Iyunolu. 2004. "Narrative Memory and Identity in Alex Haley's *Roots*." *CLA Journal* 47 (June): 391–408.

Ottaway, Mark. 1977. "Tangled Roots." *London Sunday Times*, April 10, 1977.

Page, Clarence. 1993. "Alex Haley's Facts Can Be Doubted, but Not His Truths." *Chicago Tribune*, March 10, 1993.

Raeside, Julia. 2017. "*Roots* Review: This Remake Is Brutal and Harrowing but It Needs to Be." *The Guardian*, February 9, 2017.

Reynolds, David S. 2011. *Mightier Than the Sword: Uncle Tom's Cabin and the Battle for America*. New York: W. W. Norton.

Reynolds, David S. 2020. *Abe: Abraham Lincoln in His Times*. New York: Penguin Press.

Ruane, Michael E. 2017. "Lost Slave Freedom Papers Tell of the Tortuous Paths out of Bondage." *Washington Post*, February 20, 2017.

Ryzik, Melana. 2016. "Roots Remade for a New Era." *New York Times*, May 15, 2016.

Saunders Redding, J. 1988. *To Make a Poet Black*. Ithaca: Cornell University Press.

Schaffer, Matt. 2005. "Bound to Africa: The Mandinka Legacy in the New World." *History in Africa* 32:321–69.

Schickel, Richard. 1977. "Television: Viewpoint: Middlebrow Mandingo." *Time Magazine*, January 24, 1977.

Van Arragon, William. 2012. "Fort Pillow, a Civil War Massacre, and Public Memory." *Canadian Journal of History* 47, no. 2 (Autumn): 454–55.

Variety Staff. 1977. TV Review: "*Roots* Miniseries a Remarkable Presentation." January 21, 1977.

Washington, Angela. "Afrofuturism in the Stacks: Watson's Library Collection of Afrofuturist Books." The MetMuseum.org, June 15, 2022.

Wright, Donald R. 2014. "Uprooting Kunta Kinte: On the Perils of Relying on Encyclopedic History in Africa." Cambridge University Press, May 13, 2014.

Wyatt-Brown, Bertram. 1986. *Honor and Violence in the Old South*. New York: Oxford University Press.

Chapter 4

Sankofa (1993)

Sankofa (1993), written, directed, edited, and produced by the Ethiopian American filmmaker and retired Howard University professor Haile Gerima (1946–), is a sprawling and searing Pan-Africanist epic film about American slavery. It's the time-traveling story of a contemporary Black model, Mona, played by Oyafunmike Ogunlano, on a photography shoot at the slave tourism site Cape Coast Castle in Ghana, a former fortress that held Africans before they were forced on ships during the transatlantic slave trade. The self-appointed guardian of the castle, the Divine Drummer, or Sankofa, played by Kofi Ghanaba, a.k.a. Guy Warren of Ghana (1923–2008), a high priest in real life, compels Mona to go back into her past life as an enslaved American. Sankofa, a mythical bird, means in the Akan language of Ghana to return to one's past to find what is useful to move forward in one's life.

The film opens with intense, hypnotic drumming and chanting. The incantation spoken and repeated is "Spirit of the dead, rise up and possess your bird of passage, and claim your story." Images of wooden African sculptures float across the screen. Details of the history of slavery, the African Holocaust, also known as the Maafa, are referenced, while images of tall sugarcane stalks against pink and lavender skies fill the screen.

Mona frolics in the ocean near the castle wearing an animal-print bathing suit, while a white male photographer captures her image, urging her to be sexier. The Divine Drummer is playing the drums, calling to Mona to confront her past, to go "back to your source," while a group of tourists are being shown the castle. The guide informs them that a row of ships waited for the human cargo. The Divine Drummer lashes out at the tourists telling them they are on "sacred ground. Our people were snatched and taken by the white man. It was here we were bought and sold to Jamaica, Trinidad,

Jamaica. It was genocide. They treated us with contempt." He claims he brings his stolen people back across the ocean to Africa.

The Divine Drummer taunts Mona, getting her attention. She follows the tourists to the dungeon, the portal to the past. Darkness ensues, and then Africans chained together stare at her. She screams, "You're making a mistake! STOP! I'm not an African! Don't you recognize me? I'm Mona! I'm an American!" She is dragged out by white men who cut her clothes off and brand her shoulder with an iron. The Sankofa bird appears and flies, and the sounds and images of chained Africans forced across the ocean morph into plantation images. Mona, who narrates the film, becomes Shola, "a house slave raised in the big house with Joe and Lucy," when she arrives in antebellum Louisiana.

"If you're born a slave," Mona says, "it was easier to accept things as they was (sic), but on the Lafayette Plantation we had people like Nunu and Shango." Shola lives in the house where, as shown in several flashbacks, she is brutally raped by the plantation owner. She befriends Shango, played by Allan Hope, a.k.a. Mutabaruka (born 1952). Mutabaruka is a Jamaican Rastafarian dub or reggae poet from the West Indies. Shango (the Yoruba god of thunder and war), who was sold to the Lafayettes because he was a militant "troublemaker," encourages Mona to resist, rebel, get revenge, and poison her white enslavers. At first, she refuses, claiming that mistreating others is evil.

Shango's Jamaican/West Indian accent is so strong that there are subtitles. This is quite unusual in films about enslaved African Americans where the spoken language, broken and/or grammatically incorrect English, is usually uniform. Mona attempts to run away, and Shango helps heal her after she is viciously beaten by the Catholic priest, Father Raphael, played by Reginald (a.k.a. Reggie) Carter (1936–95) in the church after being caught. Several scenes are set inside a church near the plantation.

Nunu, played by Alexandra Duah with an African accent (died in 2000), was raped on the ship coming to America when she was fifteen. Her biracial, blue-eyed son Joe, played by Nick Medley, the enslaved headman, is and always has been at odds with his mother; Mona says the two "couldn't set horses together." Nunu is firmly rooted in her native African culture, but Joe has been indoctrinated into Christianity and is disgusted by his mother's "heathenism." Joe is under the sway of Father Raphael's religion, Roman Catholicism; Joe is referred to by an enslaved man as "Bible Boy." The film is suffused with visual imagery of crosses, a confession room, robes, vestments, and iconography of the Virgin Mary, including paintings in the church and the locket Joe wears around his neck.

After Kuta, a pregnant woman played by Alditz McKenzie, gets caught running away to the people who have escaped to the hills to live free—she wanted to have her baby in a free place, Joe asks Noble Ali, an enslaved man played by Afemo Omilami, Nunu's friend and potential love interest, to punish and beat her. Kuta is hoisted up on a whipping post, and her arms are tied up. Noble Ali at first refuses to beat her, saying he cannot count, and he is dizzy, but he is forced by the white overseer to do it.

After Noble faints, Joe takes over the whipping. Nunu confronts her son for whipping Kuta, who dies. Led by Nunu, the women take Kuta's body down. Nunu recites incantations to the ancestral spirits. She cuts the baby out of the dead woman and names him Kwame, meaning, she says, witness. Noble Ali tells Nunu he had always vowed to find his mother who was sold away from him. Instead of doing that, he says with profound shame and self-recrimination, "he took someone else's mother."

Despite Kuta's public punishment, the spirit of rebellion and resistance is not quashed; in fact, it is made stronger. The community depicted outside the plantation is vibrant and vital as is the call recruiting the enslaved still on the plantation. One leader, Mussa, played by Jimmy Lee Savage says, "We'll take all of you to the hills, one by one. We serve our own god in the hills. The snake shall have whatever is in the belly of the frog." A rebellion is planned—some enslaved people are going to light the plantation on fire even though they risk getting caught and being, in the words of an enslaved person, "put on the tops of trees for vultures to feed on. Hung up there for days until to die, one by one."

Nunu is being sold; Noble Ali cries out and begs the powers-that-be to not take her. She tells him not to worry; she is coming back. Shola is devastated by the news and runs to Nunu, hugging her and crying. Nunu does come back—upon her return, she jubilantly tells Noble and Shola that she was "too old to be sold, too old to be bought." Shola, who can no longer endure being raped by the enslaver, runs away. In voice-over, she reports that she was taken back by the overseer and dogs. She is called a heathen for attempting to escape and for associating with the Africans who live outside the plantation. She is stripped naked by Father Raphael in the church, while Joe watches. Her arms are tied up, and she is beaten. She is forced to swear her allegiance to Jesus Christ. Shango helps her to heal by lovingly spreading soothing leaves on her skin.

Lucy, an enslaved woman played by Mzuri, has made it clear to Joe and others that she is attracted to him. She goes to his cabin and seduces him, but he rejects her and forces her out when she touches his Madonna and Child necklace as they are about to make love. Devastated by Joe's rejection of her, Lucy asks Shango to mix a potion that will make Joe "come around" and love her. Shango warns her to only put a little bit of it in his food, but she puts a lot. Lucy brings Joe his altered food, and after eating it, he gets dizzy and nauseated. He acts like a madman, starts beating Lucy up, and then runs to the river. Nunu runs to his rescue down to the river after him and rocks him like a baby, calling him by his African name, Tumey. They tousle in the water, and in a fit of rage, Joe strangles Nunu after she rips off his Virgin Mary necklace. A contrite and devastated man, Joe carries his mother's body to the church and places her on a table with her arms outstretched. She is a Christ figure. Father Raphael warns Joe, "[T]he devil is trying to get to you through your mother."

Joe contradicts him and replies "Ain't she a saint?"

Shola reveals that the church was burned to ashes. Joe and Father Raphael perished, but a trace of Nunu was never found; "a buzzard came, rumor has it, and swooped her up and flew her back to Africa." Shola, with Shango's help and guidance, kills her sexually abusive master with a machete and is transformed back to the present in Africa, where the film begins. Mona is one of a group of formerly enslaved people sitting on the coast in Ghana looking out across the ocean at America and the past. She is shocked to see Nunu, who smiles as a tear falls down her face. Shola/Mona's spiritual journey has come full circle. She has confronted her past and is able to move on.

Made on a $1 million budget with money that took Gerima nine years to raise from American foundation grants as well as funders in Europe and Africa and filmed in Ghana, Burkina Faso, Jamaica, and Louisiana, Gerima sought but could not get equitable distribution for his seventh film (McKenna 1995). An outspoken critic of Hollywood's racism against Black films and filmmakers, Gerima said in 1993 that the ugly side of slavery, unlike the Holocaust, had not been embraced by Hollywood and that Hollywood for most of its history was only interested in Black exploitation stories (Henderson 1994). Gerima was not able to persuade the major movie theater chains to get behind it; the film has no movie stars or actors familiar to audiences. Consequently, he and his wife, his creative and business partner, Shirikiana Aina, decided to distribute the film through their own company, Mypheduh Films.

Coproduced with his wife, who is also a documentary filmmaker, Gerima formed a committee of local supporters who helped organize and present a fundraising Washington, DC, premiere that pulled in more than $20,000. They rented a movie theater in October 1993, and the film played there for eleven weeks after having its U.S. premiere in Baltimore, outlasting many other discount-priced films at the theater. *Sankofa* became a word-of-mouth phenomenon and was screened successfully in many cities, including New York, Philadelphia, Atlanta, Baltimore, Chicago, Detroit, Boston, and Washington, DC, where it had long runs and grossed more than $3 million.

Gerima, whose father was a well-known playwright in his native Gondar, Ethiopia, came to America in 1967 to study drama in Chicago, where according to his wife, he experienced "intense racism." After realizing that films had a much wider audience than plays, Gerima eventually decided to become a filmmaker. As a graduate student at the University of California, Los Angeles (UCLA), he made *Child of Resistance* (1973), a short film about the wrongful imprisonment of Black women, starring Barbara O. Jones, a.k.a. Barbara-O, and Barbarao, an actress with a close resemblance to Angela Davis, the iconic scholar/activist/Black Panther member;

Harvest: 3000 Years (1975), about a poor family in Ethiopia; and *Bush Mama* (1976), his thesis, a "landmark" quasi-documentary black-and-white film about police brutality and systemic racism. It is the story of a Black woman on public assistance in Watts, Los Angeles, and her relationship with a Black Vietnam War veteran who is wrongly convicted of a crime after returning home from the war. Her journey "dramatizes the development of political awareness, the rise of desire for political knowledge, and the burgeoning impulse toward political action" (Brody 2017).

Gerima's other films include *Teza* (2008), about Haile Mariam Mengistu's brutal dictatorship in 1970s Ethiopia, which won the equivalent of Africa's Oscar award; *After Winter: Sterling Brown* (1985), a documentary about the Black African American folklorist, scholar, and poet Sterling Brown; and *Ashes and Embers* (1982), an urban drama about an aggrieved Black Vietnam War veteran with posttraumatic stress disorder (PTSD), "possibly one of the best films on the psychological trauma of a Vietnam War veteran ever produced" (Kai 2016). Before the release of Spike Lee's *Da 5 Bloods* (2020), it was also, like *Bush Mama*, one of only a few films to feature an African American Vietnam veteran protagonist. An unscripted, revelatory moment was caught on film when in 1976 a Los Angeles Police Department squad interrupted and stopped Gerima's shoot of a scene in *Bush Mama*; they were suspicious of a Black filmmaker (*Spirits of Rebellion* 2016). You can watch this unscripted scene in Zeinabu irene Davis's documentary *Spirits of Rebellion* and witness a rarely seen aspect of systemic institutional racism. The police did not treat Gerima and his crew brutally; it was a disrespectful and insulting inconvenience.

Gerima was one of the founding members of the L.A. Rebellion, also known as the Los Angeles School of Black Filmmakers, a group who met as graduate students while studying film at UCLA. These talented and visionary artists attended the university's Master of Fine Arts (MFA) program from the 1960s until 1992. Gerima enrolled in 1971. The impetus was "Ethno-Communications," an innovative program created by Elyseo J. Taylor, a filmmaker, and the only Black professor at UCLA at that time, for multicultural students to investigate and expand the curriculum to document Native American, African American, Asian American, and Latin American lives. An outgrowth took root in the film department, and a multicultural lens was developed and put into motion, launching a masterful deep reservoir of careers and films.

The New York University film professor, scholar, and writer Clyde Taylor coined the name "LA Rebellion" in 1986 to convey the enduring, pioneering work of the collaborative vision and energy of the filmmakers, the first collective of Black and minority filmmakers. Taylor, in 1997, compared the L.A. Rebellion to the Renaissance humanist movement of the fourteenth and fifteenth centuries. He says, "While this may sound strange, it was a flawless analogy. Both movements tried to free images from cultural imprisonment with style" ("Humanism, Cinema, and Engagement" 2011). In addition to Haile Gerima, the Rebellion claims among others Charles Burnett, Julie Dash, Billy Woodberry, Jamaa Fanaka, Larry Clark, and Zeinabu irene Davis as founding members.

Though mostly Black, as Gerima notes, there were also "Chicanos, Asian, gutsy white left-wing and other filmmakers" who created a new, "Third Cinema"—one that was politically driven and nonconforming of commercial Hollywood fare, telling humanistic and dimensionalized stories of Black lives, highlighting Black pride and dignity (Kai 2016). The filmmakers, most of whom are still making films, shared a vision of storytelling infused with cultural diversity and inclusivity of subject matter, including gender and childhood themes, Black and minority family and working-class life, and Third World revolutionary movements.

In 1991, Julie Dash was the first African American woman to direct and theatrically release a full-length movie, the independent and experimental *Daughters of the Dust*, about the West Africanist Gullah culture outside of South Carolina; this film's intergenerational themes focusing on Southern women influenced Beyoncé to make her visual album *Lemonade*. Other notable L.A. Rebellion films include Jamaa Fanaka's *Penitentiary* (1979), the highest-grossing independent film of 1979; Charles Burnett's *Killer of Sheep* (1978); his award-winning *To Sleep with Anger* (1990); and *The Glass Shield* (1995), about police corruption, a Black cop, and the arrest of a Black man; and *Nightjohn* (1996)—see chapter 5.

The L.A. Rebellion filmmakers' mission was to "create an alternative—in narrative, style, and practice—to the dominant American mode of cinema" (Field, Horak, and Stewart 2015). Gerima was frustrated that students were not taught by filmmakers of color and that consequently, so many minority-themed stories were not being told. Professors urged students to "conform to Eurocentric standards of how films should be made" as well as upon whom they should focus, largely excluding people of color (Turner and Kamdibe 2008, 970). The films about Black lives being green-lighted in Hollywood in the 1960s and 1970s featured stereotypical characters and stories with a few exceptions that were one-dimensional. Gerima and his peers set out to write and film anything but the "Blaxploitation" films of the early 1970s "with their lurid emphases on sex and violence" (Field, Horak, and Stewart 2015). While there was pushback by organizations, including the National Association for the Advancement of Colored People (NAACP), who deemed Blaxploitation offensive and some filmmakers continue to bemoan Blaxploitation's legacy, it is also acknowledged as a "subgenre that acted as a kind of film backwater for black film-makers who were not going to get mainstream films to direct" (Anthony 2017). The actor Leon Isaac Kennedy, the lead in *Penitentiary*, claims that for him and other actors and storytellers, Blaxploitation was a "great training ground for Blacks in film" (*Spirits of Rebellion* 2016).

Meanwhile, an independent film revolution outside of Hollywood fomented, and myriad masterworks about the complexity of contemporary Black stories as well as historical films about slavery were made: Gerima's *Sankofa*; Davis's half-hour film *Mother of the River* (1995), a mesmerizing film about an enslaved young girl and her relationship with a magical older woman; and Burnett's eloquent and moving television film *Nightjohn* (1996), about how the enslaved achieved literacy.

Hollywood since the beginning of the film industry depicted slavery. Gerima has spoken out against Hollywood's versions of slave stories, what he calls "the plantation school of literature" (Gerima 1994, 100), in which the enslaved appear to be happy in their bondage and dancing and singing. His films present diasporic and mystical Pan-African perspectives, examining "the physical, cultural, and psychological dislocation of Black people during and after slavery." Gerima says that "Slavery was a scientific adventure, an attempt by an industrialized society to create a robotic society of mindless human beings, pure labor" (Gerima 1994). The attempt failed, and Gerima in *Sankofa* is interested in showing resistance, an outlier community, organizing, and the self-determination the enslaved managed to grab despite society's constraints.

He humanizes enslaved Africans. They are emotionally complicated people who refuse to "happily" accept their enslavement. They refuse to beat their brethren; they express rage; articulate resistance in drumming, music, potions, shelter, and spoken and unspoken language; plan rebellions; and kill their oppressors. A mother and son are depicted as fatal adversaries. He charts the arc of Mona's spiritual awakening, showing how she evolves into a person who believes killing for revenge is justified. Gerima created a graphic, revelatory, and mystical film.

In 1993, *Sankofa* won the Grand Prize at the African Cinema Festival in Italy and Best Cinematography, by Augustin Cubano, at the FESPACO Pan-African Film Festival in Burkina Faso, and it was nominated for the Golden Bear Award at the Forty-Third Berlin International Film Festival (Tassy 1994). The film's pulsating and rousing score was composed by David J. White. The strikingly lush cinematography by Augustin Cubano juxtaposes beautiful images with the horrors of slavery; the clay, earthly colors of Africa contrast with America's polychromatic skies.

Production design is credited to Kerry Marshall, the distinguished African American artist now known as Kerry James Marshall. A production designer directs and coordinates the visual elements of storytelling, the way the film looks, the style of location, costumes, and time period; s/he also oversees the art department. The colorful clothing worn expresses individual quirks of character more so than in other films depicting slavery, and the bright red headbands of the rebellious slaves symbolize their fire and fury to break free of the chains of slavery.

Richard Brody claims, "The central dramas of *Sankofa* are dramas of consciousness—the consciousness of the enslaved, and the consciousness of modern Black Americans of the origins and import of their culture. *Sankofa* depicts the appropriation of violence by its victims—and the movie itself is an act of history, a bearing of witness, and a reminder and reinforcement of dignity" (2019).

HISTORICAL BACKGROUND

Tourist visits to the more than forty slave river and coastal forts where Africans spent their last moments is known as ancestral tourism or heritage offerings and tripled in 2019 following the release of the Afrofuturist film *Black Panther* in 2018 (Prentice and Sibeko 2019). More than five hundred thousand people visited these sites in 2019, the four hundredth anniversary of Africans arriving in America. President Barack Obama visited the Cape Coast Castle in Ghana in 2009. He remarked, "[I]t reminds us of the capacity of human beings to commit great evil" ("Remarks" 2009).

Cape Coast Castle was a holding place for history's "largest forced human migration." The dungeons created and known by the British as "hot holes" would hold as many as fifteen hundred Africans, most of whom were male. Tourists can visit the "Door of No Return," out of which Africans walked onto the ships that transported them against their will to enslavement in the Americas. This is known as the Middle Passage. The boats took many months; it is estimated that "close to 15 percent of the twelve million Africans died aboard, en route." Some Africans in their first act of resistance against slavery jumped off the ship (https://www.atlasobscura.com/places/cape-coast-castleou).

The writer and African American studies scholar, Saidiya Hartman, in her book *Lose Your Mother: A Journey along the Atlantic Slave Route* (Farrar, Straus and Giroux, 2007) includes a chapter, titled "So Many Dungeons," documenting her numerous visits to Cape Coast Castle. She describes a brochure for the castle featuring children "costumed as slaves" (Hartman 2007, 133) and wonders if they can comprehend the severity of the children who were forced to leave their homes. Although she makes numerous visits to the castle, she "failed to discover anything." What she hoped to do was be able "to reach through time and touch the prisoners" (Hartman 2007, 119), as Mona does to the hypnotic beat of the Divine Drummer.

Keeping alive the practice of drumming, an intrinsic and essential aspect of West African culture, was another life-affirming act of resistance as well as an ancestral touchstone for the enslaved. Drumming was outlawed in some states when whites feared the enslaved were using drums to send messages of planned rebellions. In America, when it was still owned and controlled by the British, drumming fueled the Stono Rebellion, the largest rebellion of the enslaved before America achieved its independence ("Breaking the Silence" 2009). The 1739 rebellion, which took place at the Stono River, near Charleston, South Carolina, was also known as Cato's Conspiracy or Cato's Rebellion. Jemmy Cato (or Cater), who was able to write freedom passes for many of his brethren as he was literate, unlike the majority of the enslaved at this time, led twenty enslaved people in a protest march. They demanded their freedom, while beating drums and heading to Spanish Florida, also known as La Florida, for asylum. It did not end well for the enslaved; more than sixty were killed.

Starting in 1693, Spain's king Charles II offered refuge and citizenship in Spanish Florida for runaway enslaved British colonists from South Carolina and Georgia; it was contingent upon them to join a militia to fight for Spain or claim Catholicism as their religion. The Spanish relinquished control of Florida to the British in exchange for Cuba in 1763, but the newly freed Blacks created a community in the 1730s and built in St. Augustine, the oldest city in America, what is now a tourist destination, Fort Mose Historic State Park, also known as America's Black Colonial Fortress of Freedom.

The rebellious Maroons were escaped enslaved people who formed communities outside of plantations. The word "Maroon," like the French *marron,* derives from the Spanish *cimarrón,* originally referred to stray cattle. First recorded in English in 1666 as a reference to African American runaways, it suggested "the beast who cannot be tamed," "fierceness," being "wild," and "unbroken" (Price 2018). The legendary Nanny of the Maroons about whom books have been written, was a Jamaican resistance leader. Her face appears on the $500 bill, the largest currency in Jamaica. From the Ashanti tribe in Ghana, Nanny lived in the Blue Hills of Jamaica in an area called Nanny Town. She was an Obeah woman, a conjurer, and she led plantation raids that freed more than one thousand enslaved people. She was killed by a British soldier in 1733 (Bernard 2011).

"Marronage" is the term for the phenomenon of outlier communities that happened wherever there were enslaved Africans, Native Americans, and people of mixed race. Petit marronage refers to temporary communities, while grand marronage suggests permanent ones. Most communities ended when slavery did; however, grand marronage led to long-standing Maroon communities in, among other places, Florida and Suriname. Maroons settled in the mountainous areas of Jamaica, the caves of Louisiana, and wild land that bordered the farms and plantations and the cities and towns, places "where it was difficult for their owners to follow and catch them" (Diouf 2014, 5). There were many Maroon communities in South Carolina and in the Great Dismal Swamp—an area encompassing parts of Virginia and North Carolina. In some places, people were even able to sustainably plant crops.

Maroons were able to get what they were "denied elsewhere: autonomy, mobility, enterprise, a sense of physical security, freedom from scrutiny, control over their time and movement, and access to varied foods—interdependence, networks, and exchange" (Diouf 2014, 7). In Jamaica, they garnered so much power that the British in 1739 were forced to negotiate with them, forge a treaty, and recognize Maroon freedom (McKee 2017).

American Southern history reveals an abundance of documented stories about Maroon lives and the whites aggressively in pursuit of them. Rewards and harsh statutes, laws, and punishments erupted to police, outlaw, and curtail the Maroons' existence. Although these efforts were not completely successful, if found, Maroons were punished severely by being beaten and sold.

Gerima says traces of marronage in the caves of Louisiana and in much of the United States has been erased (Gerima 2019). Marronage, which threatened the white-controlled status quo, has, according to Gerima, been "surgically removed by the white supremacist narrative of history. In Jamaica, caves are named and marked. Georgia was created to stop maroons. History has been denied." Whites also attempted to eradicate traces of Africans' native religions.

Gerima said, "The church was the initial groundwork for slavery, miseducating enslaved Africans against their own interest to prepare them for the transportation or exploitation of their people" (Gerima 1994). The enslaved were exposed to specific teachings and various branches of Christianity and images of the Virgin Mary and child Jesus as practiced by plantation enslavers. Washington's Museum of the Bible displays a "slave Bible," published in 1807, which removed portions of Scripture, including the Exodus story, that could inspire rebellious thinking.

Some enslaver Christians used the Bible to justify slavery. Some taught that the Bible was not inherently racist, and God had previously sanctioned slavery—the Israelites owned slaves—and that He did not discriminate against African identity, and even that Christianity humanized the enslaved. Frederick Douglass condemned this hypocrisy by saying, "Between the Christianity of this land and the Christianity of Christ, I recognize the widest possible difference—so wide that to receive the one as good, pure, and holy, is of necessity to reject the other as bad, corrupt, and wicked" (Douglass 1845, 118).

Many white plantation enslavers compelled the enslaved to regularly attend their white-controlled churches, since they were fearful that if slaves were allowed to worship independently, they would ultimately plot rebellion against their enslavers. Some enslaved people believed that ministers who "promoted obedience to one's master as the highest religious ideal, as a mockery of the 'true' Christian message of equality and liberation as they knew it" (Maffly-Kipp 2005). There were Catholic bishops who publicly criticized slavery but privately condoned it. And there was a contingent of abolitionists known as the come-outers who left the church in the 1830s, inspired by the abolitionist William Lloyd Garrison, believing it should have been antislavery.

The enslaved drawn to religion created the new genre of Negro spirituals, infused with Christian beliefs but also with the pain of their mistreatment by whites. Ultimately, some enslaved forged a Christian community of faith, and "as they came in contact with this God, they found a different reality in him: the reality of Resurrection power and an ideology of resistance" (Stewart 2018). The songs and meetings provided refuge and catharsis; resistance was stirred up, and rebellions were organized.

Enslaved Africans were exposed to extrapolated teachings of the Bible even though they were not taught to read. But many religious enslaved people once they began to read felt liberated by the Scriptures and were able to challenge white-supremacist interpretations and "to validate their right to be free and function as equals in this nation" (Stewart 2018).

Non-Christian and African customs and practices were labeled "heathen" by white enslavers who unsuccessfully tried to outlaw them. Some music and "beliefs in the curative powers of roots and the efficacy of a world of spirits and ancestors did survive well into the nineteenth century," and new religions, "like Afaudou in Haiti (later referred to as 'voodoo'), Santeria in Cuba, and Candomblé in Brazirican" were formed (Maffly-Kipp 2005).

Enslaved African Americans through secret codes to which whites were not privy organized "hush harbors," where African music, beliefs, and rituals were blended with practices of evangelical Christianity (Maffly-Kipp 2005). Some enslaved men became preachers and felt chosen by God to spread the word of liberation. The prophet and preacher Nat Turner drew on the Bible's teachings for inspiration and a call to action against the injustice of slavery. He organized and led a violent rebellion in 1831 in Southampton, Virginia, that left approximately fifty-five to sixty white people dead. Turner's ultimate plan, which was unrealized, was for his follower rebels to meet in the Great Dismal Swamp, a Maroon community, to avoid capture. Turner was hanged in Jerusalem.

DEPICTION AND CULTURAL CONTEXT

This is the only feature film about American slavery that depicts the autonomous society of the Maroons, runaway enslaved African American people "serving their own god in the hills, rather than serving the white man's god," as Shango claims. People in the community are displaced by choice. They tell stories infused with African folklore. They have self-determination, and their dignity is intact. They create a stockpile of machetes, forks, pickaxes and announce how many babies have been born. They have rejected enslavement and achieved autonomy.

Tropes seen in other films about slavery are depicted in *Sankofa*. There are violent images of the enslaved being forced to beat their peers and numerous flashbacks of Shola being raped. The overseers are seen riding on horses and delegating whippings. A pregnant woman's hands are tied up in ropes, backs are bleeding and scarred, and overseers charge the light-skinned headman to whip the slaves. One unusual choice Gerima made is to eliminate any white women characters or enslaved children from the plantation life he depicts. The future is Kuta's newborn baby, who will be nurtured outside the plantation, in a Maroon community, by a woman more African than American.

When Joe in a psychotic rage, caused by the poison potion he was given, kills his African mother, Nunu, Gerima is commenting on the African American's rejection of his native culture. In contrast, Shango is connected to his native culture, as he is an Obeah practitioner. Obeah, called voodoo in Haiti, which introduced to the world the concept of the zombie, the soulless corpse that can be brought back to life by witchcraft, has its origins in a secret West African religion "that survived the period of slavery despite the colonizers' prohibition that the slaves practice any religion from which they might draw for empowerment. It is traditionally represented as a source of resistance that assisted in slave rebellions and inspired fear and awe among believers" (Mardorossian 1999, 1080). Shango defies his enslavement, and his love for and mentoring of Shola to enable her defiant act of killing the slave owner is transcendent and essential to her spiritual awakening.

Shango gives Shola the "handmade bird that he had carved out of wood. He called it a Sankofa bird, and he put it round my neck. Shango said the Sankofa was passed on to him by his Papa. But I tell you whatever that bird was all about after he put that bird on my neck, I became a rebel. No more was I scared of being flogged, burned; even death didn't scare me."

When Mona is in the dungeon at the beginning of the film and chained Africans are staring at and closing in on her, the haunting, hypnotic song "Jewe, you are the One," from the *Planet Drum* album by the Grateful Dead's drummer Mickey Hart, plays on the soundtrack. It was composed and sung by the Nigerian Babatunde Olatunji (1927–2003), a social activist and educator who composed the music for the theatrical production and film of Lorraine Hansberry's *A Raisin in the Sun* (1959 and 1961, respectively) ("The Nigerian Drummer" 2020).

When Mona is captured by the white men, her clothes are torn off, and she is horrifically branded. At this dramatic moment, Aretha Franklin (1942–2019), the Queen of Soul, sings the iconic Gospel song "Take My Hand, Precious Lord." Written in 1938 by the reverend Thomas Andrew Dorsey, an African American, it was Martin Luther King Jr.'s favorite song and a civil rights movement anthem. The last words King spoke before being assassinated on April 4, 1968, were his request for this song to be played (Adams 2018).

Nijla Mumin notes that the film offers a new type of narrative. Gerima removes slaves from "out of the one-dimensional, passive, 'victim' role, and embodies them with complications that manifest in active resistance, personal conflict, and compelling stories" and unlike most films about slavery, *Sankofa* has no "white savior" (2017). Wilkes explains the pervasiveness of the white savior film. She says, "The concept is common in slave stories where the slave must be saved from captivity by a benevolent member of the non-slave class. This idea is supremely important to the concept of sankofa because it requires the person to take an active role in reclaiming themselves" (2015).

The novelist Octavia E. Butler (1947–2006), an African American woman, was an award-winning science fiction writer, one of few Black women writing in that genre at that time. She came of age and was inspired to speak out against racism and social injustice by the civil rights and Black Power movements. There are similarities as well as great differences to *Kindred* (1979), Butler's virtuosic and mesmerizing time-travel novel about slavery, released on Hulu as an FX-produced eight episode series in December 2022. Dana, a Black woman married to a white man in 1976 returns through a portal to a Maryland plantation in the 1850s to become an enslaved person to save and protect a child, saving his life on a few occasions, who will turn out to be her ancestor. Mona while not married to the white photographer is sexualized by him during the shoot at the beginning of the film. In another parallel to *Sankofa*, Dana, like Shola in the story's cathartic climax, kills a white slave owner in self-defense when he attempts to rape her. Dana returns on numerous occasions to the past, while Mona's journey is one long sequence taking up most of the film story. Dana's trajectory and character arc is much more central and integral to *Kindred's* linear narrative than Shola's is in *Sankofa*, a mosaic narrative ultimately pitting American-born, Christian Joe against his African mother.

Kindred is taught in colleges, and a graphic version of it was published in 2017. The horror film *Antebellum* (2020), written and directed by Gerard Bush and Christopher Renz and starring Janelle Monae, is also a time-traveling and revenge story superficially about slavery. Peter Debruge's August 31 *Variety* film review references *Kindred*, and *Decider.com* asks the filmmakers if *Antebellum* is based on the novel; they say it is not; however, there is not one review that references *Sankofa*, likely due to its lack of distribution on any platform and, consequently, the general reviewer's lack of awareness about the film.

Gerima has discussed the challenges he had (and still has) distributing his films. Although in the 1980s and 1990s, more and more films about Black lives were being produced in Hollywood, he notes that Blockbuster—the DVD chain that opened in 1985 and after streaming films became the dominant platform for home entertainment—closed its stores in 2010 and did not carry his films nor other independently financed Black films. At the same time in 1993, New Line Cinema, a division of Warner Brothers, released *Menace II Society*, written, directed, and produced by Allen and Albert Hughes, African American twin brothers who were twenty-one years old at the time. Tyger Williams, who was twenty-four, wrote the screenplay from a story he and the Hughes brothers created. Its graphic violence shows urban, contemporary life in Watts, Los Angeles. It is suffused with a hip-hop soundtrack and rife with guns, gangsters, and angry young men. The film begins with news footage of the race riots in Watts that took place nearly thirty years before the film was made. During six days in August 1965, there were violent clashes in Watts between the police and African Americans militating against systemic racism.

The Los Angeles Riots of 1992 erupted in April of that year after four police officers were acquitted by a mostly white jury of their beating of Rodney Glen King (1965–2012), an African American author and activist. King was pursued in a high-speed car chase in March 1991 after being caught driving while intoxicated. This was one of the first cases where a vicious act of police brutality was caught on video. Two of the four officers in the King case ultimately, in 1993, "were found guilty of violating King's civil rights and sentenced to 30 months in prison" (Sastry and Grigsby Bates 2017).

CONCLUSION

In *Sankofa*, Gerima is calling people of African descent to connect to and reclaim their history and to cling to their culture, their mother country, and tongue, as Nunu does. The young woman who was raped by a white man during the Middle Passage and then killed by the son born of that rape is reborn and reunited with the land of her birth from which she was forced to leave. Nunu's story is juxtaposed with Mona, the model who experiences the life of an enslaved person to understand and empathize with her ancestors' experience.

Sankofa's reputation as an essential and exceptional film about slavery continues to grow; despite this, the film is not available on any streaming platform, and a DVD of the film costs one hundred dollars. It is one of the few films about slavery that depicts how formerly enslaved people resisted and rebelled, forging self-determined lives in Maroon communities outside of white control. The film scholar and curator, Aboubakar Sanogo, presenting *Sankofa* and Haile Gerima in April 2019 at the Power Plant Art Gallery in association with the Toronto International Film Festival (TIFF), said of the film that it is "invested in the decolonial project insofar as it seeks to sanction the humanity of the brutally enslaved through the impossible audacities of the imagination and imaginary through their knowledge and knowhows. The film makes clear that no amount of oppression or willful attempt at destruction will ever triumph over the rebellious and indocile creative and imaginative resources of the human. . . . Instruments of debasement become instruments of liberation—the machetes that cut the cane also chop the bodies of the perpetrators" (*Sankofa* 2019, 17:17–17:54).

The film is filled with symbolism and images of the sankofa bird. *Sankofa* humanizes the experience of the African's past and undergirds the awareness and need for American Blacks to connect to and remember it, so it never happens again. It is a complicated and layered film that tells many stories, but its Afro-centric mysticism suffuses it as does its Black rage—a rage so violent that a man kills his mother.

Gerima says, "[A]ll art is political" (1994). Mona is a beautiful young woman whose profession is as superficial as is her knowledge of African American history. Until the Divine Drummer calls her to her past, she is apolitical and unaware of and unaffected by the struggles and the pain her people endured. Like Nunu, Mona is reborn at the end of the film; when she arrives back in Africa, she is naked, and an older woman covers her with a blanket, saying, "Don't cry, my child. All is well."

FURTHER READING

Adams, Lucy. 2018. "MLK's Last Words: Play Precious Lord." *The Mountaineer*, April 11, 2018.

Anthony, Andrew. 2017. "Spike Lee: Still the Boldest and Brashest Auteur in American Film." *The Guardian*, November 25, 2017.

Beik, William. 1994. "Review of *Sankofa*." H-Ideas, H-Net Reviews, July 1994.

Bernard, I. 2011. *Queen Nanny of the Marrons (?–1733)*. https://www.blackpast.org/global-African-history/queen-nanny-maroons-1733.

"Breaking the Silence Beating the Drum." 2009. Website Development. UN Web Services Section. Department of Public Information.

Brody, Richard. 2017. "*Bush Mama*: A Landmark Film, and a Reminder of Cinema's Exclusionary History." *New Yorker*, April 26, 2017.

Brody, Richard. 2019. "Three Boldly Personal Visions of History in a Great New Black Film Series." *New Yorker*, May 2, 2019.

Davis, Zeinabu irene, dir. 2016. *Spirits of Rebellion: Black Cinema at UCLA*. Wimmin with a Mission Productions. Streaming.

Diouf, Sylviane A. 2014. *Slavery's Exiles: The Story of the American Maroons*. New York: NYU Press.

Douglass, Frederick. 1845. *Life of a Slave*. Boston: Anti-Slavery Office.

Field, Allyson Nadia, Jan-Christopher Horak, and Jacqueline Najuma Stewart, eds. 2015. *L.A Rebellion: Creating a New Black Cinema*. Oakland: University of California Press.

Gerima, Haile. 1994. "Filming Slavery: A Conversation with Haile Gerima." Interview by Pamela Woolford. *Transition* 64:90–104.

Gerima, Haile. 2019. "Post-Screening *Sankofa*." Interview by Brenda Stevenson. Hammer Museum, November 21, 2019. https://www.youtube.com/watch?v=eRfp0cJOQrQ.

Grant, Richard. 2016. "Deep in the Swamps, Archaeologists Are Finding How Fugitive Slaves Kept Their Freedom." *Smithsonian*, September 2016.

Hartl, John. 1995. "Film on Slavery Fights for Screenings." *Seattle Times*, September 22, 1995.

Hartman, Saidiya. 2007. *Lose Your Mother: A Journey along the Atlantic Slave Route*. New York: Farrar, Straus and Giroux.

Henderson, Shirley. 1994. "Filmmaker Puts Black Life Out Front." *Chicago Tribune*, September 2, 1994.

"Humanism, Cinema and Engagement: Clyde Taylor and the L.A. Rebellion Symposium." 2011. https://www.cinema.ucla.edu/blogs/la-rebellion/2011/11/16/humanism-cinema-and-engagement-clyde-taylor-and-la-rebellion-symposium.

James, Caryn. 1994. "Reliving a Past of Slavery." *New York Times*, April 8, 1994.

Kai, Nubia. 2016. "*Ashes and Embers*, the Film: A Critical Review." *Journal of the African Literature Association* 10 (2): 222–36.

Kande, Sylvie, and Joe Kanaganis. 1998. "Look Homeward, Angel: Maroons and Mulattos in Haile Gerima's *Sankofa*." *Research in African Literatures* 29, no. 2 (Summer): 128–46.

Maffly-Kipp, Laura. 2005. "African American Christianity, Pt. I: To the Civil War." *Christianity Today*. http://nationalhumanitiescenter.org/tserve/nineteen/nkeyinfo/aareligionc.htm.

Mardorossian, Carine M. 1999. "Shutting Up the Subaltern: Silences, Stereotypes, and Double-Entendre in Jean Rhys's *Wide Sargasso Sea*." *Callaloo* 22, no. 4 (Fall): 1071–90.

McKee, Helen. 2017. "From Violence to Alliance: Maroons and White Settlers in Jamaica, 1739–1795." *A Journal of Slave and Post-Slave Studies* 39, no. 1 (June): 27–52.

McKenna, Khristine. 1995. "*Sankofa*: A Saga of Slavery Reaches the Big Screen." *LA Times*, May 29, 1995.

Mumin, Nijla. 2017. "Haile Gerima's *Sankofa* Revisited." *Shadow and Act*, May 1, 2017.

"The Nigerian Drummer Who Set the Beat for US Civil Rights." 2020. *BBC News*, September 1, 2020.

Prentice, Alessandra, and Siphiwe Sibeko. 2019. "Ghana Cashes in on Slave Heritage Tourism." *World News*, August 20, 2019.

Preston, Rohan B. 1994. "Poetic Injustice." *Chicago Tribune*, August 31, 1994.

Price, Richard. 2018. "Maroons and Their Communities in the Americas." *Politika*, February 7, 2018.

Reel American History. History on Trial. Edward Gallagher. Lehigh Digital Library.

"Remarks by the President at Cape Coast Castle." 2009. White House. Office of the Press Secretary. July 11, 2009.

Sankofa, with Haile Gerima and Aboubakar Sanogo. 2019. "Resistance & Rebellion: The Cinema of Haile Gerima.TIFF." April 13, 2019. Power Plant Contemporary Art Gallery.

Sastry, Anjuli, and Karen Grigsby Bates. 2017. "When LA Erupted in Anger: A Look Back at the Rodney King Riots." NPR, April 26, 2017.

Stewart, Dante. 2018. "Why the Enslaved Adopted the Religion of Their Masters–and Transformed It." *Christianity Today*, February 12, 2018.

Tassy, Elaine. 1994. "*Sankofa* Takes a Different Route to Theaters." *LA Times*, January 24, 1994.
Thomas, Kevin. 1995. "'*Sankofa*' Delivers Powerful Indictment of Evil of Slavery." *Los Angeles Times*, May 12, 1995.
Turner, Diane, and Muata Kamdibe. 2008. "Haile Gerima: In Search of an Africana Cinema." *Journal of Black Studies* 38 (6): 968–91.
Wilkes, Niki. 2015. "'Sankofa' and Us: How Looking Back Moves Us Forward." https://blogs.bsu.edu/dlr/2015/03/09/sankofa-and-us-how-looking-back-moves-us-forward/2015.

Chapter 5

Nightjohn (1996)

Based on Gary Paulsen's award-winning seventh- to twelfth-grade young adult novel *Nightjohn* (Laurel Leaf, 1993), the exceptional feature-length made-for-television movie *Nightjohn* was broadcast on the Disney Channel on June 1, 1996. The story centers around an enslaved girl, Sarny, played and narrated by an irrepressible Allison Jones (1984–). She is taught to read and write by Nightjohn, an escaped enslaved man played with understated emotionality by Carl Lumbly (1951–), despite harsh rules against and punishment for it. It was directed by Charles Burnett (1944–), the 2017 honorary Governors Academy Award–winning African American director of many distinguished films, including *The Glass Shield* (2000); *To Sleep with Anger* (1990), also starring Lumbly; *My Brother's Wedding* (1983); and *Killer of Sheep* (1978). Coproduced by Hallmark Entertainment, the book was adapted, and the story was expanded and deepened by Peabody Award–winning playwright/producer Bill Cain (1947–).

Set on a cotton plantation in the antebellum South in 1831, the film opens with an image of Nightjohn in a prayerful pose on his knees in silhouette. Twelve-year-old Sarny in voice-over says, "This is a story about Nightjohn; I guess it is also a story about me. He told me all you got is what you remember, and I remember everything." Sarny even remembers being born, and her birth is portrayed.

The surly, cash-starved plantation owner, Clel Waller, played by Beau Bridges (1941–), stops by the cabin. He is disappointed when it is revealed the baby is a girl and says, "A boy would grow up to be worth $1,000. Can't even give away a little gal."

Sarny's mother, played by Robin Malam-Vaughn, rocks her little girl but is taken away from her four years later and will likely never see her again.

As she waves good-bye, Sarny fiercely holds onto her doll. Her mother "was a good breeder" and was therefore sold by Waller. Sarny's surrogate mother, Delie, played by Lorraine Toussaint (1960–), an enslaved house servant, grooms Sarny to be chatty, so she can work in the house rather than in the field, though Delie admits that she herself prefers working in the field; she "likes the company better." Delie teaches Sarny to listen to and smile at white people, so she can "get them to come around." Sarny assists in taking care of Weller's young son, Homer, played by John Herina (1991–). She is also charged with chewing and spitting tobacco on roses to prevent bugs and help them grow.

Nightjohn, tall and muscular, arrives in chains on the plantation. The slave trader tells Waller his price is $500, who is skeptical. Why is he underselling "this tree of a slave worth $3,000? Is he a troublemaker"? "He has good teeth," the trader says, but Waller is not interested in his teeth. He insists on looking at his back—the many raised, crisscrossing scars that are revealed prove he has endured myriad lashings for being defiant. His price is lowered to $50, but the trader tells Nightjohn to take off his pants.' For $50,' he says to Waller, "you can't have his clothing."

Nightjohn lives in the same cabin or quarters as Sarny; Delie; Old Man, played by Bill Cobbs (1934–); and Outlaw, played by Gabriel Casseus (1972–), a young man of about twenty who is in love with Egypt, played by Monica Ford, an enslaved woman who was sent to work on Clel's brother's plantation. Nightjohn asks if anyone has tobacco, and Sarny says she does, but wants to know what he is going to give her. He says, "What I got nobody can take away from me."

Sarny replies, "If they can see it, they can take it."

Nightjohn says, "They can't see it. I got letters."

They make a deal. Nightjohn tells her anytime she makes a letter she has "to get rid of it, so nobody ever sees it, just you and me." He then writes the letters in the dirt with a branch. Here is an *A*, he models.

"Where is the bottom to it," Sarny asks?

"Ain't got no bottom; stands on two feet. Just like you and me," her teacher responds and then writes a *B*. "B reminds me of my wife, who ran away." He draws a *C* and explains that "C has his mouth open like he's got something important to say." This ABC mantra is repeated a few times throughout the film.

Nightjohn tells Sarny and Delie that he was beaten for running away twice. He ran for the first time after his wife was sold for killing an overseer after he threatened to beat their son. "She chopped that man up into fine pieces. And then she killed his horse. She felt bad about the horse," Nightjohn tells Outlaw and Delie, and they laugh. The third time he "got clean away, went north all the way to freedom," but risked his freedom to come back to teach, which is extraordinary, as getting to Canada on the Underground Railroad took a lot of help and knowledge of safe routes and was an arduous endeavor.

When Old Man learns that Nightjohn is teaching Sarny to read, he is infuriated, and in one of the most powerful scenes in the film reluctantly reveals that he knows the alphabet and how to read. He shows Nightjohn the punishment he received for learning to read; his finger was chopped off. Old Man has become embittered; instead of giving him cultural power, literacy took away something from him. Nightjohn is aware of the risk and says what he says verbatim in the novel: "Words are freedom, Old Man. 'Cause that's all that slavery's made of: words, laws, deeds, passes. All they are is words. White folks got all the words, and they mean to keep them. You get some words for yourself and you be free" (Paulsen 1993, 18).

Delie expresses her fear of Sarny getting caught like Old Man was and tells Nightjohn to stop teaching Sarny. John tells Delie that she is teaching Sarny something worse than he is: to be afraid. While working in Waller's house, Sarny comes upon his ledger and realizes she cannot read it. She accuses Nightjohn of lying to her about teaching her all the letters. They are numbers, he tells her, and then tells her there are only ten of them, and he teaches her numbers. Delie says since there are only ten, she wants to learn them as well.

In church while holding the Bible, Sarny realizes she can read. She is overwhelmed and starts crying, and the preacher asks her if she has been saved. She says, "Yes, I am saved." She is saved, not necessarily by the words of the Bible, but more immediately by the ability to read them, thereby achieving the empowerment of literacy. The preacher arranges for her to be publicly baptized. Once Sarny can read and comprehend the Bible's teachings, she realizes that the preacher has been lying; contrary to how Christianity is taught in church, God is "actually on the side of the slaves."

Back in the cabin, she is reading a newspaper, the *Gazette*, about the 1831 insurrection in Southampton County, Virginia, led by Nat Turner and his "army of slaves." Old Man incredulously echoes Sarny, "Army of slaves?" Nightjohn and the others raptly gather around her to hear her read the news of the fiery revolutionary's protest and the suggestion that the insurrection was successful. They are animated, prideful, and hopeful that change is in the air.

Outlaw asks to visit Egypt, his girlfriend who works on Waller's brother's plantation, but Waller refuses his request. Old Man helps him by being a decoy to distract the overseers on the lookout for runaways. Sarny steals a Bible from Waller's house to practice reading, and Nightjohn tears a page from it to write a pass for Outlaw, prompting a character to say, "Never thought the best page in the Good Book would be the one with no writing on it!" When the Bible is discovered in Sarny's cabin by Waller's older son, Jeff, played by Joel Traywick, who says he got a licking when it went missing, Delie says she took it. But then Nightjohn insists that he took it. Waller chops off his finger in front of everyone to make an example of him. In defiance, Nightjohn teaches the slaves openly, and when Waller sees this, he picks up his gun to shoot him. Jeff Waller prevents his father from shooting him and sells him.

But when another pass is written for Outlaw, and Waller cannot figure out who did it, he interrupts a church service and threatens to shoot all the enslaved until he knows who wrote it. Sarny confronts and contradicts him, claiming that the enslaved are his wealth, and he will not shoot them because he needs the money. She then quotes prices for Waller's enslaved assets: the old man is worth $500; Delie's value is $1,000; Nightjohn's worth is $50. Mrs. Waller, fearing that Sarny will reveal her secret epistolary flirtation with the doctor, tells her husband to shoot her, but Sarny blackmails Mrs. Waller. The doctor steps up and, to defuse the situation, dishonestly claims he wrote the pass. When everyone walks away, he gives Sarny a coin, and she gives him a letter of his to Waller's wife. Sarny looks up at her fellow congregants. They smile at her and in dulcet solidarity sing the song from "Exodus," "I will sing unto the Lord for he has triumphed gloriously. The horse and rider thrown into the sea!" Sarny is sold away at the end of the film. She never found Nightjohn, she says in voice-over, but she found many people who knew and were taught by him.

Nightjohn was Burnett's first television movie. Subsequently, and also for ABC, he directed another historical-themed film, *Selma, Lord, Selma* (1999) about the 1965 protest march, known as Blood Sunday, led by the late congressman John Lewis over the Edmund Pettus Bridge, as well as *Oprah Winfrey Presents the Wedding* (1998), based on the Harlem Renaissance writer Dorothy West's 1995 novel about an interracial marriage in upper-crust Black society in the 1950s on Martha's Vineyard.

Burnett cowrote and directed the fascinating, experimental, "daring and imaginative" documentary, *Nat Turner, A Troublesome Property* (2003), also starring Carl Lumbly, playing one of the Nat Turners in the film (Brody 2020). It was funded in part by and aired on the Public Broadcasting System's Independent Lens series. It's a fifty-eight-minute film investigating Nat Turner's complicated and fraught legacy and how he has been depicted as "a great and inspiring hero and vilified as an insane fanatic" (Burnett 2003).

William Styron, the Pulitzer Prize–winning author of the controversial novel *The Confessions of Nat Turner* (Random House, 1967), discusses why the film adaptation of his novel, despite the record-breaking payment for the rights, never got made. The film includes reenactments of key scenes of Styron's novel, including the insurrection, as well as other actors playing other iterations of Turner, including from his memoir, *The Confessions of Nat Turner by Thomas R. Gray* (1832) dictated to a lawyer while Turner was waiting to be hanged. Well-known historians of slavery, including Henry Louis Gates Jr., Herbert Aptheker, and Eric Foner are interviewed. Burnett also interviews a descendant, Bruce Turner, who has heard firsthand stories about Nat Turner.

Burnett, a trailblazer in the Black independent film world, was a 1988 MacArthur Genius Award winner. Burnett, like Gerima, was also a founding member of the L.A. Rebellion filmmakers who bonded together to express "their utopian vision of a better society and create a new Black cinema non-conforming of typical commercial Hollywood fare." Their mission was to innovate, crafting new ways of telling stories focusing on the Black experience that are not only "entertaining but also meaningful" (Burnett 2020).

The L.A. Rebellion filmmakers, many of whom, like Burnett, are still making films, were in part inspired by Italian Neorealistic films to show all aspects of the quotidian Black experience, including stories about gender issues, children, work, and family. They also wanted to show their interest in social change, their "identification with the liberation movements in the Third World, and their expression of Black pride and dignity" (Field, Horak, and Stewart 2015, 9). The board of governors of the Academy Awards gave Burnett an honorary award in 2017. He has taught film, most recently in 2018, as a visiting artist in residence at Bard College.

Burnett was the first African American recipient in 1990 of the National Society of Film Critics' best screenplay award, for *To Sleep with Anger* (cinema.ucla.edu). *Killer of Sheep* (1976), set in inner city Watts, Los Angeles, is considered a neorealist class of Black lives. The film scholar Jacqueline Najuma Stewart says students comment that the film feels like "poor people's home movies," and she marvels at how apt the description is, as that reaction reveals the film's authenticity (Davis 2016).

Burnett is currently in development at Amazon with *Steal Away*, a film about an enslaved Charleston, South Carolina, man named Robert Smalls, who in 1862 managed to disguise himself as a Confederate captain and steer a steamer and its seventeen passengers to safely escaping slavery. Although a $4,000 bounty was put on his head, he was celebrated as a hero in the North, and in concert with secretary of war Edwin Stanton, Smalls initiated the recruitment of Black soldiers to fight in the Civil War and helped to enlist "5,000 men" (Gates 2013). Smalls became a Republican congressman during Reconstruction and wrote legislation that "guaranteed that all South Carolina's children—black and white, rich and poor"—could attend "a liberal and uniform system of free public schools, making South Carolina the first state to provide free and compulsory public school system in the United States" (Bowers 2019).

HISTORICAL BACKGROUND

Because there were more enslaved men than women, "slave reproduction was low," and the problem was exacerbated by "prolonged breastfeeding," "high infant mortality," and the high mortality rate of enslaved men and women (Heuman and Walvin 2003). Young, enslaved women were advertised for sale as "good breeding stock" called "breeding wenches" and worth $1,000. A Virginian slave trader bragged that his profitable breeding policies made it possible in a good year to sell as many as six thousand slave children (Simkin 2014).

Plantation enslavers urged enslaved women to start getting pregnant at age thirteen and have four to five children by twenty and often justified raping them to increase their fertility. Some enslavers promised breeding women their freedom once they "produced fifteen children" (Heuman and Walvin 2003). From when a child was born, a price was put on its head. American enslaved people brought higher prices than Africans because they had field and house training and understood English. The enslaved were examined and sold like other property, including horses and merchandise. They got higher prices if they were skilled laborers. Light-skinned enslaved women sold as sex workers garnered a higher price and were a staple of the New Orleans market (Daley 2014). Women of childbearing age or breeders were sought after and had higher value than young or older girls/women. Some were sold in public auctions; some were exchanged privately via mortgages and legal deeds.

While the central story of Nightjohn and Sarny and his memorable and repeated descriptions of A, B, and C are straight out of the thin (ninety-two-page) novel, Bill Cain's adaptation leaves out the graphic story of a young woman named Alice, brutally beaten for her defiance when she's forced to be a breeder.

Whites controlled (or attempted to control) all aspects of the enslaved mental and physical life and personhood, including their intellect, rationalizing such control with false claims. Leaders like Thomas Jefferson espoused the theory that Blacks were inferior to whites "with respect to their capacity for reason, imagine, and sentiment," even though Sally Hemings, his partner of more than thirty years and mother of at least six of his children, was a woman of color. American "craniometrists" claimed Black brains were smaller than whites', and pseudoscientists with fake science claims linking race to intelligence propagated white supremacy (Gundaker 2007).

According to Tolley, however, "despite the rhetoric about the intellectual inferiority of slaves, the South's anti-literacy laws presupposed the intellectual equality of blacks and whites," as Brown University president Francis Wayland pointed out in *Elements of Moral Science*—a text that was highly popular in Northern schools by 1835. "Such laws suppose the capacity of Negroes for intellectual culture and are an implicit confession that it is necessary to degrade their minds to keep their bodies in slavery" (2016). Still, by the middle of the nineteenth century, proslavery Americans continued to spread baseless claims and rhetoric about "the inherent intellectual inferiority of slaves. The old awareness and fear of slaves' and free Blacks' potential to achieve literacy on a par with whites became knowledge forgotten, overlooked, or relinquished—in this case, a willful ignorance of political actions in the past that served to maintain a large portion of the South's population in a state of ignorance" (Tolley 2016). It was a learned ignorance that enabled enslaving Southerners to rationalize their crime against humanity.

The human being's capacity for and evidence of learning, storytelling, humor, drama, and the love and joy of observing, sharing, collaboration, creativity, and depicting life is documented in all cultures since the beginning of modern human society. People make sense of the world through narrative; it is hardwired. While not all ancient cultures developed a written language, creation and end-of-the-world myths are universally found in oral and written traditions as are pictorial narratives and symbolic artworks about gods and goddesses to explain nature, heroes, villains, predatory animals, and shamanic practices.

Literacy for the enslaved was verboten for many reasons. When shown they were able to learn, the case for Black inferiority fell apart. Enslaved people's rights were not protected; they were considered "property and only three-fifths human," according to the U.S. Constitution written in 1787. To be able to read and therefore learn and reason was "considered after the Enlightenment what it meant to be fully, 100%, human" (Brander Rasmussen 2010).

Literacy and freedom were enmeshed from the beginning till the end of slavery. Enslaved people if literate would be able to write their passes to freedom (known as manumission). These passes were known as "freedom papers." The newly freed were mandated by law to be in the presence of a white person to "validate their presence" and papers and passes, signed by the slave owner, were required (Gundaker 2007, 1591). Also, enslavers would sometimes allow their enslaved people to work for payment at other plantations as freelancers. Slave passes, metal slave tags, or slave hire badges were required for the enslaved to move around, without which they could be arrested, jailed, and detained as runaways. This surveillance and identification system enabled plantation enslavers to have control and authority over and keep track of the enslaved's movement. Specific details of the purpose of the travel, the date and time due back, and the names of people and plantations were written on the pass ("Slavery, Institutional Racism" 2014).

Punishment could be inflicted on the enslaved person if caught without a pass. Passes were also used for illiterate, poor white indentured servants. The passes are one of earliest-known examples of numbered IDs ("Slavery, Institutional Racism" 2014). Passes were not difficult to forge. Free papers would often only mention the enslaved person's name, gender, age, and the date s/he was freed. Therefore, it wasn't hard for any person of a similar age and gender to use the same pass, although sometimes, there would be a brief description of the person's age and physical type.

Sadly, freedom papers were not a guarantee that a person of color would remain free—until slavery was abolished in 1865, a freed person of color was always at risk of being forced back into slavery. This is what happened to Solomon Northup, the author of the 1853 best-selling memoir *Twelve Years a Slave*, first adapted by the director Gordon Parks, the first African American to direct a Hollywood film for a major studio, *The Learning Tree* (1969), into the 1984 television movie *Solomon Northup's Odyssey*, and then into *12 Years a Slave*, Steve McQueen's 2013 Best Picture Academy Award–winning film.

Since the basic form of identification within the pass system was the name, naming too became a site of resistance. Mothers gave their children distinct names to keep track of them, via the grapevine, if they were sold off later in life. And truant slaves visiting distant plantations could try to evade patrollers by simply pretending to be a local of the plantation they were visiting.

The link between literacy and emancipation as a through line in African American history has often been noted (Gates Jr. quoted by Gundaker 2007, 1601). "Literacy, a term coined in the 1880s, is a fairly modern concept, one aligned with individualism, exceptionalism, social progress, cultural and economic power. And African American authors began to claim literacy as a human right, and abolitionists of both races concurred" (Barton Sweiger 2013). By 1850, the South boasted a high rate of literacy—"more than 80 percent of free people could read, 10 percent of slaves and free Blacks were literate. Like people all over the world, people achieved literacy in great numbers by the mid-nineteenth century" (Barton Sweiger 2013). The publishing industry in the Northeast was growing, and books, once a luxury reserved mainly for the rich, were becoming widely distributed and available. Most people were self-taught or taught by those who had achieved literacy. Public school, not available to every person, wasn't mandatory until the 1920s, and free Blacks were discouraged from attending schools.

Whites in rural areas, where schools were sparse, were more likely to be illiterate than urban whites. Until the nineteenth century, reading and writing were taught independently; most women could not write, although some were able to read. "Reading acquired a new sacred potential, wielding the power to bestow a rebirth and transform even unexceptional people to the very depths of self, a power it retains in our own age." Conversely, the New Orleans publisher and magazine editor J. D. B. De Bow bemoaned that to many Southerners, "Negroes, cotton, and corn rather than knowledge was power" (Barton Sweiger 2013).

And if the enslaved were able to write, and some were, they could and would, as Northup did, write books. Literacy would "expose" slavery—slave narratives were a threat to the white-supremacist enslavers. Memoirs penned by the enslaved revealed the horrors of and truth about slavery; slave narratives enabled the enslaved to "write themselves into being" (Gates 1997). More than one hundred slave narratives were published from 1760 up to the end of the Civil War. The books offered "key testimony," and many of them sold in the tens of thousands in multiple editions (Andrews 2001).

The most popular narratives were Frederick Douglass's *Narrative in the Life of Frederick Douglass* (1845); Harriet Jacobs's *Incidents in the Life of a Slave Girl* (1860); and William Wendell Brown's *The Narrative of a Fugitive Slave by Himself* (1847). Brown was the first Black writer to publish a novel: *Clotel*, about a light-skinned daughter of Thomas Jefferson, was first published in England in 1853. Brown was also the first Black writer to publish a play and a travelogue. The narratives were about escaping slavery and surviving on the run and encountering racism in the free states in the North. "Not surprisingly, in their own era and in ours, the most memorable of these narratives evoke the national myth of the American individual's quest for freedom and for a society based on 'life, liberty, and the pursuit of happiness'" (Andrews 2001). The narratives were a popular genre that "comprised a pedagogy of transformation, showing how the new futures of a few could be become the destiny of the many through the engines of hope, moral indignation, and concerted action" (Gundaker 2007).

Laws restricting literacy began after the Stono Rebellion, the largest slave insurrection in early British-controlled America, which took place in 1739 in South Carolina and during which between sixty and seventy-five people, Blacks and whites, were killed. About a hundred slaves carrying signs saying "Liberty" rose and sacked plantations, stole weapons, and killed roughly twenty whites outside Charleston, South Carolina, resulting in the 1740 South Carolina Negro Act. Any kind of "mental instruction" was outlawed, not only formal teaching, and in 1775, Georgia set new rules based on the Negro Act, and Savannah in 1818 passed an ordinance that stated anybody who taught an enslaved or free person of color to read or write would be subjected to imprisonment or corporeal punishment (Brander Rasmussen 2010). In 1830, Louisiana criminalized teaching the enslaved to read and write.

Patrols, mobs, and social ostracism faced enslavers who taught their slaves. One former slave even recalled whispered rumors that her master had been poisoned because he taught his slaves to read and write and allowed them to save enough money to buy land at the end of the Civil War (Cornelius 1983). Many literate enslaved people kept their literacy to themselves, as they were at risk of being punished and ostracized. The enslaved who worked in the house were much more likely to read that those who worked in the field. Twice as many white women than men taught the enslaved to read, and many white children taught literacy. Some enslaved people were taught, so they could assist professionals like doctors write down information. Sunday school teaching was common. One Black person talks about learning the letters as the white baby was learning from alphabet blocks. Frederick Douglass claimed that he owed as much to the bitter opposition of his master, as to the kindly aid of his mistress, in learning to read: "I acknowledge the benefit of both." Enslaved people were aware of the value of literacy; it afforded movement, social capital, and a great sense of their own value.

Literacy enabled resistance and the dissemination of antislavery writings and ideas, and therefore, there was a "revolutionary potential of Black literacy" (Williams 2005, 178). A literate enslaved person would rightfully be considered a dangerous person, one with self-determination who could transcend slavery's constraints; free minds would lead to free bodies. But still, some literate enslaved were compelled to teach. There was a free Black man of "ginger cake color," who made his living carrying his slate and book from plantation to plantation in Georgia, teaching slaves "for little what they could slip him along" (Williams 2005, 180). Teaching was hazardous for the health of the Black teacher, but it was also a terrific responsibility. Enoch Golden, known to slaves as "double-headed" because he could read and write and "knowed so much," was said to have confessed on his deathbed that he "been the death of many slaves" (quoted in Cornelius 1983, 178).

Although they were deprived of reading, the enslaved "had other ways of knowing—listening, eavesdropping, remembering, sharing." Booker T. Washington talks about the "grape-vine telegraph" by which they shared the news of current events and local gossip (Williams 2005). In a theory first espoused by psychologist Robin Dunbar, gossip, evolutionary scientists now believe, is hardwired in all human beings developing language and storytelling. The social cooperation involved in gossiping is beneficial to building a strong community. For the enslaved, the grapevine was an indispensable lifeline.

David Walker (1796–1830), an African American abolitionist and printer, who was born free because his mother was free, argued in 1829 in his privately printed (in Boston) seminal and radical *Appeal to the Colored Citizens of the World, but in Particular, and Very Expressly to Those of the United States of America*, known as *Walker's Appeal*, that the abolition of slavery by any means necessary, including the revolt of enslaved Blacks against whites and the teaching of literacy should be immediate, not gradual. "The bare name of educating the coloured people," Walker wrote, "scares our cruel oppressors almost to death." The timeframe compellingly suggests and, therefore, many scholars agree that Nat Turner, who led his insurrection in 1831, read and was influenced by *Walker's Appeal*.

Turner was a literate preacher who had visions that he claimed compelled him to fight against "the Serpent," which was slavery. His final vision coincided with the eclipse of the sun on February 12, 1831, which was a sign for him to expeditiously lead an insurrection, taking forceful action against the injustice of slavery. Known as "The Prophet," in August 1831 in Southampton County, Virginia, Turner led a bloody, four-day revolt in which his enslaved followers killed fifty-five white Virginians, including men, women, and children.

The Alabama Slave Code of 1833 forbade teaching reading or writing to the enslaved and fined between $250 and $500 if caught (Tolley 2016). By 1835, virtually all schools for Blacks were closed. A bounty was placed on Walker; his pamphlet and other publications advocating rebellion were banned in states that sanctioned slavery. "Walker's Appeal was a case in point, along with the larger abolitionist literature of which it was a part. Such documents were simultaneously protests and de facto primers and instruction manuals for self-liberation, educating the enslaved as to potential escape routes along with the informational potentials of print" (Gundaker 2007, 6).

Between twenty and thirty-nine lashes were the punishment for teaching literacy to the enslaved in some states; in some, it was cutting off fingers and toes. North Carolina's antiliteracy law permitted teaching slaves math because that was helpful with carpentry. Some thought teaching slaves to read numbers helped with weighing cotton and erecting buildings. A special law passed in Virginia in 1842 allowed an enslaved person to read, so he could best aid his white enslaver. But writing was nearly always outlawed for the enslaved, as writing would "subvert the owners' power" (Simkin 2014).

The enslaved were able to get their hands on antislavery writings and hear news of the enslaved escaping to Canada via the Underground Railroad; however, even free states like Connecticut had laws against Black education. After a New Haven school was built to educate the newly freed enslaved, some whites set it on fire. A literate enslaved person could disrupt a sale when he or she would be returned to their original enslaver. A free Virginia couple sent their daughter to school in DC until literacy was outlawed there too.

The enslaved with an urge to read would bribe and give money and trade food, candy, whiskey, and tobacco for reading material. Young and old males moved around more than females and had access to trading things. Women who worked in the house had better access to correspondence and books and would also get information about letters and numbers from white children.

There were secret hidden schools known as "pit schools," pits "in the ground way out in the woods away from the master's surveillance" and the plantation (Williams 2005). Children would sometimes read in a cave. Some enslaved children would play school with the white school children and then on their own reenact lessons and learning. There is "evidence of words and numbers written on pottery and pencils found 100 years after slavery ended when slave cabins were excavated" (Williams 2005).

Some American evangelical white women taught the enslaved to read. And twelve nuns belonging to the Catholic order of Ursulines, came from France to Louisiana, when it was still owned and controlled by the French, from 1727 to 1760 to teach literacy and Catholicism to women and girls of all races. In France, they taught servants literacy. The nuns challenged the status quo, as American girls were generally not taught nor were any Blacks, enslaved or free. The nuns were "going by practices forged in France in which class issues weren't a factor in teaching literacy, numeracy, and religion" (Clark 2007). The Ursulines prioritized a "universalist vision in the face of increasingly divisive forces on race, class, and national identity and their feminist primary goal was female education first and foremost" (Clark 2007). Although the nuns did not speak out against slavery, and, in fact, they profited from it, for them education had no color or class line.

The foundational text of literacy also had no color or class line. Noah Webster, the American educator and first person in 1828 to write and publish a dictionary, published *A Grammatical Institute of the English Language* in 1783, Volume I of which was beloved by schoolchildren, teachers, and the enslaved. The book was commonly known as *The Blue-Backed Speller*, and it helped everyone learn the alphabet and to read. There is evidence that the book was a relic of great cultural significance to the enslaved and was held by them at funerals and weddings (Gundaker 2007). Learning the ABCs and learning to read quickly, as Nat Turner did, suggested one would have "a special destiny," as reading was as potent as magic in its ability to empower the enslaved (Gundaker 2007).

Frederick Douglass learned the alphabet from an enslaver's wife and taught himself and many others to read and write. He read, and his oratory was influenced by Caleb Bingham's *The Columbian Orator*, which Douglass said was "then a very popular schoolbook" (Bly 2011). Douglass and close to four hundred other enslaved children attended the Bray Schools, started by the clergyman Thomas Bray, which ran literacy programs from the 1720s through the 1760s (Bly 2011). Some gained mobility: in Mary Colbert's Athens, Georgia, slave community, those slaves who could read and write were usually chosen to travel with their enslaver, so that if anything happened to him, they could write home (Cornelius 1983, 12). The enslaved would farm land for the literate preacher, so he could read the Bible and fill them in.

Nat Turner was born in 1800, the year of Gabriel's Conspiracy—a failed plot by the Virginian blacksmith, Gabriel Prosser, to raid Richmond and hold Governor James Monroe hostage until the enslaved were freed. The conspirators planned to sew a flag that said "death or liberty." While Nat Turner's rebellion only lasted about 24 hours, it prompted a renewed wave of oppressive legislation prohibiting enslaved people's movement, assembly—and education" (Coleman 2020).

After Nat Turner's infamous insurrection, laws against literacy were passed in all states except Maryland, Tennessee, and Kentucky ("Literacy as Freedom" 2014). There was a distinction between Bible literacy, which fostered piety, and liberating literacy, which triggered resistance and movement (Cornelius 1983). There were also different rules for teaching reading and writing. Teaching slaves reading but not writing, the powers-that-be opined, would give them agency; the ability to write themselves not only into being but into freedom, and put the social fabric of society at risk.

Enslaved people who could read stole newspapers to find out the latest news of the Civil War. When Sarny reads the *Gazette* article about Nat Turner's insurrection, the article claims that the government retreated, suggesting his insurrection was successful. Turner did manage to evade the government for six weeks during which he hid; however, he was ultimately found and hanged.

Enslavers were like monarchs and didn't always follow laws. Laws changed and were, of course, different from state to state. But it was up to the overseers' discretion, and they often didn't abide by certain unenforceable rules. Enslaved people who could read often kept their literacy secret, so it's hard to know how many in fact could read and write (quoted in Gundaker 2007, 2). The literate enslaved were often of use to enslavers, for example, helping to write down numbers and addresses of patients for doctors, and some once free became preachers, teachers, and eventually, politicians.

The enslaved wanted to learn to "expand" their world, and because it was forbidden, it sharpened their desire. The enslaved observed blacksmiths writing names and learned to write their own. Frederick Douglass gave white boys bread. They got hold of Webster's *Blue-Backed Speller*. Thousands of the enslaved learned to read and write despite the harsh laws and punishment against it, but it's hard to assess the exact number.

One man remembers when he was three years old his father being "whipped to death" for teaching reading. Religion is mentioned more than any other reason the enslaved were taught to read. Urban and house enslaved people had a better chance of being taught literacy. Literate enslaved helped other enslaved people. The belief by the enslaved in the liberating aspects of literacy as a form of resistance was not unfounded (Cornelius 1983, 15). Literacy is a basic human right as is access to education. For the enslaved, it was the possibility of freedom and the opportunity to develop the full potential of their intellect and have dignity and self-determination.

In 1903, the African American intellectual, writer, historian, and activist W. E. B. Du Bois promoted the concept of "The Talented Tenth"—the foundational pillar of Black leadership and intellectual exceptionalism. It suggests that higher education should be a mandate for the best and the brightest one out of ten African Americans. This concept was inspired by the Philosopher Rulers in *Plato's Republic* (Littleton 2014).

DEPICTION AND CULTURAL CONTEXT

Nightjohn was filmed on the Rip Raps Plantation in Sumter, South Carolina, which is included in the National Register of Historic Places, a setting that imbues authenticity. The house features six pillars, or ionic columns. It is also known as the James McBride Dabbs House. McBride Dabbs (1896–1970) was known as a civil rights leader who believed in racial equity ("Dabbs," n.d.).

Gary Paulsen dedicates his novel, which is taught in middle and high schools along with the film, to "the memory of Sally Hemings, who was owned, raised, and subsequently used by Thomas Jefferson without benefit of ever drawing a single free breath." He also writes that though there are "variations" in the timeframe and character development, "the events written in this story are true and actually happened." However, in a 2016 New York Public Library interview, Paulsen stated, "Some organizations have wanted to use the fictional character and make him an historical hero. They want to have a Nightjohn day. It's very strange, and very complimentary. I have a lot of gratitude. Many people lived through that life as slaves, but he was not a real person."

The novel sets up the main story of the film; however, its brutality is more graphic, and its depiction of the white characters quite one-dimensional. Nightjohn was bought for $1,000. He teaches Sarny to read and write and admits doing so. He gets two toes cut off instead of a finger. Delie is called Mammy and is twice John's age; in the film they are about the same age and enjoy a subtle flirtation. In the novel, Jesus is tasked with help to free the enslaved when Sarny says, "Lord Jesus, you come be making us free. Free someday. In your name, amen." She narrates, "People in the quarters weren't supposed to pray nor know nothing about God"; however, in the film, the enslaved are seen attending church and Sarny's ability to read the Bible prompts public recognition and a baptism by the white preacher.

Church services on some plantations were integrated, as it is in the film; however, in many cases and in the film, the church had different entrances for whites and the enslaved. The church in the film shows the African Americans in the balcony and the whites on the floor, although Sarny is seated in the white section, as she's taking care of the Wallers' young son, enabling the pastor to notice and interact with her.

Some enslaved were invited and encouraged to read and/or look at the Bible along with their enslavers in church. A prevailing biblical through line, even though the priest inverts its meaning and significance at one point, tells the story of the overriding of slavery that God did with horse and rider and how "[h]e overturned the escaping slaves in Exodus when horse and rider he threw into the sea." He gave safe passage to the Israelites fleeing slavery, and once they were safe, he surrounds Pharaoh and his slave masters with water, drowning them and therefore being removed from the scene, bringing the slave culture of Egypt to an end. Bill Cain is a Jesuit priest, and his repeated use of this passage is purposeful. It foreshadows the end of oppression, the triumph of freedom of the enslaved, and the imminent demise of the horse and rider of slavery in America: "Sing ye to the Lord, for he hath triumphed gloriously; the horse and his rider hath he thrown into the sea."

A character called Alice, who is "addled in the head," reacts badly to breeding and is violently beaten. She is not in the film. Sarny and Delie are not allowed entrée into the Wallers' house. Sarny talks about the dogs set on runaways—most runaways were people yearning to be reunited with separated family members; some were endeavoring to go north for freedom; some were seeking employment; some were escaping brutal enslavers. Although Sarny mentions in the novel that a character named Jim gets eaten by a bloodhound for trying to run away, no dogs are seen in the film. "Specially bred bloodhounds were clearly the dogs of choice" to hunt enslaved runaways and were trained to be so vicious that sometimes, "if not restrained at the end of the chase, they would tear their quarry to pieces" (quoted in Franklin and Schlesinger 2007, 35).

Also, in the novel but not in the film, Nightjohn leaves and gets away but comes back one night to take Sarny to a "pit school." These hidden places to learn were also called midnight schools, as they operated when whites were sleeping. Sarny looks at a "catalog" for the first time in the pit school and sees pictures of "all the things we don't have. Dresses and shoes with buttons and little gloves and pretty hats and overalls and I started crying." She is then thrilled that she can read the word "bag" over the horse's nose.

The film is accurate in its depiction of the brutal whippings of the enslaved and the horrific chopping of fingers as punishment for attempting to run away or for teaching or practicing writing and reading. Amputation was also a punishment for stealing. The raised crisscrossing scars on Nightjohn's back are realistic. The abject abuse of the enslaved is accurate. Sarny is slapped by Waller's wife in front of her dinner guests when Sarny drops a plate while serving dinner.

The characters are focused on freedom and express a "uniqueness of self-liberation"; the teaching and receiving of education and literacy affords them some self-determination (Harrington 2011, 385). The Pulitzer Prize–winning African American studies scholar Annette Gordon-Reed has claimed that field slaves, in fact, had more self-determination than those enslaved and working in the house, as in the house one's behavior and every move taken and every word spoken were scrutinized and therefore more restricted and controlled.

Bill Cain said that many moments in his script were inspired by the Federal Writers Project for the Works Progress Administration (WPA) interviews done in the 1930s with people who had been enslaved in their youth; some were the children of the enslaved. The book, *Alabama WPA Slave Narratives: From Interviews with Former Slaves* was published by Historic Publishing in 2017. Cain also drew on the controversial book *Time on the Cross: The Economics of American Negro Slavery* (W. W. Norton, 1974) by Robert William Fogel and Stanley L. Engerman for background information about the cotton business. The authors' claims of how the gears of the system of slavery worked and various material and social aspects of the enslaved's lives have been challenged by myriad articles and books, including *Reckoning with Slavery: A Critical Study in the Quantitative History of American Negro Slavery* (Oxford University Press, 1976), edited by Paul David.

It's a celebratory moment when Egypt and Outlaw are "jumping the broom." An enslaved couple who wanted to marry gathered people around them to witness and legitimize their marriage. They were given a broom a few inches from the floor to jump backward over; with each jump the broom is lifted slightly. The first one to slip was compelled to follow the wishes of the other, according to the superstitious practice, which some claim originated in West Africa. The broom warded off evil. This ritual is often depicted in illustrations and films. Dundes claims that it originated when whites forced the enslaved to marry and bear children. Children would add wealth to the slave owner. Also, it legitimized the marriage and "by the 1830s and 1840s, jumping the broom was a ritual that enslaved people understood as their own" (Dundes 1996).

In 2011, Salim Akil directed an African American–themed romantic comedy focusing on class conflict issues, titled *Jumping the Broom*, starring Angela Bassett (1958–) as an upper-class woman and Loretta Devine (1949–) as a postal worker. Both actresses appeared in the hit film *Waiting to Exhale* (1995), directed by Forest Whitaker, based on Terry McMillan's eponymous *New York Times* best-selling novel, playing African American college-educated upscale friends looking for and recovering from love in Phoenix, Arizona. An article about the film appeared on the *Times*' front page—African American women were renting out theaters to see the film, the first one to feature professional Black women. Black audiences were flocking to feature films and watching television movies, like Burnett's *The Wedding*, to see characters, settings, and themes outside of the portrayals of poverty, violence, drug use, and urban grit.

Meanwhile, the soundtrack for current events in the 1990s was rife with racial issues. In 1992, the Los Angeles Race Riots were sparked after the acquittal of the policemen who beat Rodney King. The video of King's beating was the first that went viral. And the trial of the twentieth century and one of the most publicized trials in history, the racially charged case of *The People of the State of California vs. Orenthal James Simpson*, an African American man, was playing out in the media in 1995. O. J. Simpson, a former football player and actor, was accused of and subsequently and shockingly acquitted by a mostly Black jury for killing his white wife, Nicole Brown Simpson, and her friend, Ron Goldman.

The verdict unleashed a great disparity along racial lines. At the time, many African Americans agreed with the jury's verdict, while many whites felt that justice was not served, "although in the two decades since, acquitted by a majority-black jury, the racial gap has narrowed significantly. In two recent polls, more than 50 percent of black respondents said they thought Simpson was guilty—up from about 20 percent in most polls before, during and right after the trial" (Bialik 2016).

When controversy was sparked in 2015 after secretary of state Hillary Clinton was accused of using a private email server, a pundit claimed: "Hillary Clinton is the new O.J. Simpson. She may have gotten off, but everyone knows what she did was wrong" (Kilgore 2016). And in 2016, while campaigning for president, Hillary Clinton disavowed a comment she made in 1996 depicting some African American criminal youth as "super predators." Clinton made the damaging comment while expressing support for the 1994 crime bill signed by President Bill Clinton, which some say contributed and led to the mass incarceration of Blacks, mostly young men.

The legacy of slavery and institutionally racist Jim Crow laws in the South after Emancipation fostered criminal injustice against Blacks as well as segregation and limited access to education, literacy, and voting rights. Up until 1965, Blacks were given literacy tests to disenfranchise them from voting in the South. The civil rights movement of the 1950s and 1960s sought equal rights and opportunities for Blacks, and the fight goes on with organizations like Black Lives Matter and Bryan Stephenson's Equal Justice Initiative. As the Literacy Council of Central Alabama states, "Literacy is and always has been a social justice issue."

CONCLUSION

A parable about the empowerment of the enslaved through literacy, *Nightjohn* is an enlightening and entertaining masterpiece. The *New Yorker's* film critic Terrence Rafferty called *Nightjohn* the "best American movie of 1996." The film received a 1997 Special Citation Award from the National Society of Film Critics "for a film whose exceptional quality and origin challenge strictures of the movie marketplace."

The film triumphantly with reverent wit and wisdom charts the arc of the intergenerational African American process of learning through self-education. Sarny's innate intelligence and ability to remember everything reveals her to be a quick study with a laser-sharp focus, that she is capable of being an outspoken and courageous risk-taker reveals her singular strength. The music by Stephen James Taylor stirringly blends jazz, blues, and spirituals—genres invented by African Americans. Lumbly's and Jones's performances are moving and nuanced, and Bill Cain's finely wrought and written teleplay amplifies the novel and illuminates an aspect of slavery largely unexplored in film.

Cain's fully dimensionalized characters and eloquent storytelling and Burnett's captivating and assured direction reveal how the enslaved's hunger for knowledge was not only not quashed by the restrictive brutality of slavery, but it was also galvanized. Sarny's learning to read and write enables her a modicum of self-expression and freedom from the omniscient control of the enslaver. Nightjohn's altruism and need to teach the younger generation convey how a man sacrifices his own freedom to enable the next generation to forge an unchained path of progress. *Nightjohn*, like the letter A, "doesn't have a bottom. It stands on its own two feet."

FURTHER READING

Andrews, William L. 2001. "An Introduction to the Slave Narrative." In *North American Slave Narratives*, series edited by E. Maynard Adams. Documenting the American South. https://docsouth.unc.edu/neh/intro.html.

Barton Sweiger, Beth. 2013. "The Literate South: Emancipation before Slavery." *Journal of the Civil War Era* 3, no. 3 (September): 331–59.

Bialik, Carl. 2016. "Most Black People Now Think O.J. Was Guilty." Criminal Justice. FiveThirtyEight. ABC News.

Bly, Antonio T. 2011. "In Pursuit of Letters: A History of the Bray Schools for Enslaved Children in Colonial Virginia." *History of Education Quarterly* 51(4): 429–59. http://www.jstor.org/stable/41303896.

Bowers, Paul. 2019. "Save South Carolina Schools, for Robert Smalls' Sake." https://brutalsouth.substack.com/p/save-south-carolina-schools-for-robert.

Brander Rasmussen, Birgit. 2010. "'Attended with Great Inconveniences': Slave Literacy and the 1840 South Carolina Negro Act." *PMLA* 125, no. 1 (January): 201–3.

Brody, Richard. 2020. "What to Stream: Charles Burnett's Reckoning with History in Nat Turner: A Troublesome Property." *New Yorker*, June 19, 2020.

Burnett, Charles, dir. 2003. *Nat Turner: A Troublesome Property*. Subpix.

Burnett, Charles. 2020. "American Neorealism Q & A with Charles Burnett." Interview by Ross Lippman. February 20, 2020. https://www.youtube.com/watch?v=3NV1e6EEMmY.

Clark, Emily. 2007. *Masterless Mistresses: The New Orleans Ursulines and the Development of a New World Society, 1727–1834*. Chapel Hill: University of North Carolina Press.

Coleman, Colette. 2020. "How Literacy Became a Powerful Weapon in the Fight to End Slavery." June 17, 2020. https://www.history.com/news/nat-turner-rebellion-literacy-slavery.

Cornelius, Janet Duitsman. 1983. "We Slipped and Learned to Read: Slave Accounts of the Literacy Process. 1830–1865." *Phylon* 44:171–76.

"Dabbs, James McBride." n.d. *South Carolina Encyclopedia*. Accessed August 8, 2022. https://www.scencyclopedia.org/sce/entries/dabbs-james-mcbride/.

Daley, Terri. 2014. "A Life More Terrible: The Women of *12 Years a Slave*." *The Conversation*, January 10, 2014.

Davis, Zeinabu irene, dir. 2016. *Spirits of Rebellion: Black Cinema at UCLA*. Wimmin with a Mission Productions. Streaming.

Douglass, Frederick. 2016. *Narrative in the Life of Frederick Douglass*. New York: Dover Editions.

Dundes, Alan. 1996. "'Jumping the Broom': On the Origin and Meaning of an African American Wedding Custom." *Journal of American Folklore* 109, no. 433 (May): 324–29. https://doi.org/10.2307/541535.

Field, Allyson Nadia, Jan-Christopher Horak, and Jacqueline Najuma Stewart, eds. 2015. *L.A Rebellion: Creating a New Black Cinema*. Oakland: University of California Press.

Franklin, John Hope, and Loren Schlesinger. 2007. "The Quest for Freedom: Runaway Slaves and the American South." In *Slavery, Resistance, Freedom*, edited by Gabor Boritt and Scott Hancock. New York: Oxford University Press.

Fulton-Miner, Doveanna S., and Reginald H. Pitts. 2010. *Speaking Lives, Authoring Texts: Three African American Women's Oral Slave Narratives*. Albany: State University of New York.

Gates, Henry Louis, Jr. 1997. "Introduction." In *Frederick Douglass. Narrative of the Life of Frederick Douglass, An American Slave*, x–xxiv. New York: Laurel.

Gates, Henry Louis, Jr. 2013. "Robert Smalls, from Escaped Slave to House of Representatives." PBS. https://www.pbs.org/wnet/african-americans-many-rivers-to-cross/history/which-slave-sailed-himself-to-freedom/.

Gundaker, Grey. 2007. "Hidden Education among African Americans During Slavery." *Teachers College Record* 109, no. 7 (July): 1591–1612.

Harrington, Brooksie. 2011. "The Invisible Thread: Authorial Integrity and the Trope of the Child Slave in *Uncle Tom's Cabin, Adventures of Huckleberry Finn*, and *Nightjohn*." *CLA Journal* 54, no. 4 (June): 364–86.

Heuman, Gad, and James Walvin, eds. 2003. "Family, Gender and Community." In *The Slavery Reader*, Vol. 1. London: Routledge.

Holden, Stephen. 1997. "Literacy, a Weapon for a Slave." *New York Times*, January 31, 1997.

Hunt, Aaron E. 2020. "An Incomplete Notion to Begin With: A Conversation with Charles Burnett." July 7, 2020. https://mubi.com/notebook/posts/an-incomplete-notion-to- begin-with-a-conversation-with-charles-brunet.

Kilgore, Ed. 2016. "GOP Flack. Hillary Clinton Is the New O.J." *New York Magazine*, July 7, 2016.

"Literacy as Freedom." 2014. Smithsonian American Art Museum. https://americanexperience.si.edu/wp-content/uploads/2014/09/Literacy-as-Freedom.pdf.

Littleton, La'Niece M. 2014. "High Hopes and Fixed Purposes: Frederick Douglass and the Talented Tenth on the American Plantation." *Phylon* 51, no. 1 (Fall): 102–14.

"Live Chat Author Gary Paulsen." July 10, 2003. https://web.archive.org/web/20211226073109/https://www.nypl.org/blog/2016/08/31/live-chat-author-gary-paulsen.

O'Neill Spady, James. 2011. "Power and Confession: On the Credibility of the Earliest Reports of the Denmark Vesey Conspiracy." *William and Mary Quarterly* 68, no. 2 (April): 287–304.

Paulsen, Gary. 1993. *Nightjohn*. New York: Laurel-Leaf.

Raimey Berry, Daina. 2017. *The Price for Their Pound of Flesh: The Value of the Enslaved from Womb to Grave in the Building of a Nation*. Boston: Beacon Press.

Shovo, Scott. 2011. "Interview: Filmmaker Charles Burnett." *News Nirvana Nuvo*, November 2, 2011.

Simkin, John. 2014. *Slavery in the United States*. Spartacus Educational Publishers. https://spartacus-educational.com/USASbreeding.htm.

"Slavery, Institutional Racism, and the Development of State Surveillance as a Response to Resistance." 2014. ACLU of Massachusetts, July 29, 2014. https://privacysos.org/blog/slavery-institutional-racism-and-the-development-of-state-surveillance-as-a-response-to-resistance/.

Tolley, Kim. 2016. "Slavery and the Origins of Georgia's 1829 Anti-Literacy Act." In *Miseducation: A History of Ignorance-Making in America and Abroad*, edited by A. J. Angulo. Baltimore: Johns Hopkins.

Walker, David. 1995. *David Walker's Appeal, in Four Articles: Together with a Preamble to the Coloured Citizens of the World, but in Particular, and Very Expressly, to Those of the United States of America*. Revised, with an "Introduction," by Sean Wilentz. New York: Hill and Wang.

Williams, Heather Andrea. 2005. *Self-Taught: African American Education in Slavery and Freedom*. Chapel Hill: University of North Carolina Press.

Chapter 6

Amistad (1997)

Steven Spielberg's seventeenth feature film, the deeply moving, entertaining, and enlightening historical drama *Amistad* (1997) tells the epic story of the 1839 insurrection, one of the most notable shipboard rebellions and mutinies in history. It was led by Sengbe Pieh, known in America as Joseph Cinque, and other captured Africans aboard an illegal slave ship, *La Amistad*; international slave trading had been outlawed in 1808. Three trials ensued, ending in a Supreme Court triumph for the Africans who were allowed to return home. The case strengthened abolitionist fervor, led to "the trial of the 19th century," and was a catalyst for the Civil War. While celebrated and widely reported in its time as a powerful story of African resistance to slavery, it was according to historians overlooked and understudied in the canon of American history until Spielberg's film.

Debbie Allen, the African American choreographer, actress (the *Fame* television series) director, songwriter, and producer, in 1978, read two volumes of essays about the *Amistad* she found at the Historically Black College (HBC) Howard University's bookstore (Jeffrey 2001). She was shocked that she had never read or learned about this momentous historical event and wondered why it was erased. In 1984, she optioned the rights to William A. Owens's novel, *Black Mutiny: The Revolt on the Schooner Amistad*, which had been originally published in 1953 under the title *Slave Mutiny*. After she saw Spielberg's Holocaust drama *Schindler's List* (1993), which won the Oscar for Best Picture and earned more than $300 million worldwide, she convinced him he was the right director for the *Amistad* story and that his telling an essential slavery story would be as impactful and accessible as his film about the Holocaust. He was intrigued by the story and felt compelled to film it for his two adopted African American children.

David Franzoni, who wrote *Gladiator* (2000), gets single credit for the screenplay, although Steven Zaillian, whose credits include the film adaptation of Thomas Keneally's novel *Schindler's List*, did a revision. The film acknowledges Owens's novel *Black Mutiny* as source material. Howard Jones, author of *Mutiny on the Amistad: The Saga of a Slave Revolt and Its Impact on American Abolition, Law, and Diplomacy* (1987), was one of the film's consultants, which included titans of African American studies Henry Louis Gates Jr., John Hope Franklin, and Lerone Bennett as well as Clifton Johnson, emeritus head of the Amistad Research Center in New Orleans. The late Dr. Arthur Abraham (1945–2020), a prominent University of Sierra Leone scholar in African studies specializing in Mende history and language, was on the set coaching Djimon Hounsou on Mende for the shoot.

There was immediate controversy when the novelist Barbara Chase-Riboud initiated a $10 million plagiarism lawsuit against Spielberg two weeks before the film's opening trying to prevent it from being released, claiming he "brazenly" stole from her up to that point overlooked novel *Echo of Lions* (William Morrow, 1989). A copy of her novel was, in fact, in 1988 sent to Spielberg's company, Amblin, by the author's friend, Jacqueline Onassis, a book editor at the time. DreamWorks offered Chase-Riboud $500,000 and a screen credit recommending her novel. At first, she turned down the offer, asking for $2 million, but in February 1998, she dropped her suit claiming *Amistad* is a splendid piece of work and that nothing "improper" took place (Weinraub 1998).

Chase-Riboud, who also wrote the novel *Sally Hemings* (Viking, 1987), about Thomas Jefferson's enslaved partner of thirty years, was subsequently criticized by DreamWorks lawyers who said she had "lifted entire passages" and "directly taken" material from William A. Owens's about the *Amistad* uprising (Weinraub 1998). Bruce Handy satirized Spielberg in an article titled "Steven Stealberg?" by questioning to what extent public domain history is available to all storytellers (1997).

Released on December 25, Christmas Day, 1997, by DreamWorks Pictures, the film's budget was close to $70 million, including marketing. It earned $44 million domestically and more than $58 million worldwide; therefore, it was not a box office hit (https://www.the-numbers.com/movie/Amistad#tab=summary, 1997). It received four Academy Award nominations: Best Supporting Actor for Anthony Hopkins, Best Music, Best Costume Design, and Best Cinematography but didn't win any. A historical film about another ship, James Cameron's *Titanic*, released two weeks before *Amistad*, sailed on to becoming one of the most successful films of all time, winning eleven Academy Awards, including Best Picture. Spielberg reflected on why *Amistad* didn't perform well at the box office and agreed with people who said the film "failed because it took history too seriously. With *Amistad*," he explained, "I kind of dried it out, and it became too much of a history lesson" (quoted in Jeffrey 2001).

African actors and nonactors from Mende, Temne, and Kissi tribes were cast in the film to play the *Amistad* Africans. But the key piece of casting was Djimon Hounsou, who plays Cinque. Born in 1964 in Benin, Africa, Hounsou moved to France when he was twelve. He was a model and actor for seven years—he appeared in videos with Madonna and Janet Jackson. Spielberg knew the first time he met him that he had the right qualities to play Cinque: strength of character, noble self-determination, and an expressive righteous indignation. The actor said getting the role was the most amazing thing that happened to him since his birth (*Making of Amistad* 1997).

Amistad has the distinction of being the only film in which an actual Supreme Court justice appears as a judge in a film cameo—Harry A. Blackmun, an associate justice from 1970 to 1994, is briefly on screen as Justice Joseph Story conveying the 1841 decision.

Reviews were decidedly mixed. Godfrey Cheshire called it "one of the most intelligent Hollywood movies" he's ever seen and acknowledges its "stirring profundity" (2020, 113).

Some critics compared Cinque's quest to return home to the alien in Spielberg's epochal film *E.T: The Extra Terrestrial* (1982). Susan Wloszcyzna claimed, "For what is Cinque but an alien in a strange land who is abused by authority and yearns to go home?" (1998). Some reviewers compared *Amistad* unfavorably to *Schindler's List*, including Courtland Milloy, who also questioned the filmmakers' decision to only provide subtitles when white characters are listening to the Africans. He claims "that oversight echoes a powerful historical message that Black humanity can exist only in relation to whites—and even then only in subservience. When Blacks are among their own, the film seems to say, what's in their hearts and minds is just not worth knowing" (1997). Roger Ebert found it "too much about the law and not enough about the victims" (1997).

Spielberg previously dealt with slavery in his compelling film *Lincoln* (2012), starring Daniel Day-Lewis as President Abraham Lincoln. Set during the Civil War, it is about Lincoln's and his secretary of state, William Seward's (played by David Strathairn), triumphant legislative mission to pass the Thirteenth Amendment emancipating the enslaved in 1865. Some, including the historian Kate Masur, lamented the lack of Black characters. Frederick Douglass, a vital force in convincing Lincoln to abolish slavery, is not given a role or voice in Tony Kushner's screenplay adapted from Doris Kearns Goodwin's book *Team of Rivals: The Political Genius of Abraham Lincoln* (Simon & Schuster, 2005). The Black characters in the film are "archetypal, generic"; showing Black abolitionist movers and shakers "would have suggested that another dynamic of emancipation was occurring just outside the frame—a world of black political debate, of civic engagement and of monumental effort for the liberation of body and spirit" (Masur 2012).

Spielberg's earlier African American–themed film, *The Color Purple* (1985), his adaptation of Alice Walker's Pulitzer Prize–winning edgy epistolary novel, was a celebrated box office hit. Even though he smoothed out some of the novel's rough edges, the film explores sex, love, and issues of trauma around domestic violence and incest experienced over forty years by a Black Southern woman, Celie, played by Whoopi Goldberg in her first leading film role. Coproduced by and starring Oprah Winfrey, the film also features Danny Glover and Laurence Fishburne. It was also made into a Broadway musical, and Spielberg is a producer of the upcoming musical film adaptation, which Blitz Bazawule is directing. The film is set to open in December 2023.

Academy Award–winning composer and conductor John Williams has collaborated with Spielberg on nearly all his films. Williams's lush, eclectic and swelling score for *Amistad* blends African, western, and evangelical Christian music. The first song in the film is the rousing "Dry Your Tears, Afrika," and the film ends with a reprise of it. "Afrika" is spelled with a *k* as it is in most traditional African cultures, the *k* adopted by Black nationalists. The lyrics are sung in a native language. Translated into English, the song begins: "Your children come back to you / Out of the storms and squalls / Of fruitless journeys."

Janusz Kaminski, the cinematographer who collaborated with Spielberg on many films, including *Lincoln*, *Schindler's List*, and *Saving Private Ryan* (1998), created visual contrasts, darkness, sepia tones, and bright light—vivid and bright greens, golds, and yellows permeate the African scenes. Spielberg and Kaminski were inspired by the Spanish artist Francisco Goya. The nightmarish darkness of the shipboard insurrection scene and the Middle Passage suffuses the screen, creating an immediate and visceral depth of emotion. The critic David Edelstein points out a shot in the film that "evokes Goya's *Third of May, 1808*. Cinque holds out his arms, his puffy shirt glowing white, and appeals in primitive English for freedom" (1997).

The shoot lasted more than sixty days; locations were in Newport, Rhode Island; Mystic, Connecticut; and Puerto Rico. Vivid architectural and sartorial period details evoke the nineteenth century, including horses, carriages, courthouses, clothing, and the powdered wigs and robust whiskers worn by the abolitionists, politicians, and lawyers.

Although Cinque and his fellow Africans were imprisoned, they carried their cultural practices with them; for example, when one of their brethren dies, they carry his body in the street and perform a rite. They are challenged as they adjust to American culture, but they are able, thanks to linguists and interpreters, to tell their stories to the abolitionists and legal advocates who advocate on their behalf, enabling them to secure their freedom and return to Africa.

The film's riveting opening scene centers the African's point of view and reveals a dark, lightning-strewn night on the ocean. Waves are crashing; there's heavy breathing and a close-up of an eye and then a sweaty Black man, Joseph Cinque (Djimon Hounsou), scratching a rock. He's panting, struggling while he pulls out a metal bar and loosens a nail. With the nail, he's able to unlock his chains as well as those of his brethren who grab cutlasses and sugarcane knives. He hacks a screaming captain in the pouring rain. Water rushes over the boat, on its journey from Havana, Cuba. The captain shoots a few Africans. Cinque wrestles a gun out of a white guy's hands and then stabs him. Cinque screams triumphantly and angrily.

The Africans' mutiny is victorious. The sign *La Amistad* flashes on the screen. The dialogue spoken by Cinque and his brethren is not subtitled; it will be once they arrive in America. It's 1839, daylight, and the Africans have taken charge. The African has the power; Cinque holds a knife to the white man steering the ship. To Africa—it's east to the sun, he says. Cinque takes over at the helm. Looking up at the sky, he turns the boat around. African men are singing; women and children are singing, clapping hands.

A boat passes by with musicians and a string quartet playing. Cinque tells the white guys to be quiet. The boat passes without incident. Everyone on the *Amistad* is staring. Six weeks later, the sails are shabby and full of holes. They're nearly out of water. Land is within reach. Cinque and seven others get in a small boat to shore. A man on a wooden bicycle rides by. A ship with military men and an American flag spots them. They start shooting the Africans from the small boat they're in. Cinque jumps into the water, nearly drowns, but is saved by a white man. The boat pulls up at the dock in Long Island; the *Amistad* is taken to New London, Connecticut. All the forty-four Africans are put in prison in New Haven, Connecticut; there were fifty-three when the voyage began. Cinque resists, and like others, he is screaming and crying.

Eleven-year-old Isabella II, Queen of Spain (Anna Paquin), is informed of the situation; she wants the captives turned over to her, as they were captured and transported by the Spanish. Martin Van Buren (Nigel Hawthorne) is elected the eighth president of the United States. When Van Buren is briefed about the situation, he says, "There are what three point four million Negroes in this country. Why on earth should I concern myself with these forty-four?" He was up for reelection and courting the South.

Theodore Joadson (Morgan Freeman), an abolitionist and free Black man, says, the *Amistad* is too small to be a transatlantic slaver. Joadson tells the abolitionist Lewis Tappan (Stellan Skarsgard) that the Africans have scars. Joadson reads the New Haven newspaper *Paper*, "Massacre at Sea: A Difficult Slave Case," and then the *Emancipator*, "Freedom Fight at Sea." Tappan says they'll be arrested for murder; however, he can perhaps say they were illegally arrested. Cinque resists and fights back when he and the other Africans are chained and taken to district court in New Haven. Now their dialogue is subtitled.

Roger S. Baldwin (Matthew McConaughey), a real estate lawyer assessing the contours of the case, correctly claims that the *Amistad* case is about "the wrongful transfer of stolen goods." Former president John Quincy Adams (Sir Anthony Hopkins), now Congressman Adams from Massachusetts, is seen tending to and nurturing his roses.

The judge introduces the U.S. district attorney, W. S. Holabird (Pete Postlethwaite), who presents the court with charges of piracy and murder against the Africans, but it is petitioned. Tappan points out that Holabird is not a lawyer. The secretary of state, John Forsyth (David Paymer), represents the president and Queen Isabella and Spain; he references the mutual treaty on the high seas of 1795. The "slaves" belong to and are the property of Spain and Cuba, and their sellers, Pedro Montes (John Ortiz) and Jose Ruiz (Geno Silva). The court should surrender these goods immediately. Africans see the Spaniards, get upset, and continue to protest. A receipt for their purchase of the "slaves" is produced.

Tappan approaches Congressman John Quincy Adams for help pleading the abolitionist cause. "I'm neither friend nor foe of the abolitionist cause," Adams says, "No, I won't help you." Joadson urges Adams to help crush slavery and claims that Adams's record shows he's an abolitionist. He again turns them down. Baldwin says "slaves are like livestock; the only way someone can purchase slaves is if they are born slaves on the plantation." Tappan says, "It is our responsibility as abolitionists and Christians to save these people."

There are subtitles for the Mende language the Africans speak. A group comes up to the prison and sings "Amazing Grace." The Yale linguist, Professor Gibbs (Austin Pendleton) translates for the Africans, sometimes protecting the white men from hearing the Africans calling them idiots. Cinque says the abolitionists look miserable. Anti and proslavery protests are going on outside the courthouse. James Covey (Chiwetel Ejiofor) comes onboard to translate, as he's from Sierra Leone and fluent in Mende—he was rescued by the British Navy. Baldwin needs Cinque to speak in court. Cinque, in court, says, "I have a horrible feeling he talks for us." Baldwin proves the Africans don't speak Spanish.

Holabird informs the court that the savages broke loose the collars of the white men and fell upon them with sabers and cane knives and speaks of their inhumanity. "They dismembered and mutilated a Creole cook," he says, "and Ruiz and Montes bravely steered the ship to America."

Baldwin says the case isn't about murder or mayhem and proves the Africans are not Spanish despite their Spanish names.

Joadson and Baldwin get clearance to investigate the ship. Joadson finds a small bone/token and metal chains and handcuffs and gets caught up in a tangle. He finds the ship's manifest showing the journey out of Africa of the Portuguese slave ship known as the *Tecora*, which left Freetown, Sierra

Leone, on the west coast of Africa, thirty years after England and the United States outlawed the transatlantic slave trade.

Queen Isabella says the Africans must never go free. Senator John. C. Calhoun (Arliss Howard) says this case could take America one step closer to the Civil War. He argues for slavery, with the president stating that the South relies on it for the economy.

Adams has agreed to represent the Africans. He asks Joadson, "What is the Africans' story, who are they?" Joadson answers that they're from West Africa. "Where are you from?" Joadson says he's from Georgia. "You're an ex-slave devoted to the cause of abolitionism; that's your story." An aspect of Cinque's story is that he was treated like a hero in his village for killing a lion with a rock.

Nearly halfway into the film, Cinque is showing being captured in Africa with a net thrown on him by African men. He's taken by boat to the Lomboko Slave Fortress, a massive structure.

The depiction of the Middle Passage begins an hour and sixteen minutes into the film. The captured Africans are chained on the floor naked. They are shouting, screaming, begging for food, and hungrily eating mash. Cinque's hands are flying powerfully in front of him. A baby is crying and lifted up. The Africans are washed and scrubbed in Havana.

The judge rules that the Africans will be sent home, and Ruiz and Montes are arrested. Cheering and celebration ensue. The case goes to the Supreme Court. Cinque is upset and angry. Baldwin writes to John Quincy Adams—seven of nine justices are Southern enslavers. Cinque asks if the treaty holds when it's beyond borders; Cinque will ask for the ancestors to come and help. "For at this moment," he says, "I am the whole reason they have existed at all."

Adams draws on that statement in his speech when he walks near the statues and references the founding fathers: George Washington; Benjamin Franklin; Alexander Hamilton; Thomas Jefferson; his father, John Adams. The court rules in favor of the Africans, and they're allowed to return home.

The captured Africans embedded in the Lomboko Slave Fortress are freed by British naval men, led by Captain Peter Fitzgerald (Peter Firth), in 1849. The captives run from the cavernous giant building made of stucco/clay, and once cleared of people, the British fire cannons at it. No longer imprisoned, the Africans run away from slavery, and toward freedom. Lomboko is annihilated.

The Confederate Army's defeat in Atlanta in 1864, a momentous victory for General William Tecumseh Sherman and the Union, is shown.

HISTORICAL BACKGROUND

La Amistad, which means friendship, was a sleek Spanish slave ship traveling from Cuba to the United States illegally—slave trading was outlawed in 1808. Its journey originated from Mendeland, now called Sierra Leone, when Cinque and fifty-two remaining other Africans were captured and forced onto the slave ship *Tecora*, which left Africa in April 1839. It stopped to offload some of the Africans in Havana and on June 28, 1838, sailed off to Puerto Principe, now Camagu in Cuba. "The Africans were naked, fed bad food, and beaten for not eating"; several men had died of dysentery and dehydration (Cable 1971, 52). Cinque heard that the sadistic cook Celestino said the captains were threatening that Africans' throats would be cut and they would be cooked. Cinque found a nail and unshackled himself, employing Mende military tactics, and on July 2, he killed Captain Ferrer and Celestino and staged a mutiny. Cinque took command of the *Amistad* along with Grabeau and Burnah (Jones 1987, 25). Montes was hurt but promised to help steering the ship; Ruiz was kept alive for the same reason. Both Spaniards hoped they were steering the ship toward the slavery-sanctioned states near the Southern coast. "The maritime leg of their journey included violence, suffering, and self-emancipation."

The ship was seized by Lieutenant Thomas R. Gedney, the commander of the USS *Washington* when it was sailing off the coast of Long Island. It was escorted to New London, Connecticut, and the captured Africans were imprisoned. Slavery was abolished in New York in 1827 but not until 1848 in Connecticut; therefore, Connecticut was able to claim "salvage rights" and money if they sold and enslaved the captured Africans as money.

There were fifty-three Africans, two Spaniards; "the captain's cabin boy and slave, Antonio; a mulatto cook named Celestino; $250 in cash; and cargo and provisions worth about $40,000" (Jones 1987, 23).

The Spanish captains were freed, and the forty-four Africans, including *four children, three of whom were girls, were imprisoned in Westville, near New Haven,* pending an investigation of the *Amistad* revolt. The first trial took place in the circuit court in Hartford, Connecticut; the second in the federal district court in New Haven, Connecticut; and the third in the Supreme Court, which ruled in 1841 in favor of the captured Africans, fulfilling their quest for freedom.

"The meeting of African insurrectionists and American reformers was unprecedented" (Rediker 2012, 56). The court decided who had the rights to the "cargo" of Africans. Prominent Abolitionists helped the Mende people make their case in the lower courts. President Martin Van Buren got involved, and the case went up to the Supreme Court.

Martin Van Buren, the eighth president (1837–41) was a one-term president who believed that slavery should be kept status quo. He was against the expansion of slavery, but he was also against abolitionism, viewing it as divisive. John Quincy Adams defended the Mende against Van Buren, and Southern prosecutors and lawyers represented the Cubans and Spanish.

The press was sympathetic to the Africans, especially the *New York Sun* (Rediker 2012, 9). Up to twenty-five hundred articles were published about the Africans. Learning about West African culture and the stories of the rebellion firsthand was a novelty. The public in the North was fascinated with the story; the Africans' rebelliousness was reminiscent of the heroes of the American Revolution. However, the Southern press avoided the story for fear it would inspire the enslaved to rebel and "put ideas into the minds of the slave population" (Cable 1971, 8).

The Spanish called him Joseph Cinque (spelled different ways, including with and without an accent on the e), He was a rice farmer, a married man with three children.

The Africans were from nine different ethnic groups besides Mende: Temne, Gbandi, and Loma (Rediker 2012, 5). The *Amistad* Africans studied English and theology while they were incarcerated. Students from Yale Divinity School taught them from two to five hours a day (Cable 1971, 47).

The abolitionists hired Roger S. Baldwin, a lawyer from New Haven, and two New York attorneys, Seth Staples and Theodore Sedgewick, to serve as proctors, or legal representatives, for the Africans.

Tappan

Lewis Tappan (1788–1873) and his brother Arthur Tappan (1786–1865), who was a great-grandfather of the writer Thornton Wilder, were ardent New York–based abolitionists and reformers; they were also evangelicals. With Boston-based William Lloyd Garrison, they were cofounders of the American Anti-Slavery Society. As soon as Lewis Tappan heard about the Africans' *Amistad* ordeal, he took action and also covered the story for the abolitionist publication, *The Liberator*. He was cited by the former president John Quincy Adams as being responsible for the Africans securing their freedom. The Tappans were targeted by proslavery mobs for their beliefs.

Along with Simeon Jocelyn and Joshua Leavitt, Lewis Tappan formed the *Amistad* Committee, which "hired legal counsel, made key litigation decisions, and provided support of all kinds for the Africans." The committee filed "civil suits in New York against Montes and Ruiz for assault, battery, and false imprisonment" (Linder 1995). While there was a team representing the Africans, "In historical fact, Lewis Tappan was the prime defender of the Amistad from start to finish" (Rosen 2002, 242).

Joadson

Theodore Joadson is presented as a fictional character. He was formerly enslaved and is an abolitionist. He helps convince former president Adams to argue the *Amistad* case at the Supreme Court. However, although Freeman has a lot of screen time and is a key player in gathering information from the ship, he, like Baldwin and Tappan, is somewhat of a cipher.

Newman claims that some might think Frederick Douglass inspired the character of Joadson; the character's "spiritual guide" was, in fact, the wealthy activist James Forten (1766–1842)—a Philadelphia-based member of the Antislavery Society and a "premier Black reformer of the early republic, businessman, philanthropist, Black abolitionist" who had fought in the American Revolution. Forten prospered from his sail-making business and the Forten Shipping Service. A prolific journalist and protest writer, in 1813, he anonymously (although it was an "open secret" that he penned it) published the pamphlet "Letters from a Man of Colour," a "bold and persuasive appeal to justice and common sense" in which he spoke out against a biased bill the Pennsylvania legislature was considering in which Philadelphia's borders would be closed to Black migrants (Winch 2002, 169–70).

His granddaughter, Charlotte Forten (1837–1914)—a poet, translator, and teacher—was affiliated with the Port Royal Experiment during the Civil War teaching formerly enslaved children on the Sea Islands in South Carolina. Her life and work were subject of a 1985 American Playhouse PBS movie titled *Charlotte Forten's Mission: Experiments in Freedom*.

Josiah Gibbs, a professor of linguistics and a Hebrew scholar at the Yale Divinity School, was given access to Cinque; he also met with him and Baldwin, Tappan, and the African sailor James Ferry. Gibbs learned how to count in Mende and then to find someone fluent, he walked around on the New York City waterfront counting in Mende until he found an African American sailor who understood him. He met African sailors James Ferry, Charles Pratt, and James Covey "whose cosmopolitan knowledge of multiple languages finally allowed the rebels to tell their stories of origins, enslavement, and insurrection" (Rediker 2012, 11).

James Covey was a formerly enslaved man from Sierra Leone who had been rescued by the British and taken to Freetown. He helped Gibbs prove in court the captured men were Mende—their names referred to objects in Mende; they couldn't have been given by the Spanish (Jones 1987, 23). Covey interpreted for Cinque in court.

The Lomboko Slave Fortress

Cinque told the story of his capture and time in Lomboko in February and March 1839 and that for a time his hands and feet were chained together. All fifty-three *Amistad* Africans, most of whom were under the age of thirty, spent time at Lomboko.

European traders were first captivated by Sierra Leone, West Africa, in the mid-1400s when Portuguese sailors identified the Sierra Leone River in what was known as Mendiland (also spelled Mendeland) as a viable source of food and fresh water. It was there that the notorious Spanish slave trader Pedro Blanco built, owned, and ran from 1822 to 1838 the Lomboko Slave Fortress, a "slave-trading factory on the Gallinas Coast" (Rediker 2012, 5). It was isolated and hard to find—one has to travel through a "maze of mangrove roots" to reach it (Buba 2014).

The surrounding waters were crocodile and shark filled; Rediker in the documentary *Ghosts of Amistad: In the Footsteps of the Rebels* (2014) says that due to sharks, the waters around Lomboko were "red as far as the eye could see" after captured Africans spilled out of canoes.

The fortress comprised "hastily constructed slave pens which could be abandoned quickly," small buildings, and "barracoons and sheds equipped with chains, neck-rings, and padlocks," before the Africans, children and adults, were forced onto slave ships (Rediker 2012, 49). Those interred reported that sanitary conditions were horrible and caused diseases. There was often a lack of food. Those who attempted to escape would be "hunted down by overseers using dogs, and sometimes killed," and some resisters were murdered (Rediker 2014, 51). The captured Africans were put through rigorous examinations to make sure they were healthy enough to withstand the Middle Passage and be sold for a good price in Havana. By 1839, approximately two thousand Africans a year were transported out of Lomboko into canoes and then onto slave ships. The fortress was destroyed by the British in 1849 (Rediker 2012, 44).

Lomboko's location was kept secret, as it operated long after the slave trade was outlawed—in America in 1807 and in Britain in 1808. The West African Squadron (or Preventative Squadron) comprised vigilant British Royal Navy's antislavery patrols that prowled the waters looking for slave ships. They'd capture ships and use the ships to pursue other ships and enslaved people, many hundreds of whom were freed thanks to their efforts.

Freetown, a city near Lomboko, was established in 1788, which in 1839 had forty-two thousand residents, many of them Africans liberated by the antislave British patrols. Monrovia, now the capital of Liberia, was established by the American Colonization Society; it was dedicated to returning formerly enslaved Africans to their countries of origin (Rediker 2012, 44).

Cinque, at twenty-five years old, was a celebrity in his time. He was described as "the Oseola [sic] of his race" (referring to the then-legendary Native American warrior-statesman), as possessing the character of a "Hannibal or Othello," or simply as "the Roman African" (Powell 1997).

Northern Black and white abolitionists were pitted against a proslavery president, Martin Van Buren, and the trial in the district court and then a circuit court, ending up being represented by a former president in the Supreme Court case in 1841. The Africans were freed, despite the fact that seven of the nine justices were enslavers.

Abolitionists believed that "slavery did not exist on the basis of natural law but out of man-made laws attributable to a selfish mixture of economic, political, social, and racial motivations. Such passionate issues led to the bitter conflicts between human and property rights that helped bring on the Civil War" (Jones 1987, 220).

Henry Louis Gates Jr. and Howard Jones were excited for people to learn about "the only instance in history in which captives from Africa actually won their freedom and made it back home" (Jeffrey 2001, 13). Cinque wasn't a chief or king, but he was the son of a "principal man" (Jones 1987, 43). He was captured and sold to the Spaniard Pedro Blanco, because he had a debt and wasn't able to fully pay for a business transaction. Cinque had a wife and three children and parents.

Once there were six hundred to seven hundred captured Africans, they'd be put on ships. The captain was "very cruel and beat them severely" (Jones 1987, 44). The Africans were taken outside to eat; that's when Cinque found the nail, enabling him to unchain everyone from the wall. Everyone except the children had a cane knife. Cinque killed the cook first and then the captain, but the captain killed two Africans. The two white sailors jumped ship, got the small boat, and reported to Havana what had happened. Ruiz and Montes were enchained in irons. They were treated like the Africans and given little water. Cinque told Montes to sail to Africa, but Montes sailed to Cuba. When they ask the mulatto cook for more food, he says no and that they'll be chopped up and salted and eaten by the Spanish, Cinque meets with Kin-na and others. "If we do nothing, we be killed. We may as well die in trying." Ruiz and Montes were put in prison after Cinque and his fellow Africans, Kinna, Fon ne, and Kim bo of brought charges of assault, kidnapping, and false imprisonment (Cable 1971, 55). The Africans were not slaves, they were from Africa. That they were not slaves meant they were not property.

In November 1841, the thirty-five surviving Africans along with missionaries went back to Africa on the ship *Gentleman*. They all returned to Africa three years after they arrived in America. They spent twenty-seven months in Connecticut, nineteen months in jail there. The Africans and missionaries told the *Amistad* story and published a book about it. It became known as "the trial of the century."

The Supreme Court Case of 1841

Although the former one-term (1825–29) president John Quincy Adams, the son of America's second president John Adams (1897–1901), spoke out against slavery, he did not call himself an abolitionist. According to Hopkins, Adams was an incorruptible, moral man (*Making of Amistad* 1997). The abolitionists thought he'd be the most effective person to argue the case, so they appealed to him to defend the Africans at the Supreme Court. Adams in 1841 was seventy-four years old, hard of hearing, and hadn't "argued a case in nearly three decades" (Jones 1987, 153). He agreed to take the case on and provide closing arguments. In preparation for the case, he visited the Africans in jail—and he met with Cinque. He noted in his memoirs that the two chief coconspirators, Cinque and Grabeau had "very remarkable countenances" (quoted by Jones 1987, 154).

The case was presented on February 20, 1841. There are only the lawyers present in Supreme Court cases; witnesses do not testify as they do in lower courts and trials (Zeinert 1997, 68). Roger Baldwin spoke first on behalf of the thirty-six Africans vying for "freedom and for life" and summarized the need for the court to look at the *Amistad*'s papers and analyze the international treaties.

The Africans had been brought to Cuba by Ruiz and Montes in violation of Spanish law as well as international treaties banning the slave trade. "Were their actions piracy?" Mary Cable asks. No, "pirates don't sail under any flag," and the *Amistad* was a Spanish ship, the mutiny was in Spanish waters against Spanish sailors (1971, 26). Papers covering the true intent were falsified. Therefore, "there was an irony when the attorney for Connecticut charged the Africans with piracy and murder because the captives were prima facie, free men illegally enslaved who acted with self-defense" (Wiecek 1978, 8). They were not Americans, and therefore, they could not be tried in American courts.

Abolitionists appealed to the district courts. Baldwin argued that the Africans were free when they arrived in New York and Connecticut, and therefore, the federal government could not force them into slavery; to do so would be a violation of the U.S. Constitution. Only states had the right to enslave people. He invoked the "1819 readoption of Spanish American Treaty of 1795." Adams referenced the Declaration of Independence, which guaranteed every American life, liberty, and the pursuit of happiness; however, the Constitution protected slavery.

"Justice Story ignored all contemporary restrictions based on color or race in declaring the captives free as 'kidnapped Africans' that under what he called the 'eternal principles of justice' they had the inherent right of self-defense and could kill their captors to win freedom" (Jones 1987, 219).

Popular Culture

The *Amistad* was a cause célèbre. Its tale of heroism and unique cast of characters captured the imaginations of the American and European public, and artists were inspired to create and sell images and stories about the Africans' ordeal. The first production of a play about the revolt, *The Long, Low Black Schooner*, or *The Black Schooner or the Pirate Slaver*, the title most people knew it by, written by Jonas B. Phillips, appeared at the Bowery Theater in New York on September 2, 1839—"a mere six days after the vessel had been towed into port" (Rediker 2012, 3). Shows sold out "in four theaters and took in $5,000" (Jones 1987, 156).

Thousands of people visited the Africans in jail. Many artists after visiting were inspired to create images of Cinque and his comrades that were copied and sold in newspapers in cities throughout the east (Rediker 2012, 3). The largest *Amistad*-inspired artwork, a "135-foot panorama, more than twice as long as the *Amistad* itself," was painted by Amasa Hewins—a

Boston-based artist who charged people to see it. Surprisingly, the giant painting cannot be found (Rediker 2012, 165).

John Warner Barber, a noted "engraver of New England's historic buildings and landscapes," was enraptured by the trial and began visiting the imprisoned Africans, drawing their portraits, their descriptions of the rebellion, maps and pictures of their Mende village, and Lomboko; engraving silhouettes; and writing short biographies (Rediker 2012, 160). In 1840, he successfully self-published a thirty-two-page pamphlet, titled *A History of the* Amistad *Captives Being a Circumstantial Account of the Capture of the Spanish Schooner Amistad, by the Africans on Board; Their Voyage and Capture in Long Island, New York; with Biographical Sketches of Each of the Surviving Africans: Also an Account of the Trials Had on Their Case/ before the District and Circuit Courts of the United States, for the District of Connecticut* that cost twenty-five cents (Rediker 2012, 160). The writer and poet Kevin Lowell Young, the director of the National Museum of African American History and Culture, uses Warner's silhouettes on the jacket cover of and within his book *Ardency: A Chronicle of the Amistad Rebels* (Knopf, 2011). Young lauds Barber's account as "remarkably balanced and fascinating" (Young 2011, 249).

Cinque's "outlaw charisma" also fueled interest in *Book of Pirates containing Narratives of the Most Remarkable Piracies and Murders, Committed on the High Seas Together with an Account of the Capture of the* Amistad *and a Full Authentic Narrative of the Burning of the* Caroline. Compiled for the publisher by Henry K. Brooke and published by J. B. Perry in Philadelphia in 1841, it was based on Cinque's and Grabeau's testimonies and offered a sympathetic account of the *Amistad* Africans (Rediker 2012, 118).

Notable abolitionist poet William Cullen Bryan wrote "A Poem for Cinque" and published it in the *Emancipator* on September 19, 1839, the day Cinque's first trial began. The last two lines are "A prince among his tribe before, / He could not be a slave" (Zeinert 1997, 63). African American poet Robert Hayden's poem "Middle Passage," written in the 1940s, refers to "Cinquez," an alternative spelling of Cinque. The poem ends: "Cinquez its deathless primaveral image, / life that transfigures many lives. / Voyage through death to life upon these shores."

Simeon Jocelyn was a clergyman and abolitionist whose plan to build a college for African Americans never materialized. He was a member of the Amistad Committee and collaborated with Tappan and Baldwin in using the *Amistad* story to spread details of the horrors of slavery and the illegality of the slave trade (Jones 1987, 7). His brother, Nathaniel Jocelyn, was also an abolitionist activist helping enslaved people escape in Connecticut.

The wealthy Philadelphia-based Black abolitionist Robert Purvis commissioned Jocelyn to paint the official portrait of Cinque, titled "Cinque, the Hero of the Amistad" (Rediker 2012, 224). Ennobled and determined, Cinque wears a toga-like garment which was "traditional Mende dress" (Jones 1987, 173) and "appears like a Greco-Roman divinity" (Powell 1997). He holds a cane stick; behind him are mountains and sky. Cinque's image contradicted the prevailing perception of the captive Africans as savages and became "a symbol of black resistance and activism in the face of increasing white-on-black violence and sociopolitical unrest" (Powell 1997). The artist John Sartain created a mezzotint engraving of Jocelyn's portrait, which sold for two dollars each, with the proceeds going to the Pennsylvania Antislavery Association.

Madison Washington, a self-emancipated Virginian abolitionist and Vigilance Committee member, on his "way back south to assist his wife's escape from bondage," stopped at Robert Purvis's home and saw Jocelyn's painting on the day it was delivered (Rediker 2012, 224). Purvis told Washington the story of the mutiny, and Washington, who was "captured while escaping with his wife," was inspired to lead a successful "revolt aboard the slave brig Creole en route from Hampton, Virginia, to New Orleans. In an article published in the *Philadelphia Inquirer* decades later, Purvis maintained that Washington's insurrection on the high seas was inspired by having seen Cinque's portrait and having heard Cinque's stirring story of self-liberation" (Rediker 2012, 224). In total, 128 enslaved people gained their freedom, which makes the *Creole* mutiny the most successful slave revolt in U.S. history.

Frederick Douglass wrote his only work of fiction, a "brilliant" novella, titled *The Heroic Slave* (John P. Jewett & Co., 1853), whose lead character was inspired by and named Madison Washington (Ernest 2017). This story is considered one of the first pieces of African American fiction written by an African American. The novella inspires readers to get involved in "the abolitionist cause, but also to grant Black slaves the same right to rebel against tyranny that America enshrines in its founder" (Railton 2009).

DEPICTION AND CULTURAL CONTEXT

Adams says, "Whoever tells the best story wins." He's referring to lawyerly recitations, but he's also "talking about the ownership of history, the vagaries of politics and, not incidentally, moviemaking itself" (Hornaday 1997).

Spielberg's moviemaking is all about telling the story with accurate accoutrements. The filmmakers used real chains, not "movie chains," which created chafing and hung heavy on the neck (*Making of Amistad* 1997). Chains worn for months break through the skin and create scarring. The props and locations were so authentic that Hounsou "felt so humiliated, so disrespected," and one actor felt like he had actually been imprisoned (*Making of Amistad* 1997).

The film graphically depicts the brutality of the Middle Passage and the capturing and forcing of Africans onto ships across the Atlantic on the way to ultimate enslavement in the United States and Latin America. Franzoni recalled, "[I]t was Debbie who led me to the vision of a violence so brutal and genuine that the act embodied with a single roar the timeless black American rage. When Debbie and I deliberated the Middle Passage scene, she reached down into the freezing Atlantic and from the muck and centuries resurrected for me the thousands and thousands of African souls who had perhaps until this film been lying unheralded and even unknown in anonymous graves" (quoted in Jeffrey 2001).

Allen felt Joadson was an essential character showing that abolitionism was a biracial reform movement. Born as a slave in Georgia, Joadson is portrayed as a Black abolitionist who has acquired freedom, riches, and social acceptance by the time the story begins. For Allen, who called Joadson "fact-tional," the character stood for the successful and rich African Americans in the antebellum period. Although Joadson's characterization is underdeveloped, he gets a lot of screen time, if not a lot of dialogue. His passion for the cause is forceful.

Newman groundlessly takes Rosen and Eric McKitrick to task for claiming a character like Joadson, one who influences the white abolitionists, would not have existed in 1840. Philadelphia-based Robert Purvis was an influential Black abolitionist. Newman says Black reformers used the press and "contributed columns to newspapers, published their own pamphlets and narratives and encouraged African-American communities to value the word and establish literary societies for the benefit of the race" (Newman 2000, 219–20). Black writers impacted white abolitionists like William Lloyd Garrison in the 1820s and 1830s.

CONCLUSION

The *Amistad* incident and subsequent legal decision freeing and enabling the Africans to return home remains as colossal an achievement to enslaved revolt success in America as the Haitian Revolution was in Haiti, the result of which in 1804 was the creation of the first Black republic. *Amistad* is a vivid portal into a unique and riveting chapter in American history. When Cinque twice demands during his trial to "give us free," he unequivocally calls out the crime against humanity that slavery was. Cinque and his collaborators defied their captors. For Debbie Allen, their heroic journey represented a powerful way of destroying what she called the demeaning "sambo view of Blacks who acquiesced to slavery" (quoted by Jeffrey 2001, 18).

FURTHER READING

Buba, Tony, dir. 2014. *Ghosts of Amistad: In the Footsteps of the Rebels*. Braddock Films, 51:01. https://www.ghostsofamistad.com/.

Cable, Mary. 1971. *Black Odyssey: The Case of the Slave Ship Amistad*. New York: Penguin Books.

Cheshire, Godfrey. 2020. "*Amistad* (Steven Spielberg)." In *The Press Gang: Writings on Cinema from New York Press, 1991–2011*, edited by Godfrey Cheshire, Matt Zoller Seitz, and Armond White, 111–13. New York: Seven Stories Press.

Ebert, Roger. 1997. "*Amistad* Review." Rogerebert.com, December 12, 1997.

Edelstein, David. 1997. "In the Belly of the Beast." *Slate Magazine*, December 14, 1997.

Ernest, John. 2017. "Review" [The Heroic Slave/Frederick Douglass: A Cultural and Critical Edition, edited by Robert S. Levine, John Stauffer, and John R. McKivigan]. *Early American Literature* 52 (2): 473–77. University of North Carolina Press.

Handy, Bruce. 1997. "Steven Stealberg: The Director's New Film Is Hit with a $10 Million Plagiarism Suit, but Isn't History Free to All?" *Time*, November 24, 1997.

Hornaday, Ann. 1997. "Doing Justice—Spielberg's '*Amistad*' Is a Powerful Tale of Slavery and Freedom. So We Can Forgive the Director for Taking a Few Liberties." *Baltimore Sun*, December 12, 1997.

Jeffrey, Julie Roy. 2001. "*Amistad* (1997): Steven Spielberg's True Story." *Historical Journal of Film, Radio, and Television* 21, no. 1 (March): 77–96.

Jones, Howard. 1987. *Mutiny on the Amistad*. New York: Oxford University Press.

Jones, Howard. 1997. "A Historian Goes to Hollywood: The Spielberg Touch." *Perspectives on History*, December 1, 1997.

Kellner, Douglas. 2014–15. "The Horrors of Slavery and Modes of Representation in *Amistad* and *12 Years a Slave*." *Jump Cut: A Review of Contemporary Media Jump Cut* 56 (Winter).

Linder, Doublas O. 1995. "Famous Trials." https://famous-trials.com/amistad/1229-ami-btap.

The Making of Amistad. 1997. Produced by Debbie Allen. DreamWorks and Amblin Entertainment.

Masur, Kate. 2012. "In Spielberg's *Lincoln*, Passive Black Characters." Op-Ed. *New York Times*, November 12, 2012.

Milloy, Courtland. 1997. "*Amistad* through a Different Lens." *Washington Post*, December 14, 1997.

Newman, Richard. 2000. "Not the Only Story in *Amistad*: The Fictional Joadson and the Real James Forten." *Pennsylvania History: A Journal of Mid-Atlantic Studies* 67, no. 2 (Spring): 218–39.

Powell, Richard. 1997. "How Cinque Was Painted." *Washington Post*, December 28, 1997.

Railton, Stephen. 2009. "*Uncle Tom's Cabin* and American Culture: A Multi-media Archive." http://utc.iath.virginia.edu/africam/heroslavhp.html.

Rediker, Marcus. 2012. *The Amistad Rebellion: An Atlantic Odyssey of Slavery and Freedom*. New York: Viking.

Rosen, Gary. 2002. "*Amistad* and the Abuse of History." In *The Films of Steven Spielberg: Critical Essays*, edited by Charles L. P. Silet, 239–248. Maryland: Scarecrow Press.

Weinraub, Bernard. 1998. "Plagiarism Suit over *Amistad* Is Withdrawn." *New York Times*, February 10, 1998.

Wiecek, William M. 1978. "Slavery and Abolition before the United States Supreme Court, 1820–1860." *Journal of American History* 65, no. 1 (June): 34–59.

Winch, Julie. 2002. *A Gentleman of Color: The Life of James Forten*. New York: Oxford University Press.

Wloszczyna, Susan. 1998. "Moral Compass Keeps *Amistad* Steady." *USA Today*, December 1, 1998.

Chapter 7

Django Unchained (2012)

Set in the antebellum South, Quentin Tarantino's revisionist, ultraviolent film is a revenge fantasy/love story spaghetti western about an enslaved African American. Django Freeman, played by the charismatic Jamie Foxx, is set free by and teams up with the transactional German-born bounty hunter/dentist Dr. King Schultz (Christoph Waltz) to track down and kill the vicious Brittle Brothers. Schultz promises Django his freedom once the brothers are captured. Once freed, Django becomes Shultz's sidekick. Schultz teaches Django to read. Django transforms his sartorial style; he develops his expertise with a gun. But it's his quest to find and rescue his enslaved wife, Broomhilda von Shaft (Kerry Washington), from whom he was forced to be separated, that drives and consumes him.

Hildi, as she's known, has been brought up by a German woman who teaches her to speak German. Schultz tells Django the story of Broomhilda, a popular German legend about a woman getting rescued. The men learn that Hildi is trapped in Candyland, in Chickasaw County, Mississippi, run by plantation owner Calvin Candie (Leonardo DiCaprio), his widowed sister Lara (Laura Cayouette), and their enslaved majordomo Stephen (Samuel L. Jackson).

Django Unchained was partly filmed on the historic Evergreen Plantation in Edgard, New Orleans, approximately forty-five minutes from New Orleans. A well-preserved estate built in 1777, it still functions as a sugarcane plantation. The site includes twenty-seven quarters that housed the enslaved and is a repository for ancestry research and primary documents telling the story of the four hundred people over 150 years who were enslaved there. Foxx said, "You can't walk through those places and not shed tears and feel something. I took my three and a half and my eighteen-year-old children, and I let them walk through there. I said, 'This is where you come from.' That's where we needed to be so we could really get down into the story" (quoted in Kennedy 2012).

The film was released on December 25, 2012. Its budget was approximately $100 million. Distributed by the Weinstein Company and produced by Stacey Sher, Reginald Hudlin, and Pilar Savone, it earned approximately $162 million in the United States and Canada. Its worldwide box office was $424.5 million, making it Tarantino's highest-grossing movie to date (McClintock 2013). It won Tarantino the Academy Award for Best Original Screenplay and the Golden Globe for Best Screenplay. Waltz won the Oscar and the Golden Globe for Best Supporting Actor. Waltz also started in Tarantino's previous film, *Inglorious Basterds* (2009), a revisionist World War II tale about Nazi hunters who kill Adolf Hitler. Waltz won a Best Supporting Actor Oscar for his portrayal of Hans Landa, known as "The Jew Hunter."

Django Unchained was inspired by Blaxploitation films like *The Legend of N****r Charley* (1972), starring Fred Williamson, that was, according to Eric Benson, the "only slavery film before *Django Unchained* that told a story of Black-male empowerment" (2013), and *Mandingo* (1975), as well as the spaghetti westerns of Italian film director Sergio Corbucci, whose oeuvre includes *Django* (1966), starring Franco Nero, who has a cameo in Tarantino's film.

The eclectic soundtrack blends music by the iconic Italian film composer Ennio Morricone, who worked on all of Sergio Leone's films, with Beethoven's "Fur Elise"; Americana roots artist Brother Dege's "Too Old to Die Young"; songs by John Legend, Richie Havens, and Johnny Cash; and hip-hop, including Rick Ross's "100 Black Coffins." The song "Unchained," "a mash-up of Tupac Shakur's lyrics from his posthumous release 'Untouchable' (2006) is set against an instrumental sample from James Brown's 'The Payback' (1973) that highlights Brown's signature holler and horns. The mash-up signifies Django's transition from slavery to freedom, with Brown and Shakur sonically narrating his emotional response" (Bradley 2016).

Robert Richardson's dexterous and ambient cinematography contrasts majestic Wyoming vistas with the flora, fauna, and futility of plantation life and the baroque interiors of the "Big House," with the disturbing, poetic shot of blood-splattered cotton.

A. O. Scott of the *New York Times* said the film is "a wild and bloody live-action cartoon" and "fanciful history" (2012). *The New Yorker's* David Denby said, "It's a very strange movie, luridly sadistic and morally ambitious at the same time, and the audience is definitely alive to it, reveling in its incongruities, enjoying what's lusciously and profanely over the top" (2013).

The N-word is spoken 110 times in the film, and Black filmmakers like Spike Lee and John Ridley publicly criticized Tarantino for his earlier films like *Jackie Brown* (1997) in which the word is uttered 37 times. Ridley claims that Tarantino "in some ways luxuriates in the word," adding "it's not used in particular context, it's just used to be used" (quoted in Woodcock 2020). Lee was enraged and tweeted, "American Slavery Was Not a Sergio Leone Spaghetti Western. It Was a Holocaust. My Ancestors Are Slaves. Stolen From Africa. I Will Honor Them." Tarantino's fixation on the flesh of the enslaved is relentless. The film's opening shot depicts men's legs shackled in chains, Hildi's lacerated back is shown several times; the fighters tear each other part; and Candie's Black mistresses wear revealing outfits.

The two-hour, forty-five-minute film opens with the song, "Django," from Sergio Corbucci's 1966 eponymous film about a gang of Southern racists in a power struggle with Mexican rebels. Django Freeman is one of many enslaved shirtless Black men with sweaty, lacerated backs in a coffle. They are walking in a rocky dessert, following a man on a horse with a gun. The trek continues into the cold night; the men are wrapped in blankets. It's 1858; it says, two years before the Civil War, somewhere in Texas. Dr. King Schultz, referred to as Schultz, a salt-and-pepper bearded, well-dressed lapsed dentist whose car has a giant tooth in which he keeps wads of cash attached to the top of it, pulls up. He's looking for two slave traders who purchased enslaved people at the slave auction. He matter-of-factly kills the white men when they tell him to leave.

Schultz asks each man if they know the Brittle Brothers; Django says he does. Schultz unchains the iron to which his foot is chained, claiming the iron is "nasty business." Schultz then kills one of the white men who threatens him and asks the other if he has Django's bill of sale. He doesn't, so Schultz writes one up. Schultz tells the other enslaved men: "You can kill the white man, unchain yourself and make your way to a more enlightened area of this country." He points to the North Star. Schultz, a bounty hunter, and Django ride into Daughtrey, Texas, where they kill the sheriff; Schultz proves with a warrant for his arrest that he is a wanted man and collects $200.

Schultz tells Django that being a bounty hunter is "like slavery; it's a flesh for cash business. The way a slave trader deals in bodies for cash, a bounty hunter deals in corpses." Schultz hates slavery, he says, but he's going to make this "slavery malarkey work to" his benefit.

The men will look for the Brittle Brothers on every plantation in Gatlinburg. Once they find and kill them, Schultz will reward his bounty hunter protégé Django with his freedom and pay him $25 per Brittle brother.

Django's ultimate plan is to find his wife and buy her freedom. Django tells Schultz his story, that he and Broomhilda von Shaft, known as Hildi, tried to run away to get married. When caught, their owner sold them separately. In a flashback, Django, with a cage on his face, reveals that the enslaver burned an "R" for runaway on the couple's cheeks after they got caught and took them to a "slave auction" in Greenville, Mississippi. Schultz takes Django to a haberdashery, a men's clothing store, where he picks out a new outfit to play Schultz's valet. Django picks out a fancy blue outfit with a flamboyant white bow tie, which he wears for most of the film.

They ride into the Bennett plantation in Tennessee, pretending to want to buy an enslaved woman from Big Daddy Bennett (Don Johnson) for $5,000. Bettina (Miriam F. Glover) escorts Django around. He asks her about the Brittle Brothers, one of whom beat Hildi for running away. There's a graphic flashback of Hildi hung up on a post and getting whipped while Django begs for mercy.

Django shoots one Brittle brother while he's whipping an enslaved woman for breaking eggs and then whips a white man who's trying to shoot him. Django, now holding the power of the whip, lashes and then kills the second Brittle brother. Schultz shoots Ellis Brittle and blood splatters on the cotton. Schultz produces the warrant paperwork announcing that he's a legal representative. He and Django camp out. Big Daddy orders the Ku Klux Klan to attack them. They are out to "make a lesson" of a Black man killing white men.

One hundred white-masked men ride on horses with sheets with holes for their eyes over their heads; they're holding torches. Rousing war music plays. One Klan member billed as Bag Head #2 (Jonah Hill) says he can't see anything out of his mask. Big Daddy asks, "Who made these, Willard's wife?"

Willard responds, "Make your own goddamn masks. I'm ridin' blind. I can't see, breathe or ride in this f***in' thing."

Schultz rides with Django to Greenville, Mississippi, to look for his wife's "bill of sale" to track her whereabouts, as Django knows when and from where she was sold. They find out that Hildi was twenty-seven when sold for $300 to Calvin Candie. Django tells Schultz that Broomhilda doesn't work in the field, that she's pretty, speaks well, and was in training to become a comfort girl.

The bounty hunters find out that Candie is invested in and passionate about Mandingo fighters, so they pretend to be experts seeking to buy a fighter from Candie when, in fact, they're planning to buy Hildi. They go to Candie's private Cleopatra Club. Mandingo fighters are fighting to the finish in the living room/bar area, the Julius Caesar room. Candie cheers them on. Big Fred (Escalante Lundy) is beating his opponent (Clay Donahue Fontenot) and pounds him fatally with a hammer.

Another Mandingo fighter, D'Artagnan (Atos), ran away and got caught twenty miles off the property. He says he can't fight anymore, and he's hiding in a tree. Candie tells him he paid $500 for him, and he expects five fights. Candie sics the bloodhounds on him; the dogs start to tear him apart. Schultz is mortified, but nobody stops it. The horrific images and sounds (the camera mostly cuts away) of the dogs ripping D'Artagnan apart and Schultz's horrified reaction are shown several times in flashback.

Schultz asks to meet with Hildi, as she speaks German. Candie thinks Schultz wants to take advantage of her sexually. Lara brings Hildi to him. Schultz tells her he's with Django and about their plan to purchase her.

Stephen tells Candie, Schultz, and Django that Hildi was in the hot box for trying to run away again. Hot water is thrown on her, and she screams. She looks terrified. Django has an immediate aversion to Stephen; he calls him Snowball due to his white hair, and Stephen is put off and distrustful of Django when Django and Schultz negotiate to buy a Mandingo fighter.

Candie takes out a skull of Ben—an old soul who took care of his father until he keeled over one day. Candie says, "Old Ben was unburdened by genius," and he wonders why he didn't cut his enslaver's throat. Candie gives a lecture on "the science of phrenology," what he refers to as "the separation of our species." He claims the part of the brain associated with submissiveness and servility is huge in the African, larger than any human or subhuman species. Candie saws the skull and points out three dimples or empty spaces.

He and Schultz agree on the $12,000 price tag, and Schultz tells Candie he also wants to buy Hildi. Candie gives Schultz Hildi's freedom papers and her bill of sale. Stephen informs Candie she and Django know each other. Candie confronts Schultz, and Schultz shoots and kills Candie. Candie's bodyguard Butch Pooch (James Remar) kills Schultz. Django kills Pooch, Candie's lawyer, and a few others, but after Hildi is taken hostage, he's stopped and about to be castrated by Billy Crash (Walter Goggins) when Crash is instructed by Lara to let him to go to a mining farm where he'll be worked to death. Django manages to return to Candyland with dynamite, and after retrieving Hildi's freedom papers from Schultz's corpse and killing Lara and shooting Stephen in his kneecaps so he's stuck, he places the dynamite throughout the house and Django and Hildi escape and ride off into the sunset.

The last twenty minutes of the film is a bloodbath. As Anthony Lane punned, *Django Unchained* "is a tribute to the spaghetti Western, cooked al dente, then cooked a while more, and finally sauced to death" (Lane 2012).

HISTORICAL BACKGROUND

Databases and university archives documenting the lives of the enslaved, including the National Archives Catalog, Plantation Records Online, and Duke University's Repository of "American Slavery Documents" are expanding and readily available for researchers. Not all records exist; however, some African Americans are able to research their family members back to the Civil War via censuses, last wills and testaments, vital court and legal records, and genealogical sources. Lives of the enslaved, including fugitives and those who were freed or manumitted, were enumerated in Slave Schedules kept during the U.S. Federal Censuses of 1850 and 1860. Before 1850, however, only the heads of enslaved households were listed. All at that time were identified as "Black or Mulatto" ("NARA Records," n.d.).

Eighteen states were included in the 1850 Census, called the Federation Population Schedules, the first statistical record in which all members of a household were listed by name. They were listed and numbered by "age, sex, and color [Black or Mulatto] from the oldest to the youngest, all under the name of the slave owner." Also listed were disabled slaves ("U.S. Census: Slave Schedules," n.d.).

A bill of sale "was a contract between an enslaver and a potential buyer detailing the purchase of an enslaved person. The contracts typically stated the name and location of the enslaver, the name and location of the buyer, and the gender, name, and age of the enslaved person" ("Bills of Sale," n.d.).

There were "Black slavers," free Blacks who enslaved Blacks. Historians tend to divide Black enslavers into "benevolent and commercial slave owning." Carter G. Woodson in his 1924 published report, "Free Negro Owners of Slaves in the U.S. in 1830" pioneered the idea that free Blacks enslaved people largely for benevolent or the philanthropic purpose of granting them freedom. The U.S. Census of 1830 lists 3,775 free Blacks owning 12,740 enslaved people. Most Black enslavers were women; they were granted freedom in larger numbers than men (Bassard 2008, 5). As Ira Berlin stated in his classic work, *Slaves without Masters: The Free Negro in the Antebellum South* (1974), "Many more blacks depended on their friends and relatives to extricate them from bondage. Hundreds of free Blacks used their small savings to purchase and free loved ones, especially their immediate families" (quoted in Bassard 2008, 5). However, some Black enslavers were motivated by profit, like Henry Townsend, the main character of Edward P. Jones's Pulitzer Prize–winning novel, *The Known World* (Amistad, 2003).

The Ku Klux Klan (KKK), also known in the nineteenth century as the Invisible Empire of the South, is America's oldest white-supremacist group and first domestic terrorist organization. It was assembled as a secret order in 1866 in Pulaski, Tennessee, by six twentysomething Confederate soldiers inspired by fraternity tropes, including initiation rights and a Greek name. The Greek word *kuklos* means "circle," alluding to a "band of brothers" ("Ku Klux Klan," n.d.). Its primary anti-Black racist mission was to bring down the Republican Party and undo the progressive political gains made by Blacks during Reconstruction (1865–77), the period after the Civil War (1861–65).

Other paramilitary, vigilante white-supremacist groups that sprung up, some of which merged with the KKK but were known locally by other names, included the Red Shirts, the Pale Faces, Order of the White Brotherhood, and the Knights of the White Camelias (French 2004, 156). KKK members rode at night pretending to be the ghosts of Confederate soldiers. They wore white masks, and their horses were covered in white robes made of bedsheets and pillowcases, sometimes made of satin, according to a Virginia member (French 2004, 266).

The Freedmen's Bureau, established by Congress in 1865 to help resource and situate formerly enslaved people and impoverished whites who were uprooted by the Civil War, reported in 1868 more than 336 violent attacks by Klan members, including whippings, hangings, shootings, burnings, castrations, and harsh and even unlawful imprisonments against those who supported Reconstruction or Black empowerment (Bryant, n.d.).

The KKK disbanded in 1869 and then resurged in 1915 as a result of the national release of D. W. Griffith's film *The Birth of a Nation*—a film adaptation of Thomas Dixon's novel *The Clansman*, the second in a trilogy glorifying and romanticizing the Klansmen, portraying them as heroes. Membership grew dramatically and peaked in the 1920s; estimates of membership range from three million to as high as eight million ("Ku Klux Klan," n.d.). Membership spiked again during the civil rights movement in the 1950s and 1960s. White nationalist and pro-Confederate organizations led the "Unite the Right" in Charlottesville, Virginia, on August 11–12, 2017, and the white-supremacist groups the Proud Boys and the Oath Keepers were prominent protesters on January 6, 2021, in the U.S. Capitol attack claiming that the former president actually won the 2020 election. These groups also claim that minorities are replacing them in the workplace.

Phrenology was a pseudoscience developed and introduced by German physiologist Franz Joseph Gall in 1796 in Vienna. Although it was ultimately proved to be a sham, it gained traction in the 1800s and justified racial slavery for some. It affirmed that an individual's character, mental ability, personality, and talents could be determined by examining the size and shape of the cranium and its crevices. It perpetrated disinformation and for the most part derogatory misconceptions about Blacks' difference from whites, trying to prove a propensity for servility and an innate inferiority at a time when fervent abolitionists were militating for the end of slavery. Although phrenologists O. L. and N. M. Fowler in 1859 stated that Africans "are deficient in reasoning capacity," they also stated that "Blacks have excellent memories and lingual and musical powers" (DeGruy 2017, 49).

The spreading of phrenology's unprovable discriminatory claims justified the continuation of slavery, segregation, and racism by impacting the consciousness of race in antebellum America as well as the "way scientific ideas were adopted into social, political, and cultural practices, and, in turn, how the goals of scientific inquiry and the dissemination of scientific knowledge were shaped by social and cultural circumstances and agendas" (Branson 2017). The view of people of African descent as inherently mentally inferior contributed to the continuation of systemic racist policies. As Bryan Stevenson said, "The true evil of slavery was that the Black was told he was inferior" (Olive and Goodman 2022).

James McCune Smith (1813–65), the New York–based abolitionist and writer, was the first African American to earn a medical degree and establish a pharmacy. Born an enslaved man, he was educated in Glasgow, Scotland, as American universities wouldn't accept him. McCune Smith fiercely criticized "the fallacy of phrenology" publicly, publishing widely in peer-reviewed medical journals. He "pioneered the use of medically based statistics to challenge the notion of African American racial inferiority. He scientifically challenged the racial theories promoted in Thomas Jefferson's 1832 racist tract *Notes on the State of Virginia*" (Lujan and DiCarlo 2019, 134). McCune Smith used skulls, statistics, and anatomy to refute the racist claims that the size, shape, and most importantly, the capacities of the brain could be determined by the external contours and interior crevices of the skull (Banner 2013).

McCune Smith protested the passage in 1850 of the draconian Fugitive Slave Act in his collection "Heads of the Colored People," published in *Frederick Douglass's Paper* under the pseudonym Cunnipaw. Profiling working-class Black individuals that revealed the dignity of their labor and the universality of the Black experience, McCune Smith derogatively alludes to the pseudoscience of phrenology. "Heads" is a nickname that Black people still use for each other. McCune Smith was never admitted to the American Medical Association or to any local medical society (Lujan and DiCarlo 2019, 136).

Phrenology was satirized in antebellum minstrel theatrical shows and referred to in skits and mock lectures as "Black bumpology" (Branson 2017, 191). These skits featured white performers in blackface, which is now considered offensive.

Another race pseudoscience is portrayed in Kevin Willmott's mockumentary *CSA: Confederate States of America* (2004). Dr. Samuel A. Cartwright, in his 1851 book *Diseases and Peculiarities of the Negro Race* coined a disease called "drapetomania," which he defined "as a prevalent but curable condition in runaway slaves." Willmott presents this in such a matter-of-fact, adroit way, that it might lead some viewers to think it's a spoof.

The raping of enslaved women by white men was a "routine feature of life on many, perhaps most" plantations (Kolchin 2003, 125). Black women had no legal recourse. As enslaved people were perceived as property by their enslavers, white men also "increased their wealth when 'mulatto' children" and therefore additional property were produced of rape (McDaniel 2019, 157). Therefore, it was difficult for many enslaved people to conclusively identify their male parent. One of the first enslaved women to report and write firsthand about the horror and trauma of rape was Harriet Jacobs in her autobiography *Incidents in the Life of a Slave Girl* (1860). She confesses, "I cannot tell how much I suffered in the presence of these wrongs, nor how I am still pained by the retrospect" (quoted by Kolchin 2003, 125). Enslaved women were also prostituted and provided as "comfort women" for white men visiting and doing business with a plantation owner. Some enslaved people were branded with *R*s for runaway or the name of the plantation owner. The punishment of putting someone in a "hot box" was a real torture technique used in the South.

Enslaved people's marriages were not legally binding agreements, and they were not authorized by the Christian church. The enslaved petitioned for the legal sanction of their marriage. The laws not only varied from state to state; they went through iterations (Hunter 2019, 66). Tera W. Hunter, author of *Bound in Wedlock: Slave and Free Black Marriage in the Nineteenth Century*, suggests an accurate vow would have been, "Do you take this woman or this man to be your spouse—until death *or distance* do you part?" (54). Sometimes the enslaved were forced to marry someone they didn't choose or want to marry. There were mixed status families. Sometimes a freed man would enter back into the status of the enslaved to be with his loved ones.

Django's elaborate "Blue Boy" outfit was made famous in Thomas Gainsborough's 1770 painting "The Blue Boy," which at one point was the world's most famous painting (White 2021). Tarantino's inspiration and cinematic reference for the outfit is F. W. Murnau's lost silent film *The Boy in Blue* (1919); also, Mike Myers wears the outfit in the comedy *Austin Powers: International Man of Mystery* (1997). Murnau "pioneered the unchained camera technique," developed by the cinematographer Karl Freund, used extensively in *Django*. It allowed filmmakers to get shots from cameras in motion using "pan shots, tracking shots, tilts, crane shots, etc" (Murnau 2015).

While there's not much in the film showing the enslaved laboring, Tarantino does depict the business of buying and selling of enslaved people. As in *Uncle Tom's Cabin*, "the slave traders in the film are a repellent blend of crudity, cupidity, and cruelty whose livelihood depends upon the forcible breakup of loved ones like Django and Broomhilda, for whose marriage slavery affords no legal protection" (Kaster 2013).

Kilombo claims that the metal masks worn by the enslaved were an instrument of the colonizer. A small piece sat in the mouth, "clamped between the tongue and the jaw, and fixed behind the head with two strings: one surrounding the chin and the second surrounding the nose and the forehead." White enslavers used the mask to prevent enslaved Africans from eating sugarcane or cocoa beans while working, but its main purpose was to silence the enslaved and "implement a sense of speechlessness and fear, inasmuch as the mouth was at the same time a place of muteness and a place of torture" (2008). Kerry Washington told *Vibe* that she had "initially thought the gothic metal masks seen on slaves throughout the film were Tarantino's invention" (Serwer 2013).

DEPICTION AND CULTURAL CONTEXT

The 150th anniversary of the Emancipation Proclamation (September 22, 1862), which set the enslaved free, albeit with limitations, including on people in some border states, was January 1, 2013. It wasn't until 1865 that slavery was completely and unconditionally abolished. Steven Spielberg's film *Lincoln*, released in 2012, focused on the passing of the Thirteenth Amendment to the Constitution. Anthony Hemingway's *Red Tails* about the heroic Tuskegee Black airman in World War II was also released in 2012. Unlike *Django Unchained*, these films' story lines skewed closer to the historical record.

Django Freeman is out to avenge the wrongs of slavery and, with the help of a white man, turns the tables on and treats the white man as he was treated. Tarantino envisioned Django Freeman as an "'uber-masculine black male figure of folklore'—a black Paul Bunyan or Pecos Bill . . . the film was a kind of superhero origin story" (Shone 2017, 209). In his protagonist, Tarantino wanted to veer away from the "soul-deadening victimization" he claims is endemic to films about enslaved or formerly enslaved people (Shone 2017, 211).

The character Jackson plays, "Stephen is a house slave on steroids, the self-loathing black man par excellence, who hates the field slaves almost as much as he hates his own black self" (Gates 2013).

Waltz's Schultz "bears a passing resemblance to Carl Schurz" (1829–1906), a man considered one of the most important German Americans in American history. He was appointed by Lincoln to be ambassador to Spain and, after advocating for Spain not to sympathize with the Confederacy, became the Civil War Union Brigadier General of volunteers who advocated for rights for Blacks (Von Dassanowsky 2014, 18).

Tarantino invented the name of a genre for the film. He calls it a southern, a western set in the South. His goal was not to accurately portray slavery but rather to be antihistorical (Gabriel 2018, 223). Django, "a Black Terminator" is sent back to correct the cinematic wrongs of Hollywood past. Tarantino's intent was for the film to be "a corrective to images previously presented throughout slave cinema, and a form of authenticity more real than history itself" (quoted in Gabriel 2018, 226). What kind of authenticity is Tarantino referring to, and how can his interpretation be "more real than history itself"? As Robert A. Rosenstone claims, "[T]here is not a single historical truth—not on the page and certainly not on the screen" and goes on to enumerate different kinds of cinematic truth: factual, narrative, emotional, psychological, and symbolic (2012, 32).

Tarantino questioned the authenticity of *Roots* (1977). Alex Haley's novel and the miniseries based on it, which depict slavery from the point of view of the enslaved, are in fact, suffused with authentic details about slavery, African and African American religion, and the cohesiveness of family. Haley proved that "African culture, contrary to the popular view of it as savage and primitive, was religious, mannerly, and ceremoniously formal" (Reynolds 2011, 266). Haley's insights into gender roles and the domestic,

Christian-infused world of the enslaved in America were compelling and revelatory.

Tarantino's female Black characters in this film are undeveloped celluloid stereotypes. Gabriel notes that Bettina "with her high-pitched voice and airy demeanor, bears a striking similarity to the character Prissy (Butterfly McQueen) from *Gone with the Wind*"—a childlike, inept person. The Cleopatra Club women—Coco (Daniele Watts); Sheba (Nichole Galicia), Candie's mistress; and Cleo (La Teace Towns Cueller)—fit into the Jezebel stereotype of the promiscuous temptress (Gabriel 2018, 231). Hildi is educated and literate as were some enslaved people, usually people who worked in the owner's house. She is also rebellious and attempts escaping slavery—Django affectionately calls his wife "Little Troublemaker." However, in terms of her role in the story, she needs to be rescued, a role that rarely features Black women characters therefore, "Broomhilda as a damsel in distress is revolutionary as Black women are usually not characterized as worthy of support and worth rescuing" (Horton 2018). Hildi is an anomaly; it's unfortunate that she's not fully dimensionalized. Lara, Candie's sister, has virtually no agency except when bringing Hildi as a "comfort woman" or prostitute to Schultz.

Django violently assaults enslavers, overseers, and any whites who threaten his "unchained" status. This is unrealistic for an enslaved or free Black man and would not have been tolerated. Also, revolts and insurrections were planned and carried out by groups of men.

Tarantino was inspired by the film *Mandingo* (1975). The enslaved performing bare-knuckled boxing, sometimes in battles royal or group fighting until there was one man standing, was a factor of slavery. Virginia-born Tom Molineaux, a formerly enslaved man born in 1784 who bought his own freedom with the $500 he earned for winning a fight, is considered America's first bare-handed boxing star. He moved to New York in 1804 where he earned the title of champion and then to England where another formerly enslaved man, Bill Richmond, trained him. Molineaux earned money and renown fighting and "became the first American to rise to the eminence of an international challenger," journalist Paul Magriel wrote in a 1951 edition of the journal *Phylon* (Reilly 2018).

David Blight, the Pulitzer Prize–winning author of *Frederick Douglass: Prophet of Freedom* (Simon & Schuster, 2018) claims that enslavers would never have risked an enslaved person's life in a fight. Sending "healthy slaves off to die for sport is logically flawed considering their primary use is for economic advancement through physical labor" (quoted in Bicer 2016).

The concept of enslaved men fighting to the death was likely invented in Kyle Onstott's novel *Mandingo* (Longmans, Green & Co Ltd., 1957) and the eponymous film adaptation of it released in 1975, discussed in this book. However, there's "no record of gladiator-like slave fights in the United States" nor that the enslaved fought each other until one died (Harris 2012).

There is a group of people known as Malinke or Mandingo; they are from southern Mali in West Africa. However, according to various historians, there is no evidence that Mandingo fighters were a "human version of cockfights" in the antebellum South (Harris 2012). Enslaved men were tasked with performing; however, they were not tasked with the sole purpose of fighting in a death match for entertainment.

The iconic, militant civil rights leader Malcolm X (1925–65), in a short speech he made in 1963, titled "The Parable of Modern Slavery," delineated the difference between the house and the field enslaved person. He said that the "house Negro" lived in the house and ate (what the owner left over) and dressed well, lived in the attic or basement, and "loved the master more than he did himself." They'd risk their life to save the master. The "field Negro" he said, "we, you still have them today. The field Negro—"those were the masses, ate guts or chitlin, was beaten from morning till night. He lived in a shack, in a hut, wore castoff clothes. And he hated his master. You got field Negroes today. I'm a field Negro" ("House Slave and Field Negro," n.d.).

Although some critics read Stephen as an uber Uncle Tom, his insidious and snide subservience and unconditional loyalty to the enslaver does not at all adhere to the original meaning of an Uncle Tom. Uncle Tom has come to mean something antithetical to Harriet Beecher Stowe's characterization of him in *Uncle Tom's Cabin* (1852). Stowe's Uncle Tom is a martyr, a Christ figure in his 30s, and the farthest thing from evil. He wasn't the sellout he's come to symbolize; in fact, Tom defiantly refused his master's request to provide information about an enslaved runaway's whereabouts and to beat an enslaved man, resulting in his being beaten to death. Jackson, tasked to play Stephen as an old, grizzled man, is a self-serving, power-hungry anti-Black racist.

Stephen's father was Candie's head servant, and his grandfather was Candie's grandfather's head servant. Stephen is empowered by Candie to protect slavery's status quo. The relationship is juxtaposed with the collaborative relationship between Stephen and Candie. Stephen's not Candie's equal; however, he is equally invested for his own benefit in preserving slavery, while Django is empowered by a German pseudo abolitionist to kill the white American oppressor. Schultz is Django's mentor, teacher, and friend; he teaches him how to use a gun and how to read. Schultz treats Django as an equal. Django may be hypermasculine, but like the characters in the films *Glory* (1989) and *Burn!* (1969), he's tied to a white benefactor.

The film starts in 1858, "two years before the Civil War"; however, the Civil War started in 1861. Tarantino, in his own words, was "not bound by the limitations of historical veracity" (quoted in Gabriel 2018, 230).

Tarantino's comical scene of the Ku Klux Klan members bumbling shows white-supremacist terrorists as men with flaws, feelings, and wardrobe malfunctions; the audience laughs at them, but it's uncomfortable laughter, as it humanizes them. The scene provides comic relief; it's also reminiscent of Mel Brooks's irreverent brand of race and Holocaust-based satire employed in his films *Blazing Saddles* (1974) and *The Producers* (1967), respectively.

Tarantino with characteristic hubris bristled at criticism that *Django Unchained* is too violent by reminding audiences that slavery was much worse than anything depicted in the film. He said:

> We all intellectually "know" the brutality and inhumanity of slavery, but after you do the research it's no longer intellectual anymore, no longer just historical record—you feel it in your bones. It makes you angry and want to do something. When slave narratives are done on film, they tend to be historical with a capital H, with an arms-length quality to them. I wanted to break that history-under-glass aspect, I wanted to throw a rock through that glass and shatter it for all times and take you into it. (quoted by Pulver 2012)

Tarantino is over generalizing and neglecting to acknowledge, and thus, diminishing, previous slavery-themed films that provide viewers incisive portals into slavery.

The blood splattering from the bounty hunter duo's gunfire fills up many frames, but the most horrifying and authentic scene in the film shows an enslaved man being torn apart by bloodhounds while Django and Shultz look on. The brutality of bloodhounds was a fact of slavery.

CONCLUSION

A buddy road trip film about an empowered former enslaved man morphs into a bloodbath of Gothic horror. Tarantino's unique pastiche of a screenplay is clever and entertaining; it also has a skewed historical perspective and is gratuitously violent. Tarantino accurately conveys some aspects of slavery, but it goes off the rails at the end and works metaphorically but not so much literally. If only dynamite exploded plantation houses.

FURTHER READING

"African Americans and the Federal Census." n.d. National Archives and Records Administration. Accessed September 27, 2022. https://www.archives.gov/files/research/census/african-american/census-1790-1930.pdf.

Banner, Rachel. 2013. "Thinking through Things: Labors of Freedom in James McCune's Smith's 'The Washerwoman.'" *ESQ: A Journal of the American Renaissance* 59, no. 2: 291–328.

Bassard, Katherine Clay. 2008. "Imagining Other Worlds: Race, Gender, and the 'Power Line' in Edward P. Jones's *The Known World*." *African American Review* 42, no.3 (Fall–Winter): 407–19.

Benson, Eric. 2013. "Django's Roots: Blaxploitation Star Fred Williamson on Originating the Badass Slave." *Vulture*, February 3, 2013.

Bicer, Aila. 2016. "An Analysis of Slave Hierarchies in *Django Unchained*." *York Historian*, January 4, 2016.

"Bills of Sale for Enslaved Persons." n.d. Mss.027. University of Puget Sound Archives & Special Collections. Tacoma, WA. https://archiveswest.orbiscascade.org/.

Bradley, Regina. 2016. "Imagining Slavery in the Hip Hop Imagination." *South: A Scholarly Journal* 49, no. 21 (Fall): 3–24.

Branson, Susan. 2017. "Phrenology and the Science of Race in Antebellum America." *Early American Studies* 15 (1): 164–93.

Bryant, Jonathan. n.d. "Ku Klux Klan in the Reconstruction Era." *New Georgia Encyclopedia*. Accessed August 12, 2020. https://www.georgiaencyclopedia.org/articles/history-archaeology/ku-klux-klan-in-the-reconstruction-era/.

Carroll, Rebecca. 2014. "Can Black People Really Stop White People from Using the N Word." *The Guardian*, November 11, 2014.

DeGruy, Joy. 2017. *Post Traumatic Slave Syndrome: America's Legacy of Enduring Injury & Healing*. Stone Mountain, GA: Joy DeGruy.

Denby, David. 2013. "*Django Unchained*": Put-On, Revenge, and the Aesthetics of Trash." *The New Yorker*, January 22, 2013.

"'Django Unchained' Mandingo Fighting: Real or Not?" *Huffington Post*, December 26, 2012. http://www.huffingtonpost.com/2012/12/26/djanFgo-unchained-mandingo-fighting-real-not_n_2366113.

Dunham, Jarrod. 2016. "The Subject Effaced: Race and Identity in Django Unchained." *Journal of Black Studies* 47, no. 5 (July): 402–22.

"Enslaved Couples Faced Wrenching Separations, or Even Choosing Family over Freedom." *History*, September 20, 2019. https://www.history.com/news/african-american-slavery-marriage-family-separation.

Folsom, Brad. 2013. "Yes, Mandingo Fighting Really Happened." *History Banter*, June 12, 2013.

French, Scot. 2004. *The Rebellious Slave: Nat Turner in American Memory*. Boston: Houghton Mifflin.

Gabriel, Dexter. 2018. "*Django Unchained*: Slavery and Corrective Authenticity in the Southern." In *Celluloid Chains: Slavery in the Americas through Film*, edited by Rudyard J. Alcocer, Kristen Block, and Dawn Duke, 222–41. Knoxville: University of Tennessee Press.

Gates, Henry Louis, Jr. 2013. "Were There House Slaves Like Stephen in '*Django*'?" *The Root*, April 29, 2013.

Harris, Aisha. 2012. "Was There Really Mandingo Fighting like in *Django Unchained*?" Slate, December 24, 2012.

Hendry, Erica R. 2010. "The History behind a Slave's Bill of Sale." *Smithsonian*, May 24, 2010.

Horton, Dana Renee. 2018. "'You Will Sell the Negress!': Using the Post-Neo-Slave Narrative to Revise Representations of Women in *Django Unchained* and *12 Years a Slave*." *Americana*: *The Journal of American Popular Culture* 17, no. 2 (Fall).

"Humanism, Cinema, and Engagement: Clyde Taylor and the L.A. Rebellion Symposium." 2011. UCLA Film & Television Archive. https://www.cinema.ucla

.edu/blogs/la-rebellion/2011/11/16/humanism-cinema-and-engagement-clyde-taylor-and-la-rebellion-symposium.

Hunter, Tera W. 2019. *Bound in Wedlock: Slave and Free Black Marriage in the Nineteenth Century*. Cambridge: Belknap Press.

Kaster, Gregory L. 2013. "'*Django*,' '*Lincoln*' Lessons on Slavery." *SF Gate*, January 4, 2013.

Kennedy, Lisa. 2012. "Jamie Foxx Talks *Django Unchained*, Slavery and '*Hee Haw*.'" *Denver Post*, December 20, 2012.

Kilombo, Grada. 2008. "The Mask: Remembering Slavery, Understanding Trauma." Africavenir. https://www.africavenir.org/nc/news-details/article/the-mask-remembering-slavery-understanding-trauma.html.

Kolchin, Peter. 2003. *American Slavery: 1619–1877*. New York: Hill and Wang.

"The Ku Klux Klan in the 1920s." n.d. *American Experience*. PBS. Accessed September 27, 2022. https://www.pbs.org/wgbh/americanexperience/features/flood-klan/.

Lane, Anthony. 2012. "Love Hurts." *New Yorker*, December 30, 2012.

Lujan, Heidi L., and Stephen E. DiCarlo. 2019. "First African American to Hold a Medical Degree: Brief History of James McCune Smith, Abolitionist, Educator, and Physician." *Advances in Physiology*, April 1, 2019.

"Malcolm X: The House Negro and the Field Negro." February 29, 2012. YouTube video, 23:17. Speech made on January 23, 1963 Michigan State University, East Lansing, Michigan. https://www.youtube.com/watch?v=7kf7fujM4ag.

McClintock, Pamela. 2013. "Box-Office Milestone: *Django* Becomes Quentin Tarantino's Top Domestic Earner." *Hollywood Reporter*, January 17, 2013.

McDaniel, W. Caleb. 2019. *Sweet Taste of Liberty: A True Story of Slavery and Restitution in America*. New York: Oxford University Press.

Murnau, F. W. 2015. "Der Letzte Mann AKA the Last Laugh (1924)." *Cinema of the World*, May 6, 2015.

"NARA (National Archives and Records Administration) Records Pertaining to Free Blacks in the Antebellum Period (1783–1861)." Posted by Damani Davis in African American Records on September 27, 2021. Accessed September 27, 2022. https://historyhub.history.gov/community/african-american-records/blog/2021/09/27/nara-records-pertaining-to-free-blacks-in-the-antebellum-period-1783-1861.

Olive, Jacqueline, and Barak Goodman, dirs. 2022. *Lincoln's Dilemma*. Apple TV+, Eden Productions and Kunhardt Films. https://tv.apple.com/us/show/lincolns-dilemma/umc.cmc.7003fizrrxznfhz1s20vv7ewy.

Pulver, Andrew. 2012. "Quentin Tarantino Defends Depiction of Slavery in Django Unchained." *The Guardian*, December 7, 2012.

Reilly, Lucas. 2018. "Tom Molineaux: The Ex-Slave Who Became America's First International Boxing Superstar." *Mental Floss*, December 14, 2018.

Reynolds, David S. 2011. *Mightier than the Sword: Uncle Tom's Cabin and the Battle for America*. New York: Norton.

Rosenstone, Robert A. 2012. *History on Film: Film on History*. New York: Pearson.

Scott, A. O. 2012. "The Black, the White, and the Angry." *The New York Times*, December 12, 2012.

Serwer, Adam. 2013. "In Defense of *Django*." *Mother Jones*, January 7, 2013.

Shone, Tom. 2017. *Tarantino: A Retrospective*. San Rafael: Insight Editions.

"U.S. Census: Slave Schedules, Black or Mulatto, Colored." n.d. Notable Kentucky African Americans Database. Accessed September 18, 2022. https://nkaa.uky.edu/nkaa/items/show/2369.

Vogel, Joseph. 2018. "The Confessions of Quentin Tarantino: Whitewashing Slave Rebellion in *Django Unchained*." *Journal of American Culture* 41, no. 1 (March): 17–27.

Von Dassanowsky, Robert. 2014. "Dr. King-Schultz as Ideologue and Emblem: The German Enlightenment and the Legacy of the 1848 Revolutions in *Django Unchained*." In *Django Unchained: The Continuation of Metacinema*, edited by Oliver Speck, 17–38. New York: Bloomsbury.

White, Katie. 2021. "Thomas Gainsborough's Blue Boy Painting." *Artnet News*, December 23, 2021.

Woodcock, Zara. 2020. "Quentin Tarantino Slammed by Screenwriter over His Constant Use of N-Word in Films." *Metro.com*, June 13, 2020.

Young, Kevin Lowell. 2011. *Ardency: A Chronicle of the Amistad Rebels*. New York: Knopf.

Zakarin, Jordan. 2012. "Spike Lee: *Django Unchained* Is Disrespectful. I Will Not See It." *Hollywood Reporter*, December 24, 2012.

Zeinert, Karen. 1997. *The Amistad Slave Revolt and Abolitionism*. New York: Linnet Books.

Chapter 8

12 Years a Slave (2013)

Steve McQueen's graphic, disturbing, bold, and beautiful film *12 Years a Slave* (2013), starring the British actor Chiwetel Ejiofor in a searing performance as Solomon Northup, won three Academy Awards, for Best Picture, Best Adapted Screenplay by John Ridley, and Best Supporting Actress for the magnetic and compelling Lupita Nyong'o, who played Patsey. It is the first film directed and produced by a Black filmmaker to win Best Picture. Brad Pitt, who plays Samuel Bass, was also one of its producers. It debuted and won the top prize at the Toronto Film Festival, where audience responses ranged from some viewers walking out due to the film's excessive but essential depiction of violence to others giving long, standing ovations acknowledging the film's uncompromising depiction of American Southern slavery.

Based on Northup's best-selling 1853 eponymous memoir, the film tells the story of a free African American New Yorker who at the age of thirty-three was kidnapped and sold "down the river," or sold into Southern slavery. Prior to the age of thirty-three, Northup had lived his whole life as a free man in upstate New York. Educated and literate, he was a talented fiddler and a lumber expert. He was lied to by two conmen who flattered him about his musical talent, telling him they were recruiting him to play the fiddle for their circus. They drugged him, gave him a new name, and sold him to New Orleans slave dealers. Northup endured twelve years of oppression as an enslaved man on a few plantations, the final one in Bayou Boeuf in Avoyelles Parish, Louisiana, run by a vicious, drunk slave breaker (an enslaved person who was defiant) named Epps, played by the intense Michael Fassbender, who tormented and abused him and Patsey, an enslaved woman. Northup writes several letters and with the help of a man named Samuel Bass, one gets to his lifelong friend, Henry Northup, a relative of his grandfather who was enslaved by the Northup family, who enlists Washington Hunt, the governor of New York, to help prove that Northup is a free man who had been kidnapped, and whom he releases from the nightmare of slavery.

McQueen's film compels the viewer to empathize with the day-to-day tormented plight of the enslaved. It exposes the brutal dehumanization of African and African-descended people and realistically depicts the torture meted out to them if they dared defy or resist. Film critic David Denby claimed unequivocally that "*12 Years a Slave* is easily the greatest feature film ever made about American slavery" (2013). It's the only film, except for Gordon Parks' television film adaptation of Northup's memoir, whose source material is an eyewitness account of slavery.

The film is also a film "about love," says McQueen. "It has to do with Northup's humanity. He kept hold of his humanity, his dignity, through all kinds of unfortunate situations. And it's difficult just to get through a day sometimes, but he managed to get through 12 years of the most horrific ordeal you could imagine and held onto a kind of truth, which I think is just extraordinarily beautiful and a lesson for us all" ("*12 Years a Slave*: 160 Years Later" 2013). Now titled *Half Slave Half Free*—the original title was *Solomon Northup's Odyssey*—is a television film directed by Gordon Parks in 1984.

Gordon Parks (1912–2006), *Life Magazine's* first Black photographer and the first Black filmmaker to direct a Hollywood film, *Shaft* (1971), adapted Northup's memoir first, although the filmmakers, Fox Searchlight, McQueen, and his publicists never mentioned that *12 Years a Slave* is, in fact, a remake of Parks's television film. In McQueen's foreword to Penguin Classics' 2013 tie-in reissue of the book, he says he'd never heard of the book, and not one person he knew had heard of it or Solomon Northup, although slavery scholar Eric Foner informed McQueen in a discussion with Nelson George that Northup's memoir is a well-known text. Parks's film is and has been readily available, and information about it is easily accessible.

Half Slave Half Free is a stirring and beautifully shot film. It hews closely to the broad strokes of Northup's memoir. Parks's film aired on the Public Broadcasting System in 1984 and was therefore bound by the constraints of the medium. He regretted that the film "didn't go far enough, yet it was precisely that restraint that earned the some of its strongest reviews in 1985" (Maltin 2013). Lou Potter's and Samm-Art Williams's screenplay is superb and has flashes of humor, and Avery Brooks's eloquent, deeply humane portrayal of Solomon is operatic. Although it is not graphic, it does show a realistic depiction of slavery, heartlessly ferocious enslavers as well as more lenient ones, and nuanced relationships among the enslaved. Nathan Irvin Huggins, author of the brilliant classic *Black Odyssey: The Afro-American's Ordeal in Slavery* (Penguin, 1977), was one of five historical consultants on the film.

Solomon strikes out against his master and takes a severe beating for it. More time is spent showing Solomon's life and his relationship with his wife and children before he was sold into slavery, and there are occasional flashbacks into his life as a free man. Patsey, such a pivotal character in the memoir and McQueen's film, is changed into Jenny, played by Rhetta Greene. She and Solomon have a romantic entanglement, and she tells Solomon she chooses to allow Epps to possess her, as it's in her best interest. Solomon when asked by Epps to whip her brings her into a cabin, and they fake it.

The film, for which Parks also composed the musical score, was part of a three-part American Playhouse/PBS series, executive produced by Lindsay Law, that included *Denmark Vesey: A House Divided* (1982), about an enslaved man who planned a rebellion, and *Charlotte Forten's Mission: An Experiment in Freedom* (1985), about Charlotte Forten, an antislavery activist and teacher.

Parks, who also wrote fiction and nonfiction, said in his autobiography that he would have directed this movie for free. He said, "So little is said about slavery. This was our holocaust, and it's always hushed, hushed, hushed" (quoted by Bennetts 1985). Prior to being offered the film, he did not know any story about a free man sold into slavery who survived it and reported on it so objectively. He says his sixteen-year-old daughter was quite moved by it as well at the time (Parks 2005, 333).

Parks desired and hired a crew made up of Blacks and whites so that he could show the Southerners how both races could work peacefully together. Parks noted that the local whites in Savannah, Georgia, were not used to such a mixed crew. He says, "For a few days they watched with curious eyes. Ink, amber and honey were flowing together peacefully" (Parks 2005, 336).

The memoir, the source material for the film, is a bracing firsthand indictment of slavery that fed the flames of the abolitionist movement. Screenwriter John Ridley deftly structured and wrote the vivid and compelling adaptation, and "McQueen claimed 80% of the dialogue comes from the book" (quoted in Li 2014, 326). John Ridley, who also wrote the screenplay for *Red Tails* (2012), was only the second African American to win an Academy Award for writing; the first was Geoffrey S. Fletcher in 2010 for *Precious*, based on Sapphire's novel Push (1996). Ridley, who is also a novelist and playwright, has written independent and studio films as well as television and web series; he has also directed films, including *All Is By My Side* (2013), a biopic about Jimi Hendrix. He wrote, collaborating with illustrators, the graphic novel miniseries *The Other History of the DC Universe* (DC Black Label, 2020–2021), which gives prominence to superheroes of color.

McQueen, born in London in 1969, is a Black filmmaker whose Trinidadian father and Grenadian mother immigrated from Grenada to London. He says, "Between me and an American person who looks like me is their boat went right and my boat went left" (Kerr 2013)—he's also said, "my boat went one way and theirs went another" (Weiner 2014). McQueen's edgy and provocative previous movies include *Small Axe* (2020), his five-film anthology about West Indian immigrant life in London in the 1960s–1980s, and two films also starring Michael Fassbender: *Shame* (2011), about sexual addiction, and *Hunger* (2008), a historical drama about the 1981 hunger strike staged by the Irish Republican Army's Bobby Sands. McQueen's fearless insistence on not eluding but always revealing troubling, startling, and explicit sexual and body images provides a through line in his oeuvre.

McQueen is also a prize-winning video artist (Turner Prize in 1999). His museum show in 2020 at London's Tate Museum received acclaim for its captivating projections and installations, including *Carib's Leap* (2002), a four-minute video installation depicting Grenada's Indigenous Caribs committing suicide in 1651 by jumping off high cliffs rather than acquiescing to the invading French. McQueen began his fine arts career by studying painting. This is reflected in *12 Years a Slave's* painterly and pastoral scenes of lush Louisiana's mossy treescapes and pastel skies, which are powerfully contrasted with the film's brutal depictions of lashings, lynchings, and rape.

McQueen's vision for the look of *12 Years a Slave* was, in part, inspired by the Spanish painter Francisco Goya (1746–1828), whose depictions of violence are "amazing, exquisite paintings" (McQueen, quoted by Stauffer 2014, 318). McQueen said, "Goya painted the most horrific images on battlefields, but they are the most beautiful paintings you've ever seen. He wants your attention. . . . There's no point in painting a picture which is ugly, your attention would be drawn to the form, not content." Sean Bobbitt, the cinematographer, was mindful that depicting slavery "had to feel true but also beautiful. We didn't want to layer the horrors of slavery, the dirt and mud; the reality is the locations are really quite sumptuous" (McQueen 2013). The sumptuous images, along with the ones of torture, linger on the screen. The film's Oscar-nominated editor, Joe Walker, said that the filmmakers wanted to linger on rather than "bombard" the viewer with images, enabling the audience a deeper connection to the characters (McQueen 2013). And "the candle-lit interiors and lantern-illuminated exteriors evoke the shadings of a land unfiltered by electricity" (Doherty 2013, 6).

The African American critic Armond White controversially called the film "torture porn" (2013). "Torture porn" is defined as "a genre of horror films in which sadistic violence or torture is a central aspect of the plot" ("torture porn," *Collins*). The term "trauma porn" is more often used specifically for race-based images: it's "when people share graphic videos, usually of police brutality, on social media . . . exploit a traumatic experience solely for the purpose of shock value" (Brar 2020). White's misguided claim that "Brutality, violence and misery get confused with history in *12 Years a Slave*" neglects the fact that brutality was embedded into and synonymous with America's history of racial chattel slavery.

As historian Edward Baptist states, "Torture was a factor of production," particularly on cotton plantations (2014, 141). McQueen does depict slavery as "a horror show," as White goes on to say. That's what it was. But to compare it to a horror film is specious, as the genre's tropes invoke the supernatural, which *12 Years a Slave* does not do. White says, "McQueen has made the most unpleasant American movie since William Friedkin's 1973 *The Exorcist*, but it is being sold (and mistaken) as part of the recent spate of movies that pretend 'a conversation about race'" (2013). The film cuts to the heart of the hypocritical bedrock of the history of race relations in America, whose Declaration of Independence grants "each man or person Life, Liberty, and the Pursuit of Happiness" and neglects to even mention slavery; Thomas Jefferson's reference to it in the first draft of the document was deleted.

Dede Gardner, a producer on the film along with Brad Pitt, said the film was shot in "35 days all over New Orleans in and out of the city, at plantations in the swamp and in the quarter, where you find the oldest streets in one of the oldest areas in the country." The Epps plantation still farms sugarcane. The Charles plantation where Patsey has lunch with Mistress Shaw, played by Alfre Woodard, and is treated like a human being, has a "beautiful identity" and "suggests a visual separation between the plantations" (McQueen 2013).

The film opens with a still photo-like image depicting Solomon Northup (Chiwetel Ejiofor) in the middle of a group of young and old enslaved Black men standing in front of high green stalks in a field. They are listening intently; they look stressed and unhappy. The N-word is used in the first minute by the white plantation overseer. The plantation owner tells the enslaved men they will be in a "cutting gang" and shows them how with machetes to cut stalks of cane. They work and cut, and a mass of large green leaves fills the screen.

Day turns into night, and approximately ten enslaved people in one room are getting ready to sleep on the floor. They are all sleeping except for Northup and the woman on the floor next to him who takes his hand and puts it on her body. She kisses him. Her desire for him is palpable and wordless. He pleasures her and satisfies her desire, and she sobs. This scene, showing an enslaved person in control of her own body, was invented for the film.

The next morning, Northup is eating; he's focused on the juice of a blackberry on his plate. He is cutting the edge of a small branch, making a pen. He is then seen by candlelight dipping his pen into a cup of blackberry juice to write on a piece of parchment. He squeezes more blackberry, but it is not visible enough. Frustrated and distressed, he throws the cup on the floor. A few scenes later, he is able to write using the juice.

There's a flashback to Northup lovingly looking at his wife, Anne (Kelsey Scott), and then a title card: *12 Years a Slave* typed on parchment. An elegantly dressed Northup is tuning and then playing his violin at a fancy dance with finely dressed white people. At home, he puts his two children, Alonzo and Margaret, to sleep. His well-dressed wife and the children leave the next day in a horse and buggy for her job, cooking for a white family for three weeks. Northup tells her he hates to share her cooking with others. It is Saratoga, New York, 1841.

Mr. Brown (Scoot McNairy) and Mr. Hamilton (Taran Killam) pursue Solomon, and when they find him, they lavish him with compliments on his expert fiddle playing. He agrees to their offer of a paying gig playing the fiddle in Washington, DC, where they dine luxuriously. Solomon is poured poisoned wine and wakes up chained in a brick-walled dungeon. He insists he is a free man from New York; he is told he is not a free man, but that he is a "runaway n****r from Georgia" who is told his name is now Platt. The hateful jailer tells him to produce papers if he is free. He has nothing. He is forced on the floor and brutally and repeatedly beaten by another jailer with a paddleboard and told, "You're a slave. You're a Georgia slave." Solomon screams and pants; he won't admit he is a slave and gets beaten again. Groaning and crying, he screams for help. He looks up at the window of the imposing brick building, and the Capitol building is within view.

Solomon is put in a pen with other naked captives, including a boy calling for his mother, who are washing themselves. Solomon, whose raw, lacerated back is in view, tells the boy to be silent. The boy's mother, Eliza, and his sister enter. They are taken in a covered wagon at night and placed in the lower deck of a riverboat. Robert (the late Michael K. Williams) suggests they fight, and he talks to Solomon and another man about going up against the crew. The man says, "Three can't go against the whole crew." And he says, "[T]he rest are born n****rs; they don't have the stomach for a fight. Robert, if we get where we're going, we'll wish we had died trying. Survival is about keeping your head down." The riverboat grinds on, sounding like doors slamming in a prison.

Solomon is taken to a boat where other Blacks, including Eliza, her two children, and a few men are waiting. Clemons Ray (Chris Chalk) tells Solomon to tell no one who he is and that he can read and write if he wants to survive. "I don't want to survive, I want to live," Northup responds. Robert tries to stop a white man from raping a Black woman, and the Black man is fatally stabbed. Solomon watches the white men wrap up and throw Robert's body overboard. Clemons Ray is picked up and freed by his owner.

The slave dealer, Theophilus Freeman (Paul Giamatti), shows off naked Blacks for sale. William Ford (Benedict Cumberbatch), pays $700 for Eliza, played by Adepero Oduye, who pleads with him to not separate her family. Ford wants to accommodate her request; however, Freeman tells her son to move quickly, that he will grow into a fine beast. He gets $600 for the boy. Ford wants her and buys her, but she kicks and screams saying, "You can't take my children," and Freeman punches her. Eliza's crying when she arrives at the plantation. The separation of families was a heartbreaking and cruel reality of slavery.

Mistress Ford (Liza J. Bennett) tells Eliza, "Your children will soon be forgotten."

Solomon tells Eliza to stop crying and warns her about wallowing in sorrow. "Have you stopped crying for your children?" she asks him. "You make no sounds, but will you ever let them go in your heart?" She confronts him about his fealty to Ford, known to be a kindly man.

He responds, "My back is thick with scars for protesting my freedom." An inconsolable Eliza continues crying at a religious meeting Ford presides over. Eliza is taken away. She reveals something she has alluded to before; she was a enslaver's mistress and had many comforts.

Paul Dano plays hostile John Tibeats, Ford's chief carpenter. Solomon suggests to Tibeats and Epps they clear out the timber and raft it on the canal, telling Ford of his experience in New York. Tibeats protests, saying it is impossible, but Ford wants to try it. It works, and Ford calls Solomon a marvel. Tibeats seethes with resentment and jealousy because he believes that Solomon does not know his place and has stepped outside his bounds. Ford rewards Solomon with a violin.

Tibeats orders Solomon as they build a house together and complains about his work and that he is not doing as instructed. He tells Solomon to strip, but Solomon refuses to do so. In a rage, Solomon beats Tibeats up, calling to mind, as Doherty notes, "the most famous act of rebellion in all slave narratives, when the enslaved Frederick Douglass fights back against his overseer, Mr. Covey. 'However long I might remain a slave in form, the day had passed forever when I could be a slave in fact,' declared Douglass" (2013, 7). Tibeats and two white men come and attempt to lynch Solomon by hanging him up on a noose on a large, blossoming tree. Tragically, "this punishment is 'routine' for those African Americans who dared to assert their humanity" (Hobson 2018, 262–63).

Solomon is entrapped and parched in the heat of the day for what could be minutes, hours, or an eternity. His toes, twitching in muddy shoes, scrape the ground. Enslaved people are walking around; there is silence, no music, only the sound of cicadas. Children are playing, and a girl who notices him brings him water to drink, lifting it to his mouth. There is a close-up of Solomon sweating, and then a long shot from Mistress Ford looking at him from the porch. Then, there is a long shot of Ford's overseer who disrupts the lynching, cutting the rope. He tells Tibeats and the other men they cannot harm an enslaved man because of his monetary worth and Ford owns the mortgage on him. Ford feels pity for Solomon and takes him into his house to sleep on the floor.

Solomon is sold to Edwin Epps, played by Michael Fassbender, who is a Bible-thumping, red-faced, sweaty, sneering, drunk, and abusive enslaver. Epps confronts his workers about their lack of productivity. He declares that Patsey (Lupita Nyong'o) is the "queen of the fields; she picks more than 500 pounds of cotton every day." He lavishes attention on her and places his hand on her shoulder, making her uncomfortable. "God gave her to me as a reward for righteous living," he ironically claims. Epps threatens to eliminate people who pick a low amount. Epps is possessed by Patsey, and his wife, Mistress Epps, played by Sarah Paulson, jealous of her husband's lust for Patsey, becomes obsessed with the enslaved woman's every move. In one scene, Mistress Epps from afar watches Patsey sitting on the grass making dolls out of corn stalks in her few moments of leisure.

Solomon plays the fiddle in the Epps's house party, and people are dancing. Patsey's dancing is spirited; she's gracefully moving and spinning. Mrs. Epps throws a glass pitcher at her and yells at Epps to "sell the negress, that black bitch Patsey." Patsey's wailing.

Epps says that he will not sell her, as "she's got so much vigor" and tells his wife that he would sooner do away with her than with Patsey. In the next scene, Mrs. Epps sends Solomon to the store, and he tries to run away. He sees other runaways being hanged and changes his mind.

Patsey goes to Master Shaw's to get soap from Mistress Shaw; the sadistic Mistress Epps will not give her any. Shaw's Black mistress, played by Alfre Woodard, enjoys a leisurely lunch on the porch with Patsey. It is a fascinating scene contrasting two Black women's antebellum roles: one is liberated from servitude by her white enslaver/partner; the other is abused and stalked by a crazed, abusive enslaver in lust with her. But for a moment in time, both women are ladies who lunch. Mistress Shaw brags, "I ain't felt the end of a lash in more years than I can recall. Where once I served, I have others serving me." But she knows this world built on racial slavery and capitalistic greed will not end well. She says, "The curse of the pharaohs was a poor example of what wait for the plantation class."

John Ridley says that this was the hardest scene he had to write. "There's some levity there, but then it ends on a statement of faith and hope for the future, and it's one of the few places where an individual who is in and of those circumstances can really demonstrate that they believe that there is a better tomorrow and speak to the power of the spirit for those folks who were most deeply embedded in that system of slavery" (quoted in Buchanan 2013).

Epps forces Patsey to have sex with him and then hits her and rapes her while she lays motionless. Mistress Epps says Patsey is "foul with hate.... You let it be, it's gonna come back to us in the dark of night." She pinches Patsey's ear. Patsey asks Solomon to help her kill herself and bury her in the swamp. He tells her she has melancholia, and he won't help her.

"I ain't got no comfort in this life. There is God here. God is merciful. Do what I ain't got the strength to do myself."

Solomon cries while he carves his kids' names on a box; he is desperately missing them. The group walks back to Epps. Patsey has a red eye. "A good day's labor would average 200 lbs." Armsby, a fictional character played by Garret Dillahunt, is a poor white man Epps hires. He puts a balm on and tries to soothe Solomon's back scars. Solomon asks Armsby to post a letter to Marksville and keep it confidential. Epps finds out and confronts Solomon who says he made it up. He burns his letter with tears in his eyes. Bass, hired by Epps to build a house on his land, speaks against slavery, telling Epps that the enslaved are human beings and that "there will be a day of reckoning."

Epps is screaming for Patsey. He accuses her of lying and strips her naked and forces her against a tree. Mistress Epps says, "Do it. Strike the life from her." Epps makes Solomon do it. Mistress Epps says, "He pantomimes; there's a welt on her."

Epps takes the whip, and Solomon says, "Sooner or later, someone during eternal justice will answer for this sin."

"Sin, there is no sin," Epps says. "A man does what he pleases with his property," and in the most horrific and gut-wrenching scene in the film, he forces Solomon to flog Patsey with a whip, which he does. The disturbing, unforgettable scene, which seems to go on forever is "shot from the multiple perspectives of victim, perpetrator, unwilling participant, and enthusiastic onlooker, and filmed in a virtually uninterrupted long take" (Doherty 2013, 7).

After an enslaved man dies on the field, Solomon joins his brethren and joins in the communal, religious experience of singing the Christian spiritual "Roll Jordan Roll," led by the actress and singer Topsy Chapman. He is genuinely moved.

Solomon trusts Bass and tells him his story. "I'm afraid to tell ya," Bass says, "[y]our story is amazing, and not in a good way."

"Do you believe in justice, as you say? That slavery is an evil that should befall no one." And he asks Bass to write his friends in the North acquainting them of his situation, beseeching them to forward free papers. He says freedom means everything to him; he is afraid but will do it. Bass posts the letters, which reach Henry Northup, a relative of Solomon's. Henry soon thereafter arrives on Epps's plantation with a deputy sheriff claiming the legal right to take the man who answers to the name Solomon Northup. Henry and Solomon hug. Epps threatens to lash Solomon; he is taken away, says good-bye to Patsey, and returns home. He walks into his house apologizing for his appearance.

His daughter introduces him to her baby, "Your grandson, Solomon Staunton Northup."

The postscript reads: "Solomon Northup was one of the few victims of kidnapping slavery to regain freedom." Northup lost the case against the slave pen owner James Burch, and kidnappers Brown and Hamilton were not prosecuted. Northup continued the work he did before he was kidnapped as an activist in the abolition movement and worked on the Underground Railroad. The date of his death is unknown.

The score by Hans Zimmer comprises contrasts: relentlessly grinding atonal music and celestially lofty violins. It is also suffused with silences and the sounds of cicadas and the moss on the trees moving in the breeze. There are spirituals, or "sorrow songs," coined by the Black historian and sociologist W. E. B. Du Bois in his seminal work *The Souls of Black Folk* (1903). "Roll Jordan Roll" was written by an English preacher and was appropriated by the enslaved. The song combines biblical beliefs with an expression of resistance against slavery (Ray 2016). And Paul Dano as Tibeats performs "Run N****r Run," an iconic old plantation, folkloric song, originally sung by the enslaved and inspired by a man running from a slave patrol. White singers appropriated and recorded the song in the 1920s.

The film, from the opening scene, focuses on the quotidian aspects of forced labor. McQueen noted that "there's a difference between cutting down trees and cutting down sugar cane and picking cotton. . . . Cutting down trees has a catharsis to it, a physical labor to it. It's a way you can deal with your aggression in your life. Whatever is happening, you've got hours and hours of cutting down these trees and hacking through these things. It's the same with sugar cane: It's brutal collecting sugar cane, but you are fighting something. Now, picking cotton is a completely different thing; picking cotton has no catharsis, no release, it's blindingly hot" (McQueen, interviewed by Kohn 2013).

Most Americans and viewers of the film possess general knowledge about American slavery and believe that treating people like property is indefensible and morally corrupt. Viewers can empathize with the deprivation the enslaved experienced—for example, the unfathomable pain of being separated from one's family. How can a person like Solomon Northup who has known freedom, self-determination, and literacy, at the time mostly reserved for white people, hold onto hope for freedom and the return of his fundamental human rights? By the end of the film, Solomon looks like he has aged dramatically, more like forty than twelve years. However, the steely, defiant determination in his gaze has not aged nor softened. It has only grown stronger. His burning desire to be reunited with his family and undo and militate against the injustice forced on him was not extinguished.

Solomon Northup's firm optimism was challenged in myriad ways at every turn. Northup says in his memoir, "Hopes sprang up in my heart only to be crushed and blighted" (Northup [1853] 2014, 173). But in the end, his hopes triumph over his adversity, with the help of people who had in their arsenal the will to go up against the unjust law of the land. Through the writing, publication, and reissue of his memoir, Northup transcends the enslavement of his spirit and legacy. And his story is told by a British director and an African American writer "whose roots retrace the original triangle of the slave trade [and who] have dug deep into the heart of the matter. Like the slave narrators, they have used a medium once the sole property of white men to tell a terrible story, one that can now be written—and directed—by Black artists themselves" (George 2013). This was also the case in 1984 when Gordon Parks's and Lou Potter's and Samm-Art Williams's adaptation aired.

HISTORICAL CONTEXT

The Book

Twelve Years a Slave: Narrative of Solomon Northup, a Citizen of New York, Kidnapped in Washington City in 1841, and Rescued in 1853, from a Cotton Plantation Near the Red River, in Louisiana was published by Derby and Miller in Auburn in 1853. It is dedicated to Harriet Beecher Stowe, author of the influential, mega best-selling antislavery novel *Uncle*

Tom's Cabin, published in 1852. Stowe based her novel on many true accounts of slavery. Churchwell says, Northup's "experience on a plantation near the Red River closely resembled Stowe's portrait of life on Legree's fictional plantation" (2014).

Northup's rescue was front-page *New York Times* news on January 20, 1853 (Fiske 2016). David Wilson, a lawyer, was chosen to write Northup's book and be his amanuensis, a writer who aids writing someone's autobiography. Northup dictated his life story to Wilson who wrote the book quickly. Unlike most amanuenses of slave narratives, Wilson was not an abolitionist (Eakin 2014, xiii). Northup's memoir "took five months to get published, and it sold approximately 30,000 copies overall, and 10,000 the first month it was published" (Worley 1997, 243). The book subsequently went out of print, disappearing from the public before 1900 for almost one hundred years until Sue Eakin published an annotated and historically authenticated edition published by Louisiana State University in 1968.

Eakin rescued Northup's memoir from possible oblivion. She was twelve when she was given to read and return an original copy of the book in a plantation home near the property where Northup was enslaved. It took her several more years when she was a college student in 1936 to find the book in Otto Claitor's Bookstore, where Mr. Claitor, "known as an authority on old books," told her it was "pure fiction" and gave it to her for twenty-five cents. Eakin would devote her life, she later said, to proving the bookseller wrong (Eakin 2014).

She claimed that most slave narratives were written by enslaved people "from the border states or the Atlantic seaboard" rather than Southern states. And, she says, despite being enslaved and horribly mistreated in the South, Northup was able to narrate his experience with "fairness and justice" (Eakin 2014, xv).

Frederick Douglass gave the book a rave review, saying, in part, "its truth is far greater than fiction," as did William Lloyd Garrison's abolitionist newspaper *Liberator*, claiming that "Mrs. Stowe (and her novel *Uncle Tom's Cabin*) will be acquitted of exaggeration." When Birch was arrested for kidnapping and selling Northup, the *New York Times* stated that slavery exists with features more revolting than those described in *Uncle Tom's Cabin*" (Eakin 2014, 202).

Slavery scholar Eric Foner stated, Northup's book "is one of the most remarkable first-person accounts of slavery. But it's also a piece of propaganda. It's written to persuade people that slavery needs to be abolished" (quoted in George 2013). Slave narratives, an influential best-selling genre that pushed the abolitionism needle forward, exposed the brutal horrors of slavery, enabling readers to see in granular, graphic detail how enslaved people were treated with, as Douglass said, "less consideration than mules and horses." The first American slave narrative was *The Life of William*

Grimes, the Runaway Slave Written by Himself, published in 1825. Churchwell notes that *The Interesting Narrative of the Life of Olaudah Equiano*, published in 1789, "is widely regarded as the first ever in the genre, but Equiano published his book in Britain" (2014).

Slavery is often referred to as the "peculiar institution," a term first used in 1830 by slaveholding white supremacist, John C. Calhoun, a South Carolina politician, and vice president under Andrew Jackson. The removal of a statue of Calhoun, who enslaved eighty people, in Charleston, South Carolina, took place in June 2020.

Northup claimed he was born July 7, 1808, but records show he was born on that date in 1807, in Essex County, in what is now called Minerva, New York. He married Anne Hampton in 1829 with whom he had three children (Fiske, Brown, and Seligman 2013, 27). He was a talented violinist who was also skilled in myriad aspects of the lumber business, including cutting down timber, transporting it, and woodcutting. Northup as a free man of color was educated and therefore literate; he went to school with whites, as this was the practice in New York at this time. Enslaved people were forbidden to learn to read and write and would risk getting a limb cut off if they were caught teaching or being taught literacy.

Northup and his family moved to Saratoga Springs in 1841, a growing and increasingly popular resort city made accessible by the railroad and famous by Washington Irving. When Solomon was thirty-two years old and performing and playing the violin, he was approached by two men: Merrill Brown and Abram Hamilton, who said they were connected with a circus company. They acknowledged his musical talent and promised to pay him a dollar a day for playing the fiddle and an additional three dollars a night (Northup [1853] 2014, 16).

Northup joined Brown and Hamilton, and after arriving in New York, they persuaded him to go with them to Washington, but first, they got him free papers at the Custom House. They took him to dinner and poured him poisoned liquor that first caused him a burning sensation and then to become nauseated. He spent two weeks handcuffed in a dungeon in the Williams Slave Pen. As stated in his memoir, but not shown in the film, Northup gets sick with smallpox and was interred at the hospital for a few days (Northup [1853] 2014, 26).

Northup was sold to Ford, described as a kind slave owner, who paid $900 for him. Ford never beat Northup. He sold him to Tibeats, "a universally disliked carpenter to whom Ford owed money" (Fiske, Brown, and Seligman 2013, 58). The alcoholic Edwin Epps subsequently paid Tibeats $1,500 for Northup. Epps was experienced in the cotton business. Epps tasked Solomon to be a driver and flog slaves, in addition to carpentry and fiddle playing. Northup had the will to survive, unlike Patsey who was broken and despondent. He had self-esteem and a good network—he knew the value of information. And he was a musical talent, which provided pleasure to others. He wrote a song, titled "Roaring River," which is published in his memoir. In it, he expresses his "fearless joy," an aspect of an enslaved person's survival (Fiske, Brown, and Seligman 2016, 89–91).

As was the case with nearly all plantations, it was hard for the enslaved to escape Bayou Bouf without getting caught. They needed freedom papers and passes to go to a store, and they were not allowed unless they had written permission from the enslaver to go to the post office to mail letters.

The letter Bass posted to New York was written on August 15, 1852. Bass had previously drafted three letters, none to Henry Northup, as Solomon's first letter to Henry hadn't been answered (Fiske, Brown, and Seligman 2013, 92). Henry Northup was paid $300 by the state of New York for his efforts to free Solomon. Henry Northup secured political endorsements and affidavits from many people who knew Solomon, Anne, and his family, helping to garner support in Louisiana. It took Henry Northup a month to plan to find and rescue Northup. He was driven by "the moral imperative" (Fiske, Brown, and Seligman 2013, 93). *Uncle Tom's Cabin* was published to fervent national enthusiasm and interest six months earlier, "so anti-slavery fervor was high" (Fiske, Brown, and Seligman 2013, 93).

New York governor Washington Hunt who supported Solomon's rescue was an outspoken critic of slavery and criticized President Tyler for allowing slavery to spread to the southwest. Henry Northup found Bass who confirmed he had written the letter, and he revealed where Solomon was. Henry and the sheriff arrived at Epps's house and revealed their purpose. Epps said had he had even an hour's notice, they wouldn't have found "Platt." When Henry arrived at Epps's plantation, Solomon threw his hand on Henry. Solomon is asked several questions confirming his identity. Henry says, "Throw down that sack. Your cotton-picking days are over with." Solomon was rescued and reunited with his family.

The trial against Birch began; Birch claimed he believed Northup was an enslaved man from Georgia as he was told by the kidnappers. There were baseless accusations that Northup conspired or colluded in his own kidnapping. It didn't go to trial. The Dred Scott Supreme Court case, which stated that Blacks did not have the same rights as whites, could have been an influence (Fiske, Brown, and Seligman 2013, 108).

As in most book-to-film adaptations, parts of the book are not included in the film. In his memoir, Northup's kidnapping is revealed to his family by another enslaved man, Clemens Ray, who after being captured in Williams Slave Pen is released in Washington, DC, in the first year of Solomon's disappearance. Henry Northup went to Governor Seward in 1841 to see if they could rescue Solomon, but they didn't know where he was (Fiske, Brown, and Seligman 2013).

The last part of chapter 17, titled "The Idea of Insurrection," is not included in the film. The chapter includes a discussion of an insurrection planned by Lew Cheney in Bayou Boeuf. When word about his plans got out, Cheney ended up saving his own life by betraying many enslaved people who were hanged for their involvement even though some were not involved in his plan.

The enslaved were deterred from resisting and running away by the constant threat of severe punishment. Physical abuse against the enslaved was legal, although there were laws (often ignored) against "excessive abuse and violence" and disabling, disfiguring, or endangering the life of an enslaved person (Stacey, quoted by Calautti 2014). Practices like whipping, hanging, and cutting off limbs were leveled against the enslaved when they were defiant, rebellious, accused of lying, ran away, and/or didn't follow orders and rules. These punishments were most often meted out in a public space so the "guilty" could be made examples of (Snyder 2010, 41).

Kidnapping

Free Blacks were characterized by the slavery scholar Ira Berlin as "slaves without masters" (quoted by Wilson 1994, 26). Free Blacks, in addition to "[j]ob discrimination, social ostracism, educational limitations, and residential segregation," constantly endured the threat of being kidnapped (Littlefield 1997). Some African-descended people like Solomon Northup were born free. Some enslaved people were granted freedom or manumitted in the wills of their masters, who were possibly assuaging their guilt for "owning" people like property. Some formerly enslaved people with skills were hired out and able to earn enough money to buy their own freedom.

Historians have proved false Harriet Beecher Stowe's 1853 claim that the kidnapping of free Negroes was "rare and usually fairly prosecuted" (Stowe, quoted by Eakin 1968, x). Although kidnapping was a crime, it was not often prosecuted when the victim was Black. Kidnappers were motivated by avarice due to the high demand for labor and the prices paid for able enslaved people (Wilson 1994, 45). Some whites turned a blind eye to it, but abolitionists spoke out against it and tried to stop it. Blacks living and traveling with freedom papers in free states were at risk. About the more than ten million Blacks who were kidnapped from Africa in the first place, an essay in the *Liberator* claimed in that case there was "no ransom; they were sold into slavery" (quoted by Wilson 1994, 49).

Unlike kidnapping, slave stealing, also known as "man stealing," was legal and encouraged by fugitive slave laws passed in 1793 and 1850. Confederate soldiers kidnapped Blacks, claiming that free Blacks were fugitives. Few first-person stories exist, as freedom in most cases wasn't achieved. Northup's story is the most well known. Some cases were tried, "but they rarely led to freedom as freedom was hard to prove. Only a white could testify for a Black and they feared retribution. The issue was debated in Congress, and laws were passed restricting Negro seaman, from being out and about in society; they were forced to stay in jails until their boats were back on the water. The first Negro Seaman Act was passed in 1822 after Denmark Vesey's conspiratorial plan for a rebellion was discovered" (Wilson 1994, 64).

Antikidnapping activists organized vigilance committees, like New York's Friends of Human Rights in New York and the Pennsylvania Anti-Slavery Society in Philadelphia. These groups of social justice Black and white activists gave legal assistance to kidnapped free Blacks and informed "the public via meetings, reports, and letters published in newspapers" about how they could help (Fiske 2016, 29). "In newspapers such as New York City's *Freedom's Journal* and Ohio's *Palladium of Liberty*, Black correspondents and editors denounced racism and advocated racial equality in all areas . . ." (Masur 2022, xiv).

The merciless, illegal practice of kidnapping free Blacks as well as enslaved fugitives was known as the Reverse Underground Railroad (Wilson 1994, 37). Free Blacks were at constant risk of losing their freedom. The fees necessitated by jailing a Black person, "even if exonerated were prohibitive, leading to Black insecurity, and encouraged Black resistance, solidarity, and armed resistance" (Littlefield 1997). Lynching Blacks after the Civil War is parallel to what kidnapping was before it; the white-supremacist culture committed and sanctioned crimes against humanity. As Stauffer stated, "The central metaphor of the film is Northup hanging, between life and death, representing the hundreds of thousands who were lynched after slavery ended" (2014).

Fiske Williams Slave Pen

Washington, DC, is situated between the slave states of Maryland and Virginia. Enslaved people to be sold were rounded up, "warehoused," held in "slave pens," and then "sold and sent to the cotton frontier of the Deep South, as well as to Louisiana's sugar plantations" (Forret 2020). Enslaved people provided domestic services as well as construction; they helped build the Capitol (Forret 2020). The prison system also buttressed slavery's punitive practices. The Quaker abolitionist and poet John Greenleaf Whittier condemned "the dreadful amount of human agony and suffering" in prisons and pens, referencing the "secret horrors of the prison house," which caused occasional suicides of enslaved people who had lost all hope. One man in 1838 sliced his own throat rather than submit to be sold. The presumed tragic death of a woman who fled down Maryland Avenue offered "a fresh admonition to the slave dealer, of the cruelty and enormity of his crimes" as it testified to "the unconquerable love of liberty the heart of the slave may inherit" (Forret 2020).

Williams Slave Pen, also known as Williams Private Jail, was "the most infamous establishment of its kind in the capital" (Fiske, Brown, and Seligman 2013, 51). Williams H. Williams also used a private house he owned, Yellow House. These pens operated in D.C. until 1850 when the slavery trade was abolished there. Bloodhounds, the dogs used to hunt the enslaved, guarded the house. Inside the house were sheds where the enslaved could rest on shelves. Birch's "profit for each person he sold to be enslaved was approximately $200" (Fiske 2016, 19). Churchwell said that where Williams' Slave Pen once stood is now the site of Smithsonian's Air and Space Museum (2014).

William's slave pen was not visible to outsiders. Northup describes how the camouflaged structure revealed the hypocrisy of American chattel slavery:

> It was like a farmer's barnyard in most respects save it was so constructed that the outside world could never see the human cattle that were herded there.... Its outside presented only the appearance of a quiet private residence. A stranger looking at it, would never have dreamed of its execrable uses. Strange as it may seem, within plain sight of this same house, looking down from its commanding height upon it, was the Capitol. The voices of patriotic representatives boasting of freedom and equality, and the rattling of the poor slave's chains, almost commingled. A slave pen within the very shadow of the Capitol! ([1853] 2014, 251)

James H. Birch, referred to as Burch by Northup, was a notorious slave dealer who ran the largest slave pen in Alexandria, Virginia. He tells Solomon that he bought him and is taking him to be sold. Northup tells him he is a free man; Burch beats him with a paddle and a rope. James Birch and the notorious New Orleans slave trader Theophilus Freeman began as partners as early as 1840 and were part of the Reverse Underground Railroad.

While interred at the slave pen, Solomon was brutally beaten; his lacerated back reveals raised scars. Since the Gordon photograph, also known as Whipped Peter and "the Scourged Back" of a runaway enslaved man was first published "as an engraving" in *Harper*'s magazine in July 1863, it has become an iconic and galvanizing image of slavery. The photograph taken "by two itinerant photographers, William D. McPherson and his partner Mr. Oliver in Baton Rouge, Louisiana, in 1863, shows an enslaved man's scarred back resulting from a whipping and showing a crisscrossing of welts and strafe marks (America's Black Holocaust Museum). The photograph was taken during a medical examination after Peter joined the Union army. Copies of the photograph were sold and widely disseminated and "became a rallying cry for abolition during the Civil War" (Sperling 2022).

The photograph is considered by historians to be powerful evidence of the brutality of slavery and a catalyzing factor providing abolitionists with an urgency to end it. Concurrent with the beginning of the Civil War, "[i]t was a part of a larger genre of images that chronicled the transition from slave to soldier, from bondsman to citizen. The redemptive nature of the image helped to justify the enlistment of black soldiers and later black citizenship"

(Silkenat 2014). The photograph telling Peter's story has been made into the feature film *Emancipation*, written by William N. Collage, directed by Antoine Fuqua, and starring Will Smith; Apple TV+ released it in December 2022.

Freedom and the Law

The 1840 law enabling the freeing of Solomon Northup by the governor was ratified in New York when William H. Seward was governor after first being sent to a committee led by Assemblyman Victory Birdseye of Pompey, New York. It was enacted to counter the increasing kidnappings of free New Yorkers of color into slavery in the South because of the escalating prices paid for enslaved people after the law banning any new importing of African people went into effect in 1808. A kidnapped victim "could not rely on southern laws to effect his release" (Fiske 2014).

The title of the 1840 bill is "An act *more effectually* to protect the free citizens of this State from being kidnapped or reduced to Slavery," and it implied that the existing law against kidnapping had proven ineffective. A copy of it appeared in the first edition and in every edition of Northup's memoir as an Appendix (Eakin 2014, 219).

Cotton

Beckert quotes the fugitive enslaved man, John Brown, who said in 1854: "When the price of cotton rises in the English market, the poor slaves immediately feel the effects, for they are harder driven, and the whip is kept more constantly going" (2014a, 3). Cotton is "one of mankind's great achievements," and the growth of "cotton manufacturing in Great Britain depended on violence across the Atlantic" (Beckert 2014a, 110). American merchants informed European customers that slavery in the United States, unlike in Saint-Domingue, was safe, "not least because of the presence of a powerful white militia and because slaves have no artillery nor arms. Though they are numerous they are much separated by rivers, bayous, and tracts thickly peopled with whites" (Beckert 2014a, 122).

Northup noted Patsey's extraordinarily productive technique for picking cotton: "She worked both sides of her row in perpetual motion, right and left. She reached with one hand and dropped cotton in the bag hanging from her neck with the other. "[L]ightning-quick motion was in her finger as no other fingers possessed," Northup later wrote. "She moved like a dancer in an unconscious rhythm, though of displacement rather than of pleasure" (Northup [1853] 2014, 137). "Patsey's back bore the scars of a thousand stripes."

Patsey was born in 1830. Northup describes Patsey; he says, "She shrank before the lustful eye of the one and was in danger even of her life at the hands of the other, and between the two, she was indeed accursed. . . .

Nothing delighted the mistress so much as to see her suffer, and more than once, when Epps had refused to sell her, has she tempted me with bribes to put her secretly to death, and bury her body in some lonely place in the margin of the swamp" ([1853] 2014). Calautti wonders if Mistress Epps's "request fell to someone with fewer moral scruples than Northup after his departure? It's entirely possible" (2014).

The enslaved were property, considered "very expensive livestock," and for the most part, the regulations concerning how they were treated alive and dead were not clear (McQueen 2013). "Laws were written to protect the institution of slavery." When an enslaved person passed away on a plantation, the enslaver was not obligated to inform any official of the death and "could choose where and how the body was to be interred—on their own property, in a cemetery, or elsewhere" (Stacey, quoted by Calautti 2014).

Davidson Sorkin suggests that "Patsey is not portrayed tragically, but heroically. Her honor is perfectly intact. *12 Years a Slave* has been discussed in terms of *Uncle Tom's Cabin* and other works, but if it has an animating text it may be Sojourner Truth's 'Ain't I a Woman?' speech. 'I could work as much and eat as much as a man—when I could get it—and bear the lash as well,' Truth said at the Women's Convention, in Akron, Ohio, in 1851, a year when Patsey was working in the cotton fields" (2013). Patsey endured the lash and every part of herself being violated, but she grows tired of enduring being alive.

Approximately 12.5 million Africans were transported to the Americas during the Middle Passage. Many attempted suicide and jumped off the ships, although there was netting to prevent it. Some starved themselves. Some hoped the ocean would return them to Africa. Similarly, some formerly enslaved talked about flying in the air back to Africa; this is imprinted in folklore. Many succeeded, despite harsh punishment if they were caught attempting to kill themselves, as the enslaved were considered property, and each person represented a price tag and profits (https://www.rmg.co.uk/stories/blog/curatorial/dying-on-their-own-terms-suicides-aboard-slave-ships).

The men who steered and managed the boats told tales of Africans jumping off ships. Records kept by mariners between 1792 and 1796 showed 7.2 percent of the Africans jumped overboard. Suicide might be seen as a radical response to enslavement; Michael Gomez said, it was "the ultimate form of resistance" (quoted by Snyder 2010, 40). Charles Ball said, "Self-destruction in the cotton region was more common than anyone thought" (quoted in Snyder 2010, 43).

Suicide offered solace to some of the enslaved as well as "spiritual relief . . . or a way for native-born Christian slaves to reach heaven. Suicide might also be understood as an aggressive act toward others . . . or as an escape from physical or emotional pain" (Snyder 2010, 43). For abolitionists, the suicides of enslaved people were fraught with "potent political and cultural meanings and came to symbolize much of what was objectionable about the institution of slavery" (Snyder 2010, 43). The prevalence of suicide revealed that for some enslaved people, it was the only emancipation they felt was attainable. For some, it was considered a "collective revolt" (Snyder 2010, 54), and at the same time, as the slavery scholar David Brion Davis claimed, slave rebellions "were suicidal" (quoted by Stauffer 2014).

Stephanie E. Jones-Rogers, a women's history professor, states in *They Were Her Property: White Women as Slave Owners in the American South*, that "Slave-owning women governed their slaves in the same ways that white men did, and sometimes they were even more brutal" (2019, xvii). Men at times had to hold their wives back. Male plantation owners read and adhered to prescription information they read in Southern farm publications that featured "Management of Negroes" columns about how to treat enslaved people in the field (Jones-Rogers 2019, 72). White women were trained to be physically abusive disciplinarians, and many, according to Jones-Rogers, were also as virulently racist and sadistic as men, fueling white supremacy long after slavery ended. Jones-Rogers provides evidence for historian Thavolia Glymph's claim that "enslaved people faced significantly more physical violence from their mistresses than their masters" (Sehgal 2019). A countervailing belief by feminists that white Southern enslavers' wives were themselves victims of a patriarchal society has lost favor in recent years.

White women were also idealized as pure and expected to be prudish, whereas Black enslaved women were "believed to be innately lustful beings" ("Slavery and the Making of America," n.d.). Therefore, some white enslavers were drawn to and thought it was their right to rape Black women. Some enslaved women acquiesced to advances hoping that would "increase the chances that they or their children [of these couplings] would be liberated by the master" ("Slavery and the Making of America," n.d.).

DEPICTION AND CULTURAL CONTEXT

12 Years a Slave depicts American slavery more graphically than any film before it, although Barry Jenkins's Prime miniseries *The Underground Railroad* (2021), based on Colson Whitehead's eponymous novel, includes some equally brutal slavery scenes. McQueen wanted to show the ugly, inhumane treatment perpetrated on the enslaved, but he also was intent on getting the history right. African American studies scholar Henry Louis Gates Jr. read the script and provided notes about any historical inaccuracies. Gates said, "I know Northup's narrative like the back of my hand, and they followed the text with great fidelity.... There's no question about the historical accuracy. They did a wonderful job." Gates found nothing to correct. "It's an amazing film," he says, "the best film about slavery ever made from the point of view of a slave" (quoted in Suebsaeng 2013).

McQueen noted the confluence of race issues that made the timing of *12 Years a Slave* "a sort of perfect storm of events" (McQueen, quoted by George 2013). In 2012, a young Black man named Trayvon Martin was shot by George Zimmermann, a white security guard. The acquittal of Zimmermann led to the founding of the Black Lives Matter movement and protests around the country about the high rate of incarceration and the number of wrongfully convicted Black men. People were talking about "voting rights, the 150th anniversary of the abolition of slavery, the 50th anniversary of the March on Washington and a Black president, I think people actually want to reflect on that horrendous recent past in order to go forward" (McQueen, quoted by George 2013).

Northup's journey from freedom to enslavement parallels a Black person being the victim of police brutality and wrongfully incarcerated in our time. Racist police practices like stop-and-frisk reveal "the evidence of slavery" as men of color have statistically been targeted, searched for guns, and incarcerated in greater numbers than whites. "These practices stem from centuries of legal control of Africans in America." In its earliest days as a country, America created laws "specifically to control Africans, enslaved and free. Slave catchers culled the woods in search of those Africans who dared escape" (Browne-Marshall 2013).

New York City mayor Michael Bloomberg advocated stop-and-frisk to fight crime, and in 2013, a federal court ruled "the stop-and-frisk tactics of the New York Police Department breached minorities' constitutional rights in the city" (Browne-Marshall 2013). The racism laced into these practices posed a problem for Bloomberg when he briefly ran for president in 2019, and he stopped defending it.

Solomon's patience pays off when Bass is able to get his letter into the right hands. Kaisary notes that "Slave resistance is non-existent in the film but 'ever present' in the book" (2017). However, survival *is* resistance. *12 Years a Slave* ends with Northup's rescue, but his capture and experience as a deceived and abused enslaved man torn from his freedom and family whose survival depends on his not letting it be known that he can read and write reveals the dehumanization of slavery and the abject cruelty of Southern white-supremacist culture fueled by an economy where capitalism, especially cotton and corn, had more value than human life.

CONCLUSION

12 Years a Slave recounts Solomon Northup's eyewitness account of slavery from 1841 to 1853, although it is mediated by a modicum of artistic license taken and a few scenes added by the filmmakers. When history is portrayed on film, Pierre Sorlin said that the essential question to ask is "Is history presented with integrity?" (1980, 6). *12 Years a Slave* shows "slavery for what it was, a system that treated people not as a subaltern class but as a different species" (Doherty 2013).

When Solomon in frustration smashes his violin, a moment not documented in his memoir, he is rejecting the one thing that throughout his ordeal enabled him self-expression. Stanley Fish claims that "the point of the relentless sequence of physical and psychological degradation in *12 Years a Slave* is to withhold from the audience an outlet for either its hope or its sympathy" (2013), mirroring the plight of the enslaved.

FURTHER READING

Baptist, Edward E. 2014. *The Half Has Never Been Told: Slavery and the Making of American Capitalism*. New York: Basic Books.

Beckert, Sven. 2014a. *Empire of Cotton: A Global History*. New York: Knopf.

Beckert, Sven. 2014b. "Slavery and Capitalism: Excerpt." *Chronicle Review*, December 12, 2014.

Bennetts, Leslie. 1985. "TV Film by Parks Looks at Slavery." *New York Times*, February 11, 1985.

Berlatsky, Noah. 2013. "How *12 Years a Slave* Gets History Right: By Getting It Wrong." *The Atlantic*, October 28, 2013.

Berlatsky, Noah. 2014. "*12 Years a Slave*: Yet Another Oscar-Nominated 'White Savior' Story." *The Atlantic*, January 17, 2014.

Brar, Kiran. 2020. "Trauma Porn: Misguided 'Activism' on Social Media Harms More Than It Helps." *Butler Collegian*, September 8, 2020.

Brody, Richard. 2013. "Should a Film Try to Depict Slavery?" *New Yorker*, October 13, 2013.

Browne-Marshall, Gloria J. 2013. "Stop and Frisk: From Slavecatchers to NYPD, a Legal Commentary." *Trotter Review*, July 21, 2013.

Buchanan, Kyle. 2013. "The Toughest Scene I Wrote: John Ridley's on *12 Years a Slave* WTF Moment." *Vulture*, December 20, 2013.

Calautti, Katie. 2014. "'What'll Become of Me?' Finding the Real Patsey of *12 Years a Slave*." *Vanity Fair*, March 2, 2014.

Churchwell, Sarah. 2014. "*12 Years a Slave*: The Book behind the Film." *The Guardian*, January 10, 2014.

Cohen, Lara Langer. 2017. "Solomon Northup's Singing Book." *African American Review* 50, no. 3 (Fall): 259–72.

Davidson Sorkin, Amy. 2013. "Jezebel and Solomon: Why Patsey Is the Hero of '*12 Years a Slave*.'" *New Yorker*, November 5, 2013.

Denby, David. 2013. "Fighting to Survive." *New Yorker*, October 14, 2013.

Doherty, Thomas. 2013. "Bringing the Slave Narrative to Screen: Steve McQueen and John Ridley's Searing Depiction of America's 'Peculiar Institution.'" *Cineaste*, December 1, 2013.

Eakin, Sue Lyles, ed. 2014. *Twelve Years a Slave*, by Solomon Northup. Monee, IL: Eakin Films & Publishing.

Eakin, Sue Lyles, and Joseph Logsdon, eds. 1968. *Twelve Years a Slave*, by Solomon Northup. Baton Rouge: LSU Press.

Fish, Stanley. 2013. "No Way Out: *12 Years a Slave*." *New York Times*, November 25, 2013.

Fiske, David. 2014. "The Law That Saved Solomon Northup, and Others." *New York Almanack*, May 6, 2014.

Fiske, David. 2016. *Solomon Northup's Kindred: The Kidnapping of Free Citizens before the Civil War*. Santa Barbara: Praeger.

Fiske, David, Clifford W. Brown, and Rachel Seligman. 2013. *The Complete Story of the Author of Solomon Northup's Odyssey*. Santa Barbara: Praeger, an imprint of ABC-CLIO.

Forret, Jeff. 2020. "The Notorious 'Yellow House' That Made Washington, D.C. a Slavery Capital." *Smithsonian*, July 22, 2020.

George, Nelson. 2013. "An Essentially American Narrative: Interviews." *New York Times*, August 13, 2013.

Gilroy, Paul. "*12 Years a Slave*: In Our 'Post-racial' Age the Legacy of Slavery Lives On." *The Guardian*, November 10, 2013.

Hobson, Janell. 2018. "This Film Called My Back: Black Pain and Painful History in *12 Years a Slave*." In *Celluloid Chains: Slavery in the Americas through Film*, edited by Rudyard J. Alcocer, Kristen Block, and Dawn Duke, 262–75. Knoxville: University of Tennessee Press.

Jones-Rogers, Stephanie E. 2019. *They Were Her Property: White Women as Slave Owners in the American South*. New Haven: Yale University Press.

Kaisary, Philip. 2017. "The Slave Narrative and Filmic Aesthetics: Steve McQueen, Solomon Northup, and Colonial Violence." *Melus* 42, no. 2 (Summer): 94–114.

Kerr, Euan. 2013. "'*12 Years a Slave*' Director Steve McQueen Sees Slavery as a World Story." MPR News, November 9, 2013.

Kohn, Eric. 2013. "*12 Years a Slave* Star Chiwetel Ejiofor Explains Why He Was Worried about Whether He Could Pull Off the Role." *Indie Wire*, September 12, 2013.

Krauss, Theresa L. n.d. "Was FAA HQ the Site of a Notorious Slave Pen." Accessed August 28, 2022. https://www.faa.gov/about/history/milestones/media/Was_FAA_HQ_the_Site_of_a_Notorious_Slave_Pen.pdf.

Li, Stephanie. 2014. "*Twelve Years a Slave* as a Neo Slave Narrative." *American History Review* 26, no. 2 (Summer): 326–31.

Littlefield, Daniel C. 1997. "Review of *Freedom at Risk: The Kidnapping of Free Blacks in America 1780–1865*." *American Historical Review* 102, no. 3 (June): 890.

Livesay, Andrea. 2014. "A Life More Terrible: The Women of *12 Years a Slave*." *SBS News*, November 1, 2014.

Maltin, Leonard. 2013. "Before There Was '12 Years a Slave' There Was 'Solomon Northup's Odyssey.'" October 17, 2013. https://www.imdb.com/news/ni56313357.

Masur, Kate. 2022. *Until Justice Be Done: America's First Civil Rights Movement, from the Revolution*. New York: W. W. Norton.

McQueen, Steve, dir. 2013. *12 Years a Slave*. Performances by Chiwetel Ejiofor, Lupita Nyong'o, Michael Fassbender, and Brad Pitt. Searchlight Pictures.

Northup, Solomon. (1853) 2014. *Twelve Years a Slave*. Quebec: Magdalene Press.
Parks, Gordon. 2005. *A Hungry Heart*. New York: Atria.
Ray, Sadie. 2016. "'Roll, Jordan, Roll': A Critique of Slavery and a Story of Hope." https://core152eray.wordpress.com/2016/04/30/roll-jordan-roll-a-critique-of-slavery-and-a-story-of-hope/.
Sehgal, Purhal. 2019. "White Women Were Avid Slaveowners, a New Book Shows." *New York Times*, February 26, 2019.
Silkenat, D. 2014. "'A Typical Negro': Gordon, Peter, Vincent Colyer, and the Story behind Slavery's Most Famous Photograph." *American Nineteenth Century History* 15 (2): 169–86. https://doi.org/10.1080/14664658.2014.939807.
"Slavery and the Making of America." n.d. Accessed August 28, 2022. https://www.thirteen.org/wnet/slavery/experience/gender/history2.html.
Smith, Valerie. 2014. "*12 Years a Slave*: Black Life in the Balance." *American Literary History* 26 (Summer): 362–66.
Snyder, Terri L. 2010. "Suicide, Slavery, and Memory in North America." *Journal of American History* 97, no. 1 (June): 39–62. Oxford University Press on behalf of Organization of American Historians. https://www.jstor.org/stable/40662817.
Sorlin, Pierre. 1980. *The Film in History: Restaging the Past*. Totowa: Barnes & Noble Books.
Sperling, Nicole. 2022. "Apple Shot an Oscar Contender Starring Will Smith. That Was Before the Slap." *The New York Times*, September 18, 2022.
Stauffer, John. 2014. "12 Years between Life and Death." *American Literary History* 26, no. 2 (Summer): 317–25.
Stevens, Dana. 2014. "My Problems with *Twelve Years a Slave*." Slate, January 14, 2014.
Suebsaeng, Asawin. 2013. "Henry Louis Gates Jr. Fact-Checks *12 Years a Slave*." Mother Jones, October 16, 2013.
"*12 Years a Slave*: 160 Years Later, a Memoir Becomes a Movie." 2013. Renee Montagne, host. NPR, October 17, 2013.
"Violence in Art: Goya and *12 Years a Slave*." Same Old Art. Accessed September 27, 2022. https://sameoldart.tumblr.com/post/67053577728/violence-in-art-goya-and-12-years-a-slave.
Weiner, Jonah. 2014. "The Liberation of Steve McQueen." *Rolling Stone*, March 3, 2014.
White, Armond. 2013. "Can't Trust It." *City Arts: New York's Review of Culture*, October 16, 2013.
Williams, Chad. 2014. "From American Playhouse to *12 Years a Slave*." *Humanities* 35, no. 1 (January/February). https://www.neh.gov/humanities/2014/januaryfebruary/feature/solomon-northups-odyssey.
Wilson, Carol. 1994. *Freedom at Risk: The Kidnapping of Free Blacks in America, 1780–1865*. Lexington: University Press of Kentucky Press.
Worley, Sam. 1997. "Solomon Northup and the Sly Philosophy of the Slave Pen." *Callaloo* 20:243–259.

Chapter 9

The Birth of a Nation (2016)

The Birth of a Nation (2016) tells the searing story of the mystical enslaved preacher, Nat Turner, leader of the 1831 bloodiest (though not largest) and most legendary slave rebellion in American history, which took place in Southampton County, Virginia. The actor Nate Parker (born in 1979) directed, starred in, wrote the screenplay, and cowrote the story with Jean Gianni Celestin. Parker cobbled myriad investors together, adding $100,000 of his own money to the film's $10 million budget. The film debuted at the Sundance Film Festival in January 2016; a bidding war erupted after it garnered a deeply emotional response; the audience was "celebratory and euphoric. There was sobbing, cheering, and a sustained standing ovation" (Buchanan 2016). Hollywood was reeling from the second year there was a profound lack of nominations for people of color, #OscarsSoWhite. It won the Audience Award and the Grand Jury Prize (Buchanan 2016). Fox Searchlight paid a record-breaking $17.5 million and released the film on October 7, receiving sweeping press coverage, some of which about Parker was damning.

Parker echoes the title of D. W. Griffiths's notoriously racist but cinematically pathbreaking *The Birth of a Nation* (1915), based on the novel *The Clansman* by Thomas Dixon. Griffiths's controversial film sparked protests at theaters and was banned in some cities. Set during Reconstruction (1865–77), a time when African Americans aced the political opportunities for representation they were finally given, the film was infused with anti-Black and white supremacy propaganda, depicting the Ku Klux Klan (KKK), the terrorist group, militating against African American accomplishments. The film stars Lillian Gish and white actors in blackface playing malicious rapists and killers.

"I've reclaimed this title and re-purposed it as a tool to challenge racism and white supremacy in America to inspire a riotous disposition toward any and all injustice in this country (and abroad) and to promote the kind of honest confrontation that will galvanize our society toward healing and sustained systemic change," Parker told *Filmmaker Magazine*. The film depicts the brutality and oppression of the enslaved and a man whose vision and plan for ending the "peculiar institution" were inspired by the Bible.

Much excitement was initially generated by Parker's labor of love about the most iconic and controversial revolutionary martyr figure in African American history. The film offers a sympathetic view of Turner and an African American–centric depiction of slavery. "The iconography of West African spiritual beliefs saturates the film as does Christian imagery" (Fanto Deetz quoted in Parker 2017). It depicts how the enslaved loved, married, nurtured, and survived against dehumanization and how they preserved aspects of African culture, defied, rebelled, and sometimes transcended the brutal constraints of chattel slavery.

The film's production values are high. The acting is first-rate, the cinematography by Elliot Davis superlatively re-creates the pastoral and the interior day-to-day lives of the enslaved in their cabins and in their working lives in the field and plantation house as well as the violent clash of Turner's army with the white militias. The score by Henry Jackman blends soaring music with African percussion and African American spirituals.

But the film's reception and box office earnings were a crushing disappointment, vexed by mediocre reviews and controversy after details of rape charges against Parker and his cowriter and then college roommate, Celestin, were released. As Penn State University students in 1999, they were suspended from the wrestling team after a white woman brought rape charges against both men. While Parker was acquitted, Celestin was charged with sexual assault and sentenced to two to four years in prison; after serving some time, his conviction was vacated, but no punishment was meted out. She claimed they continued to harass her; she tried to commit suicide twice. Fox Searchlight revealed they knew about the incident but also knew that Parker was absolved. Parker refused to apologize (Redden 2016). The tragic pièce de résistance—when it was for the first time publicly revealed in August—was that the victim, her name unknown, had committed suicide in 2012.

The American Film Institute canceled its screening of *The Birth of a Nation* on August 24. Parker was scheduled to appear in public for the first time since news of the scandal was released. Sharon Loeffler, the rape victim's sister, spoke out against the film, particularly a scene in which Turner's wife is raped by a group of white men, in *Variety*. "This is fiction," she writes, noting that the event does not show up in the historical record. "I find it creepy and perverse that Parker and Celestin would put a fictional rape at the center of their film, and that Parker would portray himself as a hero avenging that rape" (quoted by Jones and Bashein 2016). Parker's choice to portray Turner's wife being raped as the catalyst motivating him mitigates Turner's righteous indignation and religious justification for his acts against slavery. That Cherry isn't given a line or any voice to express herself after the rape renders her an inert and passive victim.

Parker's film is the first full-length feature film to tell the Turner story, although, a high-profile studio project came close to getting green-lighted in the late 1960s. A year after the publication of William Styron's 1967 Pulitzer Prize–winning novel, *The Confessions of Nat Turner*, inspired by Thomas Gray's *The Confessions of Nat Turner* (1831), A-list directors including Norman Jewison and Sidney Lumet were set to direct an adaptation of it. Though Black actors were at first reluctant to take the role, James Earl Jones, riveting audiences on Broadway in *The Great White Hope* was cast as Turner. Styron, a white Southerner born in Newport News, Virginia, near Turner's revolt, also drew on Frederick Law Olmstead's *A Journey in the Seaboard Slave States* (Dix and Edwards, 1856); however, he also fictionalized Turner's life, creating for him an obsession and love for a white woman named Margaret Whitehead. William Drewry wrote the first in-depth book about the revolt, and from Drewry's book, *The Southampton Insurrection* (1900), Styron learned that the only person Nat Turner had no problem killing was Margaret Whitehead; she's the only person he actually killed (Casciato and West 1981, 565).

Film rights to Styron's novel were sold to Twentieth Century Fox and David Wolper (who ten years later produced the blockbuster miniseries *Roots*) for a then record-breaking price of $600,000. After considering many white screenwriters to adapt the book, the producers settled on Louis Peterson, an African American playwright and the first Black screenwriter in Hollywood. *Time* magazine's review claimed, "This novel goes beyond a mere retelling of history to show how the fettered human spirit can splinter into murderous rage when it is goaded beyond endurance."

However, Styron's novel generated pushback from Black writers; treatises outraged by it were gathered in the book *William Styron's Nat Turner: Ten Black Writers Respond*, edited by John Henrik Clarke (Praeger, 1987), republished under the title *The Second Crucifixion of Nat Turner* by Black Classic Press in 1997. Comprising historians, including Lerone Bennett, Dr. Alvin Poussaint, Vincent Harding, and Ernest Kaiser, whose overarching claim is that Styron's novel is racist, it misinterprets Turner's life and legacy, and "distorted his message and downplayed his rebellion" (Clarke 1997).

Says Parker, "Styron's reimagining [of Turner] played directly into white America's fear and anxieties surrounding the intention and potential of the contemporary Black male" (quoted in Tanenhaus 2016). The film adaptation of Styron's book never got made; however, in 1999 filmmaker Spike Lee discussed adapting the book with the African American studies scholar Henry Louis Gates Jr., who felt Styron's novel had merit.

Gates makes an appearance in Charles Burnett's fascinating one-hour quasi-documentary, *Nat Turner: A Troublesome Property* (2003). The experimental pastiche includes dramatic reenactments as well as interviews with Turner's descendants, activist-actor Ossie Davis, and the slavery scholars and historians, including Herbert Aptheker and Eric Foner.

The Birth of a Nation opens with a quote from Thomas Jefferson, 1785: "Indeed, I tremble for my country when I reflect that God is just, that his justice cannot sleep forever." It's night, and to intense drumming, a mother and son, the young Nat Turner (Tony Espinos), are running toward a man who's speaking in an African dialect. He's surrounded by women covered in white ash, sitting, swaying, and praying—signifying the ancestors swaying to the beat outside in the elements.

The man says children with marks on their bodies were brought before the elders. They were given titles that would last a lifetime. The young Nat has three raised marks on his chest, and the man names for the ancestors each "holy" mark a quality: wisdom, courage, vision, claiming "[H]e is a leader. He is a prophet. We should listen to him. This boy holds the holy marks of our ancestors." It's 1809 in Southampton County, Virginia.

Nat's playing with the slave owner's son. His father, Isaac (Dwight Turner), is shot after he shoots a slave catcher chasing him for stealing food. Isaac escapes, never to return. White hired hands like Raymond Cobb (Jackie Earle Haley) come to Nat's cabin threatening to hurt his family if they don't reveal Isaac's whereabouts. This is the first of many scenes in which Nat witnesses brutality against Blacks.

Bridget (Esther Scott), Nat's grandmother, and his mother, Nancy (Aunjanue Ellis), see him off and hug him. Nat takes the Bible off the rocking chair and reads it in bed. When Elizabeth Turner, the slave owner's wife (Penelope Ann Miller) tells Nat's mother about Nat's literacy, Nancy says she will beat him for it. There were laws and punishments prohibiting and punishing literacy. Mistress Turner tells her not to do that and takes Nat to her library. Mistress Turner says these books are not for you, but the Bible is.

Nat learns that the plantation owner on his deathbed demands that Nat be a field hand. In a quick cut, Nat Turner transforms into a grown man, played by Nate Parker. He is picking cotton with his mother; the African American Christian spiritual "Swing Low, Sweet Chariot" is sung in the background. Nat is preaching to a small group of the enslaved. Samuel (Armie Hammer) and Reverend Walthall (Mark Boone Junior) are talking about their economic hardships and that "talks of insurrection got folks scared." The reverend suggests that people might pay good money to have "someone like them" preach to and tell them to calm down a bit. Samuel agrees and chooses Nat to preach. The two men travel together to neighboring plantations.

Nat preaches at Joseph Randall's plantation to an intrigued but traumatized group of enslaved people. He reads from First Peter 2:18: "Submit

The Birth of a Nation (2016)

yourself to your masters with respect, not only those good and considerate but also kind and harsh" and quotes Joseph, who says, "[I]f you listen to him, perhaps you'll get into heaven." Nat sees some enslaved men hanging by their wrists and refusing to eat. A white man knocks out an enslaved man's teeth, putting in a funnel for him to eat. Nat observes an enslaved group in a barn; the men have been brow and body beaten. Nat trembles: it's hard for him to see their suffering. Nat has been sheltered from these horrors. Nat's sermons grow more intense. A white girl skips and prances while walking a Black girl on a leash—Nat is incredulous. This image is repeated throughout the film; its deepening effect on Turner's revulsion of slavery is palpable.

At Randall's, Nat encounters a young man named Jasper, who will take part in the revolt but eventually alert his owner to Nat's revolt and at the end of the film become a Union soldier. Back at the Turner's, when Nat is being hit by a white man who's upset Nat spoke to his wife, Samuel threatens the guy, forcing him to stop it. Nat and Samuel stop at an outdoor "Slave for Sale" opportunity. Nat suggests Samuel buy the raging, raggedy woman for $275 for his wife, and he does. Cherry-Ann (Aja Naomi King) is broken in and delivered to Samuel's wife. She and Nat fall in love, though Cherry is taken to a different planation to work. Nat gives Cherry a gold mask he says his mother got from her "granddaddy in Africa"; and was "the only thing that kept his mom free." Fanto Deetz says, it "represents more than a family heirloom. That gold signifies the kingdoms that ruled West and Central African" (quoted in Parker 2017). Bridget officiates when the couple marries. Cherry is covered in cowry shells, which represent the spiritual world of the ancestors (quoted in Parker 2017).

Nat's friend and coconspirator, Hark Travis (Colman Domingo) "jumps the broom"—marrying Esther (Gabrielle Union). The enslaved celebrate by dancing; the song playing is "You Got a Right; You Got a Right to the Tree of Life."

Cherry tells her husband about being sold from her mother when she was thirteen. Her mom said," I'll always be here loving you." Nat teaches Cherry to read and continues to ride with Samuel to preach, making coins, now bills. An overseer throws his whip, forcing a woman to pick cotton faster. His teeth are hammered; a funnel to feed him is forced. Nat's watching.

He's moved to tears. Raymond confronts Cherry while she's getting water from a well demanding a pass. Cherry is raped and viciously violated by a group of white men. Nat bleeds after he sees his wife for the time after she's raped. A newfound conviction takes root in Nat. Isiah (Roger Guenveur Smith), the head house-enslaved man, tells Samuel that Nat needs to talk to him. Nat borrows Samuel's horse to visit his wife.

Mistress Turner says God's going to punish whoever did this. One of Turner's friends, Joseph, wants Esther. Hark resists capitulating his wife, but he has no choice. "Where is he, Nat?" Hark says. "Where is God now?"

Nat baptizes an unkempt white man while enslaved people watch. He tells Nat he's been rejected by other preachers. Samuel is displeased; however, Nat stands his ground and gets publicly whipped for it. His mother and grandmother watch. He's on the cross like Christ being crucified; blood is dripping from his lips. He gets out of his handcuffs. He is risen.

Nat's mother and grandmother balm his lacerated back. Nat announces his plan to "slay the enforcers of slavery" and meets men in the forest to plan. Nat says, "Now go and smite Amalek. And utterly destroy all that they have, and spare them not, but slay both man and woman, infant and suckling, ox and sheep, camel, and ass." He says, "Going back to the bible Every word to support our bondage, there's one demanding our freedom. Every verse they use to justify our torture, there's another damning them to hell for those actions. The Lord has spoken to me; visions of what is to come. We've been chosen."

Nat says, "Six of to us start, and then others will join. Start here at Turner's and fight our way. Grapevine's ablaze with fightin', slaves all over having meetings." Isiah tries to talk Nat out of his plan. Nat tells Cherry of his plan. First one Nat kills is Samuel. Samuel dies; a cross is seen on the window. His mom says she's proud of him and is crying.

Isiah, however, cautions, "If you kill them, you kill us."

Nat says, "Your earthly master is gone; you're now free men and women, servants of only the Lord, our supernatural power of God. As the sword bears down on our enemies, our ancestors and unborn children rejoice. We are now alive seeing through eyes that have been denied us since being born into the darkness of bondage." The enslaved are moved. Nat says, "I've gone back to the verse with new eyes. Every line there's a line demanding our freedom, to rise good against evil. Slaves all over having meetings, waiting for something waiting for us. We'll cut the head from the serpent."

Isiah cautions again, "He is a god of love. He's also a god of wrath."

Carrying torches, he and his followers begin the violent, deadly rampage in the middle of the night. They go to the Travis house first and machete people while they're sleeping; most of the people killed were sleeping. A Black man cuts the head of a white man. The white militia confronts the enslaved; there's a choreographed fight scene. Turner gets shot but not shot dead. Nat's followers continue going into white people's homes and axing them to death. Blacks are overtaken by whites' guns. Hark is shot. "Strange Fruit" plays. A butterfly, a symbol of transformation, appears on the shirt of a young man being lynched. Nat's voice visits Cherry.

Nat and Hark are covered in ash, a reminder of the ancestors. Nina Simone's cover of "Strange Fruit" plays. The anthemic antiracism song about lynching Billie Holiday made famous when she recorded it in 1939, written by the New York Jewish science teacher, Abel Meeropol, under the pseudonym Lewis Allan, is arguably the most well-known song about American racist practices. The tracking shot depicts Black men and women hanging from trees on a rope. It's a surreal image; the people's eyes are mostly closed, but they aren't frothing or looking pained. A few have their eyes open; most look like they're sleeping. Nat's voice visits Cherry again. She tells him, "They killin' people everywhere for being black." The authorities find him soon after. Nat is captured; he's beaten by militia men who are told to stop it by their general, so he can be hanged for all to see.

Nat marches to his execution to a jeering crowd. When asked if there's something he'd like to say, he says he is ready. The noose is placed on his neck. He exchanges a look with Jasper who ratted him out. Nat's face fills the screen; he sees his wife as an angel with wings above him.

Intertitles at the end reveal that the rebellion lasted nearly forty-eight hours and caused the deaths of sixty slaveholding family members, stirring up panic throughout America and the vengeful murder of hundreds of enslaved and free African-descended people being murdered. "Nat Turner's body was flayed and dismembered, his skin sewn into relics, his flesh churned into wagon grease. All in hope of preventing a legacy."

HISTORICAL BACKGROUND

The dehumanizing and horrific American hereditary chattel slavery had claimed two million souls by 1830 (Dunbar 2019, 36). It was a "human Hell" that many Southerners felt was a necessary evil (Bennett 1968, 84). Out of slavery came the white supremacy movement and virulent racism; both still prevail. Plantations and small farms were the bedrock of the economy in the South and fueled industrialization in the North. There was mounting antislavery fervor as the abolitionism movement (1830–70) grew stronger. Abolitionism was a hot-button issue all over America; however, while some opposed slavery, they didn't support full emancipation.

Some admonished that Virginia enslavers were too lenient, enabling the enslaved to partake in church meetings and travel to farms and as far as Jerusalem to visit loved ones. Some whites felt that "permissiveness was the best way to prevent rebelliousness." While the enslaved showed resistance every day, mostly manifest in "individual acts of vandalism, sabotage, or escape" (Oates 1990, 15), there were planned American attacks, most of which were stopped before they began.

No slave rebellion since the Stono Rebellion in 1739 (discussed in *Sankofa*) had resulted in more than one or two deaths The Gabriel conspiracy in Richmond was revealed in 1800. Gabriel Prosser was a literate enslaved man inspired by the American and French revolutions and the hypocrisy of only white men having the right to freedom. Gabriel and thirty-four collaborators were sentenced to death. Prosser planned his eponymous conspiracy in Richmond, Virginia, 1800, the year Nat Turner was born. Prosser, a dynamic and literate twenty-four-year-old enslaved man, was going to capture the Virginia governor James Monroe and demand freedom for the enslaved, but his plan was foiled by the delay a heavy rainstorm caused. In the interim, some enslaved revealed the plan to their masters, and he and twenty-five others were hanged (Library of Virginia).

The 1811 Louisiana slave revolt known as the German Coast Uprising is considered the largest slave revolt, even though it was stopped by a militia within forty-eight hours after two white men were killed. Charles Deslondes of Destrehan's Plantation led approximately five hundred enslaved men who didn't have guns (Smith 2021, 54). Deslondes was cut up and mutilated (54). The artist Dread Scott staged a community reenactment of this uprising in 2019, titled "We Are Going to End Slavery: Join Us!" (Michael 2021).

Denmark Vesey's plan for a rebellion in Charleston, South Carolina, was revealed in 1822. When word did get out, slaves would be tortured till they revealed information and sometimes sold. Some people who opposed slavery didn't support emancipation; the colonization movement, the American Colonization Society, believed that the enslaved should be set free by their enslavers immediately and taken back to Africa. Abolitionists were gaining traction; Harriet Beecher Stowe's antislavery novel *Uncle Tom's Cabin* (1852) was a huge best seller. The come-outers in the 1830s were religious people who left their places of worship out of frustration with their church's proslavery position. There were abolitionists who advocated the "moral suasion" argument to end slavery: slavery was immoral and the antipathy of religion and the principles built into America, that every person had the right to life, liberty, and the pursuit of happiness ("Margaret Washington," n.d.). It caused virulent racism against African-descended people that lasted long after slavery was abolished, and it unleashed a white supremacy movement that pervaded and still exists today.

Nathaniel, a biblical name that means "given by God," was born on October 2, 1800, in Southampton County, Virginia, on Benjamin Turner's plantation. He was known as Nat Turner; the slave owner's surname was given to the enslaved. It is said that Nat's African-born mother Nancy tried to kill her newborn rather than see him be enslaved (Oates 1990, 11). Nat had bumps on his chest and scars, a sign of being special in his mother's Akan African culture. The opening scene depicts a ritual of the outlier community, known as Maroons, acknowledging the signs on this young boy. Maroons comprise a community of runaways living outside the plantation; these were formerly enslaved African and African-descended people. Maroon communities are found in many parts of the world where slavery was enforced.

Some thought Nat was destined to be a prophet; he himself felt he was "ordained for some great purpose" (Bisson 1998, 36). He was a precocious child who learned how to read and write when he was quite young. The Bible was the main text he had access to, and he knew it well. It instilled in him an intense religiosity. When he was twenty, he ran away from an overseer and stayed away for thirty days until he had one of his first visions, a visitation from a spirit who told him to return to his "earthly master" ("Nat Turner's Rebellion," 1831). He returned to the plantation to fulfill his destiny.

Virginia was in an economic depression when Nat was twenty. Blacks outnumbered whites (Oates 1990, 32). Southampton County was famous for its apple brandy. Jerusalem was the "county seat." It was a tidewater community; the average farm owned ten or eleven slaves. Farms raised tobacco, corn, and apples; not much cotton was grown.

Nat received Methodist training with "its emphasis on free will and individual salvation"—the Turners, like many, broke away from the Anglican church (Oates 1990, 9). American Methodists had more members than any other Christian denomination in 1840. Its founder, John Wesley, proselytized a robust antislavery stance, as did the Quakers, when it was established in 1785. By 1824, Methodists encouraged enslavers to bring the people they enslaved into the church. However, the Methodists walked it back gradually and ultimately condoned slavery. By 1840, there was a split in the church—some members were so virulently proslavery they threatened ousting abolitionists from the church (Barringer Gordon 2020). Whereas the Quakers never wavered from their fierce belief that slavery should be abolished. They were criticized by some who cautioned that the Quakers' zeal could lead to planting "dangerous notions in the slaves" (Oates 1990, 9).

By the early 1800s, there was a groundswell of Christian churchgoers who felt freedom for the enslaved wasn't an option, yet they were compelled to formally teach the oppressed their religion. They believed the word of the Bible would keep slaves in their place, put the fear of God into them, save them, and make them happy; they were not, in the Christians' words, in "savage, heathen Africa." Literate enslaved people studied the Old Testament; however, in the "heavily redacted Slave Bible," the parts about Moses leading the Israelites out of Egypt were intentionally left out, lest the text could stir up rebellion (Little 2019).

Nat had another vision, a revelation in 1825. Inspired by biblical passages, he started planning his revolt and waited for a sign from God.

Nat claimed to be in communication with "the holy spirit" in the same way God in the Old Testament visioned Ezekiel (Oates 1990, 35). Ezekiel, whose name means "strengthened by God," was a prophet and a priest. Nat knew that for every Bible lesson religious white men found to justify forcing African and African-descended people into slavery, "the Scriptures contained an opposite injunction against human bondage" (Oates 1990, 36).

He traveled to plantations and Black churches from 1825 to 1830 on Sundays to preach to the enslaved and was known as the best slave preacher in the area (Oates 1990, 37). He was known as "Prophet Nat." Nat sought enslaved men he could trust with the mission he was planning. It was said that the Holy Ghost was in him. "While laboring in the field, I discovered drops of blood on the corn as though it were dew from heaven—and I communicated it to many, both white and black, in the neighborhood," he told Gray—or so Gray recorded him "fully and voluntarily," as he put it in *The Confessions of Nat Turner* (quoted by Tanenhaus 2016).

Whites felt enslaved preachers could boost morale and inspire their own and help "discipline" them (Oates 1990, 38). But some whites accused Turner of being a "witch doctor" (39). "He felt signs that Judgment Day was coming. He baptized a troubled white man named Brantley. People were outraged after word got out." He had a vision on May 12, 1828, that time was running out. He converted E. T. Brantley to Methodism and baptized him.

"He was like a powerful angel whose wings were nailed to the floor" (Oates 1990, 41). Thomas Moore gave him a lashing when he said the enslaved should be free. Vigilance committees to watch the enslaved were formed (Oates 1990, 3).

On May 12, 1828, there was a celestial eclipse, a major eclipse of the sun. Celestial eclipse!—"Just as the black spot passed over the sun, so shall the blacks pass over the earth," said Turner (quoted by Bisson 1988, 60). Turner planned his rebellion, collaborating with four enslaved men—Will, Hark (short for Hercules), Sam, Henry, and Nelson, his close friends—and Billy Artis, a free man of color who collaborated with Turner and took his own life rather than surrender (Bisson 1988, 66). They all kept Turner's plans under wrap. Will, Hark, Sam, Henry, and Nelson, all referred to him as general. Turner showed them his elaborate written plans.

At two o'clock in the morning on Monday, August 22, 1831, Nat began the insurrection, killing his owner Joseph Travis and his wife, striking them with his sword. His men killed everyone else in the house; Nat ordered them to spare "neither age nor sex." They took rifles and gunpowder, but they didn't loot nor take anything else of value. They didn't humiliate or torture anyone. They walked to the next town, Salathial, and then ten miles to Jerusalem, and kept going, picking up enslaved people along the way (Bisson 1988, 68). They told all who joined them to not give anyone information. A thief entered the ranks and stole; some men found and drank apple brandy. The plantation where Cherry worked was spared as was a childhood friend's farm (71). An enslaved man named Aaron told Nat it was time to turn back. "He rode at the back, he had 60 followers. They wanted to take over Jerusalem and then flee for the Great Dismal Swamp 20 miles to the east." Word got out; people were barricading themselves (78). It lasted between for a day and a half at which point Nat Turner and his army had killed more than fifty-five white men, women, and children. No women were raped. The enslavers were unprepared but created militias; they also outlawed the killing of slaves. Breen says few were killed after the insurrection than most think: "fewer than 40 slaves" (2015, 10); "the revolt did not have broad support in the black community" (11).

One of the most troubling things about this revolt was the killing of ten children under the age of five. Nat and his men didn't want to break the door down with an axe; in one case, they went in through the upstairs window and went back to kill a sleeping infant for fear it would cry and wake up the neighbors.

Hark was sentenced to death; the state "had to pay the estate of his owner $450" (Bisson 1988, 93). Neighboring counties in North Carolina as well as federal military resources helped fight against Turner and his men.

Nat Turner's men carried forth "with orders to approach the houses as fast as they could ride for the purpose to carry terror and devastation wherever they could" (Drewry 1900). This was the first time white militias confronted weaponized enslaved men (Bisson 1988, 83). The white militias got closer to Turner and his men, and Turner yelled, "Charge/Fire on them." "Five of Turner's best men fell wounded. Turner had about 20 men left. Turner had a few backup plans. Turner and Hark rode to the Ridley Plantation—he had 40 men. But there was an ambush, and some slaves joined the side of their masters" (Bisson 1988, 84).

Turner was hiding in a cave he made underground and had his sword with him. He was almost caught two times. On October 30, more than two months after the revolt began, he crawled out and was caught by Benjamin Phipps. Phipps was not an enslaver; he was a poor white man. Turner was carried in chains to Jerusalem, taken before two judges who questioned him; he answered honestly and calmly and showed no regret for the deaths of fifty-five to sixty whites. He said he would have spared all who didn't resist. He had no remorse; he said he was carrying out God's will. His hearing was held for November 5, 1831.

Turner's army sent a shockwave through America and opened many eyes to the bitter hatred that the enslaved felt for their oppressors.

Much of what is known about Nat Turner comes from the original *The Confessions of Nat Turner: The Leader of the Late Insurrection in Southampton, Virginia*, dictated by Turner and written by Thomas Ruffin Gray. Published in New York in October 1831, *The Confessions*, a small pamphlet, quickly sold out its first printing of more than forty thousand copies. Gray was a local attorney and enslaver whose fortunes had nearly dried up by the time he defended some of Turner's insurgents. He agreed to hear Nat's confessions and "the true story behind the rebellion." Turner omitted all the names of the rebels except for the ones he knew were dead (Bisson 1988, 101).

Gray interviewed the incarcerated Turner in the days before he was hanged in 1831. Turner, waiting to be judged and executed by the court of law, "confessed" his crime and provided details of its motivation and planning. Turner's religious fanaticism and fierce intellectualism were layered in, while Gray writes in a voice more consistent with his own; most of the facts have been corroborated. Gray was impressed with Turner's intelligence, but he also may have put some words in his mouth and in *The Confessions*. Breen claims that it does retain Turner's voice as well as conveys accurate details about Turner's trial (2015, 171). "On November 11, 1831, a white man with a rope broke Nat Turner's neck on a gallows in a town in Virginia called Jerusalem. But ideas cannot be killed with ropes" (Bennett 1968, 96).

Breen also claims that *The Confessions* is a "unique narrative that may be the most important work on slavery written and published in the slaveholding South" (2015, 1). Rael suggests that "Like Augustine's, Turner's detailed a spiritual journey. Unlike Augustine's, it had an unmistakable and practical political purpose, which was nothing less than to continue the revolution he had begun" (2015). "Their nightmare (had) come to life—the slave who had seized back his own humanity with the sword" (Bisson 1988, 102).

Many scholars have investigated the reliability of Gray's narrative and whether and in what ways he may have embellished Turner's remembrances. The jury is out.

The fact is that *The Confessions* was used as evidence against Turner in his trial. He entered a plea of not guilty at the trial and said he had no guilt (Bisson 1988, 103). He was calm during the trial; Gray was horrified at how calm he was.

Not much is known about Nat's wife, Cherry, but she was beaten and tortured when questioned about her husband's whereabouts. The family was separated when Nat's enslaver Samuel Turner died in 1822. The separation of family, one of the cruelest practices of slavery, was common. In his confessions, he didn't mention Cherry or his three children from whom he was separated, to spare her (Bisson 1988, 38). "Cherry was part of Nat's inner circle. She was entrusted with maps written with pokeberry ink (made from a purple berry that grows wild in the South), lists in code, and strange ciphers that have never been deciphered to this day" (56). The insurrection was scheduled for July 4, but Turner was sick.

William Lloyd Garrison—the fervent abolitionist who with his collaborator, Isaac Knapp, published the *Liberator* (1831–65) in Boston, Massachusetts—found *The Confessions* incendiary (Oates 1990, 145). The weekly paper advocated a nonviolent and quick end to slavery—a merciless institution that was hypocritical to American and Christian ideals. However, Garrison warned in his first issue that if Southerners didn't outlaw slavery immediately, the enslaved would militate against their bondage and "[w]oe if it comes with storm and blood and fire" (Garrison, quoted by Oates 1990, 130). The *Liberator* article chose to view the revolutionaries as merely "deluded wretches" (Bisson 1988, 90).

Some claimed that Turner was influenced by the *Liberator* as well as *Walker's Appeal*, written by David Walker, a free Black man, who urged slaves to revolt against enslavers, and the *African Sentinel* and the *Journal of Liberty* published by free Blacks in Albany, New York. Copies of these publications were sent to Governor Floyd's office to be scrutinized as "manifestoes of *Insurrection!*" (Oates 1990, 130). Floyd thought the revolt was fueled by a conspiracy. *Freedom's Journal*, founded by John Russwurm and Samuel Cornish, published in New York by the reverend Peter Williams Jr. from 1827 to 1829, was the first Black-owned antislavery Negro newspaper. David Walker, a free Southern Black man, wrote and published his revolutionary pamphlet *The Appeal* in 1829 advocating the enslaved to revolt—"a pamphlet which challenged Blacks worldwide to unify and combat whites in the fight to end slavery," declaring that whites were an "unjust, jealous, unmerciful, avaricious, and blood-thirsty set of beings" (Dunbar and Ramey 2016, 47). A year before Turner's revolt, "Walker predicted a future leader of a great rebellion" (47) just one year before Turner's insurrection.

Turner became a "martyred soldier of Black liberation who broke his chains and murdered whites because slavery had murdered Negroes. He was a man for war" (Oates 1990). For Blacks, Turner was a "legendary Black hero" who led the "first war against slavery, the Civil War being the second" (145).

Deetz laments that there's no memorial to Turner. She's researched where the bodies are buried and bemoans that people can't pay homage to Nat nor memorialize him or the tree he was hanged on.

Frederick Douglass said Turner is essential to American history. Descendants and slavery scholars note that Nat Turner isn't taught in schools. Nate Parker said, "Nat Turner is taught as a killer not a freedom fighter driven by faith. Black people who stand up for themselves and kill whites are never considered heroes" (2016).

Thomas Wentworth Higginson, an abolitionist and Civil War colonel of the Union's first Black regiment, described Turner in 1861 as a "short, stout, dark mulatto" who "felt himself singled out" for important work, of great "moral character." He notes that "55 whites were killed but not one single slave and there was no rape, just murder. Turner was persuaded by his followers to stop at the Turner plantation, but there he was doomed, and the whites prevailed upon him and his followers. He dug a hole in the Dismal Swamp and lay there for 6 weeks, avoiding capture."

The Nat Turner project, created in 2015 by Sarah N. Roth, is a digital collection of original documents about the rebellion.

Nat was "a man capable of love and hatred, doubt and thundering visions, sensitivity and messianic rage" (Oates 1990, ix). He was in possession of a sword when he was found.

It was reported first that the British were the perpetrators, although they hadn't been in Virginia for twenty years (Breen 2015, 212). It was also noted that Turner's followers were "armed with guns, axes, swords, clubs, and other weapons" and some were drinking alcohol (Drewry 1900). Governor Floyd authorized a $500 reward for Turner; seaport cities of Portsmouth and Norfolk were seized by panic (Bisson 1988, 91). "3,000 armed whites assembled and marched toward Southampton, North Carolina cavalry killed forty Blacks, decapitating fifteen and placing their heads on poles." More than 120 Blacks were killed over the next four days. General Richard Eppes proclaimed martial law on August 28, 1831.

Nat said "freedom or death" was his motive, not money when asked what he did with all the money his followers stole. Enslavers didn't understand. The judge delivered a speech about "the horrors of rebellion" and ordered Turner to be hanged by the neck on November 11, 1831.

The myriad reverberations after the attack included vigilante violence, insurrection scares, and policy triage. Following the Turner insurrection, Virginia passed a law prohibiting the enslaved to read or learn how to read. The state also "came within seven votes of taking the first step that could have led to abolishing slavery" in 1832. However, the general assembly's lively debate "ultimately reinforced the status quo, and its monumental deliberation has receded into the historical arcana of the American South" (Ahrens 1994).

For Blacks, he was a "legendary Black hero," and his revolt was the "first war against slavery, the Civil War being the second" (Oates 1990, 145). He was a "martyred soldier of black liberation who broke his chains and murdered whites because slavery had murdered Negroes" (145). "The public would long argue whether Turner left the world a hero or a villain. Turner, for his part, had said all he had to say" (French 2004, 50).

"Nat Turner's strike for liberty was the outburst of feelings of an insane man—made so by slavery" (William Wells Brown, quoted by Foner 1971, 145).

Ossie Davis said, "Nat was our secret weapon, our ace in the hole, our private consciousness of manhood kept strictly between us" (1968).

Black Leaders decried, "Remember Denmark Vesey. Remember Nathaniel Turner" (Foner 1971, 139). "While resistance historians have celebrated Nat Turner as a hero," his legacy among the Black community remains controversial and not "monolithic" (Breen 2015, 6).

Aptheker was one of the first scholars to grapple with Turner's revolt. He quotes W. E. B. Du Bois: "You are nobody. Why strive to be somebody? Be reasonable." Nat Turner was one who "refused to be reasonable, and it is believed as the present-day stirrings of the American Negro people grow, the significance of the Turner Revolt as a tradition of progressive struggle will increase" (2006, 107).

Lerone Bennett wrote in 1968 that Turner "still sears the subconscious of the nation, because the gaping wound he opened still runs" (Bennett 1968, 84). That is still true though it was written more than fifty-five years ago. The controversy about the teaching of slavery and critical race theory is on the mind of politicians and voters. It was ludicrous to speak of the kindness of enslavers; slavery was a "human hell." Nat Turner came into a world that defined him violently, and there was no other way for him to define himself except in reaction to that violence. Nat saw that it was necessary for the oppressed to confront the violence of the system directly" (91).

DEPICTION AND CULTURAL CONTEXT

12 Years a Slave won the Academy Award in 2013 for Best Picture, and Fox Searchlight thought there was an appetite for slavery-themed films and that lightning might strike twice for them when three years later they acquired another "Sundance sensation."

The Black Lives Matter movement, advocating against police brutality and systemic racism, went global in 2016. Donald Trump's 2016 presidential campaign, Make America Great Again (MAGA), resonated for the white supremacy movement. Nat Turner interpreted the Bible in a fundamentalist way, which has parallels in jihad.

Parker claimed that although there have been slavery-themed films showing the enslaved physically and mentally triumphing over crushing adversity; "we have rarely seen those dealing with resistance and self-determination from the position of the enslaved. It is through this angle I hope audiences will continue to engage; having their eyes further opened regarding both those who endured and those who resisted."

Vanessa Holden explores the role of women and children in the rebellion, in her new book, *Surviving Southampton: African American Women and Resistance in Nat Turner's Community*. "Enslaved men rebel while enslaved women resist."

Both Nate Parker and Armie Hammer whose meteoric careers were taking off in 2016 have been publicly disgraced, Parker for the rape and Hammer for accusations of sexual assault and a cannibalistic fetish. Their careers were subsequently stalled. Parker wrote, directed, and starred in the poorly reviewed *American Skin* (2019).

The actor Colman Domingo said, "We had a lot of night shoots on a plantation where you knew there was blood in the soil. . . . [Y]ou were calling on all this trauma in the air, in the land, in the things that we touched. We created a sense of 'well-protected danger.' About slavery—it's art, but it's a useful tool for there to be more examinations of our collective history" (quoted in Parker 2017).

CONCLUSION

Nate Parker asks, "How do you judge what's moral or immoral in a system that is so immoral?" The film is searing, stirring, powerful, and flawed. It shows the enslaved in multidimensional ways and juxtaposes the violence of Turner's insurrection with a humanistic through line of a people joyfully loving, nurturing, imagining freedom, and desperate for dignity.

FURTHER READING

Ahrens, Frank. 1994. "The Slave Revolt That Shook Virginia." *Washington Post*, December 14, 1994.
Aptheker, Herbert. 2006. *Nat Turner's Slave Rebellion Including the 1831 Confessions*. New York: Dover.
Barringer Gordon, Sarah. 2020. "Why the Split in the Methodist Church Should Set Off Alarm Bells for Americans." *Washington Post*, January 16, 2020.
Bennett, Lerone, Jr. 1968. *Pioneers in Protest*. Chicago: Johnson Publishing.
Bisson, Terry. 1988. *Nat Turner: Slave Revolt Leader*. New York: Chelsea House Publisher.
Bradshaw, Peter. 2016. "*The Birth of a Nation* Review: Biblical Passion and Cheesy Emotion." *The Guardian*, December 6, 2016.
Breen, Patrick H. 2015. *The Land Shall Be Deluged in Blood: A New History of the Nat Turner Revolt*. New York: Oxford University Press.
Brody, Richard. 2016. "The Cinematic Merits and Flaws of Nate Parker's *The Birth of a Nation*." *New Yorker*, October 9, 2016.
Buchanan, Kyle. 2016. "After Months of Scandal, Let's Remember Why *The Birth of a Nation* Started as Such a Sensation." Slate.com, October 6, 2016. https://slate.com/culture/2016/10/5-reasons-that-the-birth-of-a-nation-began-as-a-sensation.html.
Casciato, Arthur D., and James L. W. West III. 1981. "William Styron and the Southampton Insurrection." *American Literature* 52 (4): 564–77.
Clarke, John Henrik, ed. 1997. *The Second Crucifixion of Nat Turner*. Baltimore: Black Classic Press.
Coffin, Joshua. 1860. *Slave Insurrections*. New York: American Anti-Slavery Society.
Davis, Mary Kemp. 1999. *Nat Turner before the Bar of Judgment: Fictional Treatments of the Southampton Slave Insurrection*. Baton Rouge: LSU Press.
Davis, Ossie. 1968. "Nat Turner: Hero Reclaimed." *Freedomways* 8, no. 3 (Summer): 230–32.
Drewry, William S. 1900. *Nat Turner's Insurrection*. Washington, DC: Neale Company.
Dunbar, Erica Armstrong. 2019. *She Came to Slay: The Life and Times of Harriet Tubman*. New York: 37 INK, Simon and Schuster.
Dunbar, Erica Armstrong, and Daina Ramey. 2016. *The Birth of a Nation: Nat Turner and the Making of a Movement*. Edited by Nate Parker. New York: Simon & Schuster.
Foner, Eric, ed. 1971. *Nat Turner: Great Lives Observed*. Englewood Cliffs, NJ: Prentice-Hall.
French, Scot. 2004. *The Rebellious Slave: Nat Turner in American Memory*. Boston: Houghton Mifflin.
Haygood, Wil. 2021. *Colorization: One Hundred Years of Black Films in a White World*. New York: Alfred A. Knopf.
Holden, Vanessa M. 2021. *Surviving Southampton: African American Women and Resistance in Nat Turner's Community*. Urbana: University of Illinois Press.

Jones, Nate, and Rachel Bashein. 2016. "A Timeline of the Nate Parker Rape Scandal, and the Damage Control That Has Followed." *Vulture*, October 3, 2016.

Kaiser, David. 2016. "*The Birth of a Nation* and Nat Turner in His Own Words." *Time*, October 28, 2016. https://time.com/4524172/birth-of-a-nation-nat-turner-confessions/.

Kaye, Anthony. 2007. "Neighborhoods and Nat Turner: The Making of a Slave Rebel and the Unmaking of a Slave Rebellion." *Journal of the Early Republic* 27, no. 4 (Winter): 705–20.

Little, Becky. 2019. "Why Bibles Given to Slaves Omitted Most of the Old Testament." *Museum of the Bible*. https://www.history.com/news/slave-bible-redacted-old-testament.

"Margaret Washington on Moral Suasion." n.d. *Africans in America*. PBS. Accessed September 22, 2022. https://www.pbs.org/wgbh/aia/part4/4i2981.html.

Michael, Taylor. 2021. "Dread Scott Celebrates a Long-forgotten Rebellion as a Moment of Resilience." *Hyperallergic.com*, November 17, 2021.

"Nat Turner's Rebellion." 1831. *Africans in America*. PBS. Accessed September 22, 2022. https://www.pbs.org/wgbh/aia/part3/3p1518.html.

Oates, Stephen B. 1990. *The Fires of Jubilee: Nat Turner's Fierce Rebellion*. New York: New American Library.

Onion, Rebecca. 2016. "How The Birth of a Nation Uses Fact and Fiction." *Slate*, October 24, 2016.

Parker, Nate, dir. 2017. *The Birth of a Nation*. DVD. BRON Studios, Creative Wealth Media Finance, and Follow Through Productions.

Rael, Patrick. 2015. "Why Did Nat Turner Confess?" *Black Perspectives*, April 29, 2015.

Redden, Molly. 2016. "The Story of Nate Parker's Rape Accuser and a University's Cold Shoulder." *The Guardian*, August 19, 2016.

Rezayazdi, Soheil. 2016. "Five Questions with *The Birth of a Nation* Director Nate Parker." *Filmmaker Magazine*, January 25, 2016.

Ryfle, Steve. 2016. "Nat Turner's Hollywood's Rebellion." *Cinéaste* 42, no. 1 (Winter): 31–33.

Smith, Clint. 2021. *How the World Is Passed*. New York: Little, Brown.

Tanenhaus, Sam. 2016. "The Literary Battle for Nat Turner's Legacy." *Vanity Fair*, August 3, 2016.

Van Der Werff, Emily. 2016. "Nate Parker's Birth of a Nation Is Almost Good Enough to Withstand Its Controversy." *Vox*, October 7, 2016.

Wagner, Lon. 2003. "Nat Turner's Skull Turns Up Far from Site of His Revolt." *Baltimore Sun*, June 15, 2003.

Wang Yuen, Nancy, and Joshua D. Smith. 2016. "Birth of a Controversy: The Legacy of Nat Turner." *Huff Post*, November 1, 2016.

Warren, Kenneth W. 2016. "Why We Don't Need Another Hero (Film): Nate Parker's 'The Birth *of a Nation*.'" *Los Angeles Review of Books*, November 4, 2016. https://lareviewofbooks.org/article/why-we-dont-need-another-hero-film-nate-parkers-the-birth-of-a-nation/.

Wentworth Higginson, Thomas. 1861. "Nat Turner's Insurrection." *The Atlantic*, August 1861.

Williams, Jakobi. 2012. "Nat Turner: The Complexity and Dynamic of His Religious Background." *Journal of Pan African Studies* 4, no. 9 (January): 114–47.

Chapter 10

Harriet (2019)

The first feature film solely devoted to the life of the iconic American liberator of the enslaved, the Underground Railroad (UGRR) conductor Harriet Tubman (1822–1913), *Harriet*, was released by Focus Features on November 1, 2019, two months after premiering at the Toronto International Film Festival (TIFF). Starring Cynthia Erivo (born in 1987), the Tony, Emmy, and Grammy Award–winning British actress; written by Gregory Allen Howard and Kasi Lemmons; and directed by Kasi Lemmons, the film received two Oscar and two Golden Globe nominations in the same categories. Erivo was nominated for Best Actress and Best Original Song "Stand Up," which she cowrote with Joshuah Brian Campbell and performed at the Oscar telecast. The song, played during the end credits, includes Tubman's last words, "I go to prepare a place for you," which John says in the Bible. The rousing score was composed by Terence Blanchard, who's worked on most of Spike Lee's films.

"There are 30 films about General Custer," said the festival's director Cameron Bailey, introducing the film. "This is the first film about Harriet Tubman" (quoted by Coyle 2019). The late legendary actress Cicely Tyson (1924–2021) played Tubman in the two-part, 240-minute 1978 miniseries *A Woman Called Moses*, narrated by Orson Welles and directed by Paul Wendkos. HBO was developing an adaptation of historian Kate Clifford Larson's 2004 book, *Bound for the Promised Land*, which Viola Davis was attached to star in and produce. However, it never happened. According to Davis, speaking with *Entertainment Weekly* in 2016, "The reason her life has not been honored, the reason people don't know what she contributed, is because she's a Black woman. She was born a slave. If you look up the history of anyone who contributed to the country who were not white males, their contributions are always minimized." (quoted in Sperling 2016).

The actress Aisha Hinds played Tubman in an episode of the WGN TV series *Underground* (2017), which depicts Tubman telling her story to a group of white antislavery activists while outlining where the abolitionist movement is and should be going. Before it was even scripted, the episode was known on the show's set as "Harriet Tubman's TED Talk" (Berman 2017). And the British actress Zainab Jah plays Harriet Tubman in episode 4 of *The Good Lord Bird*, Showtime's 2020 miniseries about John Brown based on James McBride's eponymous novel.

Despite the backlash of the #NotMyHarriet controversy sparked in 2018 after the British actress Cynthia Erivo announced on Twitter that she would be playing the American hero, *Harriet's* opening weekend surpassed expectations, grossing more than $12 million. The film's $17 million budget was close to tripled; it earned $43.1 million in the United States and Canada and $200,000 in other territories for a worldwide total of $43.3 million, plus $4.2 million with home video and university sales (McClintock 2019).

Kasi Lemmons, a former actress, wrote the libretto for Terence Blanchard's 2021opera *Fire Shut Up in My Bones*, based on Charles M. Blow's memoir. It is the first opera by a Black composer in the Metropolitan Opera's 138-year history. Lemmons directed the first two episodes of Netflix's *Self Made: Inspired by the Life of Madam C.J. Walker* (2020), starring Octavia Spencer as America's first African American female millionaire; *Black Nativity* (2013), an adaptation of Langston Hughes's 1961 musical drama starring Forest Whitaker, Angela Bassett, and Jennifer Hudson; *Talk to Me* (2007), starring Don Cheadle and inspired by the life of the Washington, DC, radio deejay, Ralph Waldo "Petey" Green; and *The Caveman's Valentine* (2001), starring Samuel L. Jackson, based on George Dawes Green's novel about a former piano prodigy who becomes a mentally ill and homeless man; and she wrote and directed *Eve's Bayou* (1997), her lauded, atmospheric debut Southern Gothic horror film infused with a slavery theme.

Harriet was for the most part favorably reviewed. Richard Brody (2019) said, "The movie relates Tubman's story, and the story of her times, with the exalted power of secular scripture." Peter Bradshaw/the *Guardian* (2019) raved, "History, heroism and leadership are the stuff of Kasi Lemmons' rousing and heartfelt film about the life and times of Harriet Tubman, the Spartacus of the American south." "So often, historical films are stale and mired in misery, but *Harriet* has a rare buoyancy. . . . [I]t's a remarkable biopic," said Simran Hans (2019). Hornaday (2019) claimed the film "is an ideal introduction—or reintroduction—not just to Tubman, but to the inhumane system that she refused to accept. Clear, linear, sometimes bluntly obvious, *Harriet* is a rich, enlightening portrait—as sturdy and straightforward as the title character herself." However, Mark Jenkins/NPR claimed that Erivo's dynamic performance shows Tubman as a superhero that "[l]ike most monuments, the biopic is somber, well-intentioned, and fundamentally inert" (2019).

Lemmons said the time was "not only the right time for a film about Harriet Tubman, but the right time to have the story told by three women: herself and the producers Debra Martin Chase and Daniela Taplin Lundberg" (Lemmons 2019). Martin Chase is one of Hollywood's first and most successful Black women producers. Taplin Lundberg's company, Stay Gold Features, is a female-led film production and finance company. Lemmons said Erivo was uniquely qualified on a spiritual level to play this part. Howard saw her galvanic Tony Award–winning performance in *The Color Purple* on Broadway and knew she had to play Harriet.

Howard, who also wrote the screenplay for *Remember the Titans* (2000), started pitching a movie to Hollywood producers and studios about Harriet Tubman in 1994. He recalls a studio executive suggesting that Julia Roberts play her, claiming "No one will remember Tubman was Black." Howard was intent on a film that showed Tubman as "an action figure. I wanted to *entertain* people, not *preach* to them." His first draft was titled *Freedom Fire*. He didn't find any takers; he says that Hollywood's decision-makers at that time not only underestimated the knowledge the moviegoing public had of abolitionist agitators but also of its appetite about a Black woman savior. Hollywood wasn't making many Black-themed movies, and one featuring a Black woman faced an even harder challenge.

Lemmons's and Howard's screenplay foregrounds Tubman's resistance and transcendence of her oppression and achievement of freedom through activism and abolitionist agitation. The atrocities, pain, trauma, and humiliation the enslaved experienced are portrayed in swift, horrific flashpoints; however, the film is focused on resistance, rebellion, and the empowerment of people of color to document and control their own destiny.

The picture only recently discovered of Tubman as a young woman was Lemmons's inspiration. She says, "There was this very small, young woman who managed to do incredible things" (Lemmons, quoted by Coyle 2019). Lemmons wanted to tell a story about the young "badass" Harriet. She was a "superhero who lived outside the ordinary limitations, it's story of a leader with purpose and courage." Cynthia Erivo was excited to play "a woman who changed history."

Howard, who wrote *Remember the Titans* (2000) and *Ali* (2001), wanted to make Tubman's life into a "kick-ass adventure movie" rather than give history lessons" ("Print the Legend" 2019). He and film executives felt that the success of *12 Years a Slave* (2013) and the Afro-futurist *Black Panther* (2018) helped pave the way for the story of a real-life superhero and make her story accessible to a mass audience. He wrote it as "a valentine to Black women, showing this young Black woman take on this incredible power structure and triumph over it. Lemmons was also interested in showing how Black women use pain to make themselves stronger" (Fagerholm 2019).

Lemmons and the film's editor, Wyatt Smith, wanted Tubman's seizures to look "simple and kind of shocking, almost piercing in the way a seizure might be, or a flash of insight" (Fagerholm 2019). When Harriet walks into the river, it's like Moses parting the Red Sea. Nina Simone's song "Sinner Man" is played. It's a traditional "African American spiritual inspired by the book of Exodus. It tells the tale of man running from God ('the Lamb') and begging for forgiveness on Judgment Day, but ultimately, man cannot escape his wrath" (Jefferson 2022).

Several characters in addition to Harriet and her family, her husband John Tubman, plantation owner Edward Brodess, Reverend Green, William Still, and William Seward are based on real people; however, some supporting characters, including Bigger Long, a Black slave catcher; Walter, a reformed bounty hunter; and Marie Buchanon (Janelle Monae), a free, entrepreneurial Black are fictional. Producer Debra Martin Chase was sobbing at the climax of the Combahee River Raid scene when approximately two hundred extras are shown running to freedom. "It's like they're channeling something from their great-great grandparents, and it's incredibly powerful. It's the right moment in history to be exploring this story," Lemmons noted (Lemmons 2019).

The film opens with the young Harriet, called Minty, short for Araminta, in Dorchester County, Maryland in the 1840s. The area is called Cambridge today. She is lying on the ground having a sleeping spell and visualizing memories of family members sold away. Her husband, John Tubman (played by Zackary Momoh), a free man, brings her a lawyer's letter for the freedom suit her family is pursuing, and the couple jumps with joy. Led by the reverend Samuel Green's sermon "Keep your hand on the plow." Ben Ross, Harriet's dad, and John tell the slave owner, Edward Brodess. That they hired a lawyer claiming that Minty's mother was supposed to be freed at forty-five; "She's nearly fifty-seven," he says, "and her daughter was illegally sold away from her. Her daughters were all supposed to be free."

Harriet says, "We want our babies born free like they're supposed to be." Brodess rips up the document.

Harriet prays to God to kill Brodess. Brodess's son, Gideon, played by Joe Alwyn, overhears her, and says, "God, don't listen to n****rs." He reminds her that hers was the first face he saw when he was sick with typhoid, praying it "scared the fever right out of me. I got used to your face."

Brodess dies soon after. While he is being buried, the enslaved sing, "Keep your hands on the plow. Hold on." Gideon's pasting a newspaper ad on a tree. It says, "Negro at sale, a fine-looking Negro girl, Minty between 24 & 25 years of age fine looking and very capable." Harriet is compelled to escape; she worries that John who's free will be captured, but he insists on going.

She looks at her fellow enslaved and sings, "I'm going to leave you, I'm bound for the promised land." Some sing along. John on his way to meet

Minty gets stopped by Gideon. Minty goes to see her dad, Ben Ross, played by Clarke Peters, and tells him she must run because she knows she'll be sold down the river, meaning south. He insists she stop at Reverend Green, played by Vondie Curtis-Hall (Lemmons's husband), to pray for her journey. Her father gives her a small carving he made. The reverend asks if she can read; she can't.

He says, "Fear is your enemy. Trust in God. Follow the north star. If you can't see it, follow the river; if you can't see the river, listen for it. Follow it to Wilmington. After it splits, the Delaware River be on your right, look for a merchant, the blacksmith Thomas Garrett." Thomas Garrett was one of the most prominent figures in the history of the UGRR. He has been called Delaware's greatest humanitarian and is credited with helping more than twenty-seven hundred slaves escape to freedom over a forty-year period.

Harriet is on the run. She wakes up to slave catchers on horses and bloodhounds chasing her through the forest. Gideon corners her on a bridge; she threatens to jump. Gideon tells her that suicide is a sin against God. He tells her that his mom decided not to sell her, that he misses her and that "You've been there all my life, like yo mama was for my daddy. Daddy vowed never to free your mama, and I'll vow never to sell you."

"I'm going to be free or die," she says, and jumps in.

Gideon scours the river looking for her. She wakes up shoeless, throwing up, and clutching the wooden head her dad gave her. She runs and climbs into a horse and cart with hay. She hops on and finds a freed Black man who gives her directions to find Thomas Garrett, a white man with a dark, large-brimmed Quaker hat. She asks him if he knows Reverend Green; he says, "I do," and she faints and wakes up in a beautiful bed. The Quaker drops her off at the Pennsylvania border and asks if she wants him to accompany her or "walk alone to freedom," and she says, I'll walk with the Lord." The momentous shot of her jumping into freedom with the sun gloriously setting on an autumnal expanse reflects her joy. Philadelphia is twenty-five miles away. Harriet is in search of the Pennsylvania Anti-Slavery Society, and in particular, William Still, whose photograph or "likeness" Garrett shows her.

Black and white people are intermingling on a busy city street. Harriet stops to ask a Black man selling apples for directions. He says, "Walk like you got a right to." She walks into the Anti-Slavery Society office and meets William Still, played by Leslie Odom Jr., and tells him Garrett sent her.

Still gets out a book to write in, asking her for her full name and where she's from. "This book," he says, "is full of slave histories."

"Brodesss is dead," Harriet says. "His wife owns me and my family."

Still tells her, "Not you anymore," and asks her who journeyed with her.

"Just me and the lord," Harriet says.

"By some miraculous means, you have made it 100 miles to freedom." He asks her if she'd like to pick a new name to mark her freedom as most formerly enslaved people do.

She says, "My mama name Harriet. I want my mama and husband name. Harriet Tubman."

"Did your master harm you physically, wounds or scars?"

She tells him how the overseer cracked her head open when she was about thirteen. He was pursuing an enslaved man who refused to work. He threw a two-pound weight at the runaway, but it hit Harriet, breaking her skull. She slept for two months, she said, and the next thing she remembers is seeing her sister sold off. We see the images of this in flashback. "Except I saw it before it happen. God showed me. The hole in my head made God's voice more clear."

Still writes down "Possible brain damage." He brings her to Marie's boardinghouse. The elegant, Ms. Marie Buchanon, played by Janelle Monae, tells Harriet her mother was freed when her master died and pregnant with her, so she was born free in Philadelphia. She also tells Harriet she "stinks like a barnyard animal."

Harriet replies, "Guess you never had the stink of fear. Of running for your life."

Marie gives her a bath and gets Harriet work as a maid. Harriet tells Marie she'd like to get word to her husband that she's okay. Marie tells Harriet about the boatmen called the Black Jacks who travel up and down the Chesapeake carrying messages to enslaved people to get word to John Tubman, and Harriet does.

One year later, Harriet asks William if she could have use of his "angels" to go to get John and her family. He tells her things are getting tougher—their work has gotten much more dangerous, there are more slave catchers, and that Congress is passing laws to appease the South. "Catching slaves requires careful planning and reading. Can you read a sign, a map?"

She says indignantly, "Don't tell me what I can and can't do.... I'm going back; without my husband and family, I'm just a stranger in a strange land."

Marie gives her advice to not look a white man in the eye and helps her with a dress to help her look like a free lady, and she gives her a gun. "If trouble comes, you'll be ready," Marie says.

She gives Harriet papers and says they may not match her exactly, but the authorities are more worried about Blacks headed north than they are about those headed south. After getting off the train, a white man asks for her papers and says, "They say she's five and a half feet tall; you ain't more than five feet."

"Must have been wearing my high boots that day," she replies.

Mrs. Eliza Brodess claims she must sell slaves. "Our stature in this community is measured by Negroes. Robert alone is worth six or seven hundred dollars."

Harriet shows up singing to John, "I'm sorry I had to leave you." He tells her he thought she was dead after he heard she jumped off the bridge and that he remarried and is expecting a child. A devastated Harriet cries and asks God why he let her live. She reunites with her dad and siblings and takes them with her. Reverend Green reveals to her people hiding in his basement, under the floorboards.

Gideon runs into Walter, played by Henry Hunter Hall (Lemmons's and Vondie Curtis-Hall's son). He offers to work for pay to help him find the slave stealer. Bigger Long, played by Omar J. Dorsey, is another man of color who earns money to help slave catchers. Gideon agrees to pay them $200 if they return Harriet to him unharmed.

Harriet faints while leading a group to freedom. "She's talking to God," one of her brethren says.

"We can't go this way," she says, "there's danger." They are being followed. Harriet leads them to cross a river, but most can't swim. She pulls a gun out and forces her fellow slaves to "be free or die." She walks in the water holding the gun up. She walks in, prays to the Lord to let the river go through her; she keeps walking, and her head sticks up and then the water again gets shallow. The others follow.

Walter, after being roughed up by Gideon, offers Harriet his services to protect her. Slave catchers catch up to her, and she, gun blazing, and Walter ride off on a horse.

Baltimore, Maryland. A meeting of men desperate to find Moses and to pass the Fugitive Slave Act, allowing slave catchers without a warrant to go after and seize the enslaved in every state, even free states. Bigger tells Gideon that Moses is Harriet, but Gideon doesn't believe him. The act is passed, and people of color near the dock in Philadelphia are running around panicked. Still tells everyone to go north to Canada for safety. Gideon and Bigger Long and a few other white men break into Marie's place. They rough her up and demand to know where Harriet is. Marie says, "She's gotta live long enough to do God's work and that Harriet is smarter than they are." She resists, and the more she does so, the harder Bigger kicks and beats, finally killing her. Harriet enters but hides, knowing they will kill her. Harriet runs and is helped onto the boat after running into her owner. Gideon shoots at but misses her.

Harriet is in Saint Catharines, Canada, when she learns that her sister Rachel has died and then in upstate Auburn, New York, when William Seward, secretary of state (from 1861 to 1869) expresses his condolences. There's talk of civil war; Harriet says, "We can't give up." At an abolitionist meeting, she tells the men they don't know what slavery was like. Some were born free, and they "don't know slavery firsthand; you got comfortable and important. I'll do whatever I have to do until this beast, this monster called slavery is slain dead. Children beat for not working before they understand what work is. Girls raped before their first blood, brothers ripped, sisters sold from their babies."

It's 1858 at the New York/Canada border. Harriet sees her mother and tells her she's not an angel; she's come to take her north. She tells her she's

Moses, the slave stealer. White men with blazing torches confront the Brodess plantation asking for restitution, as Moses was their slave. Harriet rescues her niece and pulls her gun on the white people as does Walter. Mrs. Brodess says, "We need to find her and burn her at the stake like Joan of Arc."

Harriet, her niece, and Walter tie up the whites, and Harriet sings "Let My People Go." A man says, "Moses must be found and prosecuted by the law." They hide out in a cart and get stopped when crossing a bridge, but a white guy recognizes the kid driving the cart and lets them go without being inspected.

The owner and Black man corner Harriet—she shoots the Black man. "God don't mean people to own people, Gideon," Harriet says. She mentions the "Lost Cause" and dying on a battlefield and says, "God has shown me the future, and my people are free."

It's two years later, and the Civil War is in full swing. It's 1863 at the Combahee River in South Carolina. Harriet in uniform is addressing the soldiers; she's declaring that slavery has to end. She's in the water singing "Wade in the Water," while hundreds of enslaved people are carrying their possessions and running toward her. They're running to freedom.

Title cards reveal that during the Civil War, she became a spy for the Union Army and led 150 Black soldiers in the Combahee River, freeing 750 formerly enslaved people who sailed to Beaufort. She remains one of the few women in the United States who led an armed expedition. The credits roll and the song "Stand Up" is played. On the screen is written: "Harriet was the most famous conductor on the Underground Railroad bringing 70 slaves to freedom."

"She fought to change a nation," reads the crawl at the end of the film. "Be free or die."

HISTORICAL BACKGROUND

Araminta Ross, nicknamed Minty, was born into slavery on March 6, 1822, in Dorchester County, on the Eastern Shore of Maryland. She had eight siblings. She was often beaten as a child on the tidewater plantation owned by Edward Brodess. She was hired out and had to work full days when she was only five, babysitting and cleaning houses for white people (Sernett 2007).

The young Tubman suffered a skull injury when she was thirteen and in a store. An overseer threw a two-pound weight at an enslaved person escaping. Tubman protected him and endured the blow. The weight struck Harriet, tearing a hole in her skull, pressing a portion of it against her brain. Though she bled profusely, no medical care was granted. Ever afterward, she suffered from seizures and what was called a "stupor" or "sleeping sickness," also known as hyposomnia, what today would likely be diagnosed as "temporal lobe epilepsy" or narcolepsy (Clifford Larson 2003, 43). After her injury, Tubman had powerfully prophetic, revelatory visitations from God.

"I grew up," she said, "like a neglected weed—ignorant of liberty, having no experience of it. . . . Every time I saw a White man I was afraid of being carried away. 1 had two sisters carried away in a chain gang—one of them left two children. We were always uneasy. . . . I think slavery is the next thing to hell." Her sisters Linah and Soph were sold down the river, down south, in 1845. She never saw them again (Dunbar 2019, 20). Although slavery was in decline in Tubman's youth, the enslaved were still and even more valuable. The number of free Blacks increased as the number of enslaved decreased. More enslaved escaped from Maryland than any other place, according to the 1850 census (Bordewich 2005, 347).

As she grew, Harriet was forced to perform hard labor, including flax harvesting, releasing muskrats from traps for their pelts, and rigorous housekeeping. She learned how to cut logs for lumber from her father, a timber inspector, and clear land, and she became physically strong (Dunbar 2019, 26). And it "put her in touch with free Black sailors who shipped the wood to the North, and she learned about the secret communications that occurred along trade routes" (Hobson 2014).

She married John Tubman, a free, mixed-race man, at nineteen in 1844. The couple, married for five years before she escaped, did not have any children. Tubman married again but didn't have biological children. Tubman "earned the $5 to pay for the attorney to investigate an old will" stating that when she turned forty-five years old, her mother was to be set free, "insisting that her family's freedom had been promised by the landowners' great-grandfather" (Clifford Larson 2003). Tubman changed her name to Harriet to honor her mother and as a spiritual conversion after marrying John.

When she learned she would be sold, she and her brothers tried to run away, but John did not want to escape with her because he was free (Clifford Larson 2003, 15). Harriet and her brothers tried following the North Star and the Big Dipper; however, they got lost and returned (Bordewich 2005, 349).

Edward Brodess's death in 1849 elicited an urgency. His financially strapped widow was selling the enslaved. Harriet's niece and grandniece were sold for $375 (Dunbar 2019, 32). There were "horsemen coming for her, like the riders of the apocalypse; she heard the terrifying screams of women and children. She dreamed of flying over fields and towns, rivers and mountains, and looking down up them like a bird," reiterating a phrase that appears in the Bible in Psalm 124.7: "We have escaped like a bird out of the fowler's snare" (Bordewich 2005, 349). Tubman was twenty-seven years old when she successfully ventured out of slavery in 1849.

The Dorchester County Methodist preacher and farmer Reverend Samuel Green advised Tubman about traveling and helped put her in touch with the Quakers. He was actively involved with the UGRR in the 1850s. Born in 1802, Green received an education, unusual for the enslaved. He bought his and his wife's freedom, but their children remained enslaved. He knew the Black activists Frederick Douglass, Stephen Myers, and John S. Rock. Although he was never arrested for aiding and abetting Tubman and other fugitive slaves, he did serve jail time for possession of a copy of a best-selling book, Harriet Beecher Stowe's antislavery *Uncle Tom's Cabin*, shown in a scene deleted from the film (Taylor 2019).

Reverend Green gave Tubman the names of the Quakers Thomas Garrett and Hanna Leverton, operators on the UGRR. The eighteenth-century Quakers, also known as the Society of Friends, was the first white American group to publicly reject slavery, spread the word and initiate actions of abolitionist agitation, and to help the enslaved escape to Canada via the water and land routes of the UGRR. Quakers sometimes "provided cover for fleeing slaves by posing as white slave traders, for example, or offered hiding places on their farms or in townhouses during the daytime. George Washington, shortly before he became president, complained that one of his enslaved people had disappeared; Washington wrote that "he suspected 'a society of Quakers formed for such purposes' had helped the runaway" (Foner 2015, 128).

Tubman was helped by Black and white people giving her directions, providing money as well as protection in safe houses and connecting her with other people she could trust. After receiving instructions, she "followed rivers that snaked northward." The moss grew northward, and Tubman followed the moon, the stars, and other natural phenomena to guide her north. She recognized "every creek, every cove, every hiding place, every curve in the road" (Petry [1995] 2007). She wore and was a master at disguises—she sometimes dressed as a man, a field hand, and/or as an elderly woman or man. She paid bribes. However, "she did not as some have claimed use coded quilts; that is an urban legend" (Clifford Larson 2016).

The discovery in April 2021 of the rural house near the shore Tubman lived in with her father, Ben Ross, and the finding of artifacts like brick and glass fragments, nails, and a rare coin, confirmed that living in this area "was the opportunity she had to learn about how to navigate and survive in the wetlands and the woods. We believe this experience was able to benefit her when she began to move people from Maryland to freedom" (Schlabitsky, quoted by Owens 2021). Tubman's direct knowledge of the land, the marshes, the birds, the plants, and even the night sky was key to her and her fugitives' survival.

Tubman experienced "prophetic visions," what she described as mystical trances during which directives from God compelled her to make her first escape. She would "occasionally burst out into religious song and rhythmic dance, what some call a spiritual shuffle" (Gersen 2021). She had a dream she could fly "like a bird" (Grady 2016, 5).

When leading her charges, she would alter the tempo of certain songs like "Go Down Moses" and "Bound for the Promised Land" or "mimic the hoot of an owl, to signal whether it was safe or too dangerous to reveal their hiding places." She also used dictated letters she had people write. In December 1854, for instance, she had a letter sent to Jacob Jackson, a literate, free Black farmer and veterinarian, instructing him to tell her brothers that they needed to be ready to "step aboard" the "Ol' Ship of Zion." In other words, she was coming to rescue them (Clifford Larson 2016).

Tubman rescued her niece and her children when she heard in 1850 that they were being sold and her seventy-year-old parents in 1856. By 1860, Tubman had made thirteen trips from Maryland and escorted close to seventy enslaved people in their life-changing odyssey from bondage to freedom, although Sarah Bradford in her book exaggerated and claimed Tubman had made nineteen trips and brought three hundred people to freedom (Clifford Larson 2016). It was unusual for the enslaved to escape in groups, as it was more likely one would get caught. William Wells Brown, the notable African American abolitionist and writer, said "fugitives in Tubman's care were never captured" (Clinton 2004, 87). Tubman would leave on Saturday evenings because newspapers were not printed on Sundays, and therefore, no advertisements for runaways could appear before Monday (Clifford Larson 2003, 100). Advertisements offering one hundred dollars for her capture described her as "of a chestnut color, fine looking, and about 5 feet high" (Clifford Larson 2003, 100).

Tubman carried fake freedom passes describing a variety of enslaved people. Tubman made her way to selected plantations where the enslaved were informed of her presence by songs and prayers; "selected enslaved people were then apprised of the rendezvous area and the time of departure." General Tubman, as she came to be called, insisted her fellow travelers be on time. She carried a gun and fresh ammunition. Tubman carried a pistol during rescue missions, "telling her charges to go on or die, for a dead fugitive slave could tell no tales." Carrying these "tools" hidden on her person, she slipped across the Mason-Dixon line, the line that separated slave from free states. It separated four U.S. states, forming part of the borders of Pennsylvania, Maryland, Delaware, and West Virginia (Sernett 2007, 127).

Tubman's example encouraged many enslaved people to flee from Delaware. Thomas Garrett provided clothing (enslaved clothing was detectable), shoes, forged free papers, carriages, and directions to safe houses throughout Delaware. Tubman journeyed by night and slept by day. Tubman had a special angel, many thought, and divine intervention (Clinton 2004, 91). She was illiterate, but she knew the Bible, and she retained and recited detailed passages on the journey. Her entry into Pennsylvania "was the salvation she sought, not only a physical place but a profoundly spiritual one" (Bordewich 2005, 350). Tubman networked and traversed from Maryland through Delaware to Philadelphia to New Jersey, and from New York City to Albany, Rochester, Auburn, over the Niagara Falls Suspension Bridge and into Saint Catharines, Canada.

When she was not traveling, she cooked in kitchens and hotels in Philadelphia and Cape May, New Jersey, the first summer resort in America, to "build up her war chest" (Clinton 2004). Tubman, whose mother was a cook, was a resourceful and excellent cook. Private carriages cost money as did bribes, food, and other supplies. Tubman was a tireless fundraiser and networker who collected money from places as far away as Scotland and Ireland.

Although none are written in her own hand, letters about Tubman's clandestine escapes exist. Thomas Garrett's 1868 letter describes the old horse she commandeered when she took her elderly parents out of slavery, claiming that she "drove to town in a style that no human being ever did before or since; but she was happy at having arrived safe." Sydney Howard Gay, a New York–based abolitionist journalist and editor of the *National Anti-Slavery Standard*, interviewed "Captain Harriet Tubman" (he alone called her that) when she brought a group of fugitive enslaved people to his office in 1856 and published stories of her exploits in his *Record of Fugitives*. Frederick Douglass, who escaped from slavery and became an eloquent writer and leader of the antislavery movement, claims in a letter he wrote about Tubman in 1868 that "excepting John Brown, no one's risked more perils or hardships to serve our enslaved people" (Foner 2015, 194).

The first protest against slavery took place in 1688 where Philadelphia is now. Known as the Germantown Quaker Petition Protest Petition, it was "the first American document of its kind that made a plea for equal human rights for everyone." The quest for equality accelerated "in Pennsylvania and the other colonies with the Declaration of Independence and the abolitionist and suffrage movements, eventually giving rise to Lincoln's reference to human rights in the Gettysburg Address." This petition was written out of history until 1844 when it was reclaimed, becoming a catalyst for the blossoming abolitionist movement. It was rediscovered after being excavated from a vault in March 2005 (https://www.nps.gov/articles/quakerpetition.htm).

Pennsylvania's Abolition Act in 1780 made it the first state in America to pass a law, one of gradual emancipation, against slavery; it applied only to children born after March 1, 1780.

Pennsylvania was founded by William Penn, a Quaker. Maryland was close to a free state; therefore, it was easier than states in the Deep South to escape from.

The Underground Railroad was not an actual railroad, but instead, a secret network of people known as abolitionists who helped between thirty thousand and sixty thousand African Americans escape slavery by 1860. Many "movement centers" and "elaborate system of songs, symbols, secret communications, and bold movements" were employed, including couriers to disseminate information and news (Newman 2018, 82). Enslaved people who were being helped were called cargo. Most were conductors; some white men before Harriet who helped the enslaved to escape were also called abductors. Harriet started escorting enslaved people in the 1850s from Maryland through Wilmington, Delaware (Sernett 2007).

Liberated formerly enslaved people would find sanctuary in free Northern states and ultimately in British Canada, where slavery was abolished in 1834. Best-selling revelatory slave narratives, also known as captivity literature, were published in the 1840s and 1850s for a great many readers horrified but eager to read the evils of slavery. The books helped spread abolitionist fervor.

Abolitionism was the "world's first social movement" (Newman 2018, 3). It was "part of a communications revolution that allowed ever-more people to learn about, and join, the burgeoning movement. From slave narratives ... to anti-slavery newspapers, abolitionists used the media in stunningly modern ways. They were ahead of their time" (6). Although the name "Underground Railroad" was given in the 1830s with the advent of the new rail system, and "stations" and "depots" were homes, businesses, churches, etc. where the enslaved were hidden, secret networks were in place long before then (87). Some historians claim that abolitionism and other reform movements were influenced by the Protestant revival in the early nineteenth century known as the Second Great Awakening, which highlighted the belief that, to God, everyone is created equal.

As Herbert Aptheker says:

No people anywhere in the world have shown greater ingenuity and heroism than did the American Negro people in connection with the many types of activities arising from efforts to flee the land of sorrow. First are the heroes who started out, often knowing no more than that somewhere north was freedom, having no guide but the north star, no road but the forest and swamp, seeing in every white person a probable enemy, and leaving behind folks whom they loved. They went; thousands went. Many (how many will never be known) failed, dying in the attempt or being recaptured and suffering lashes. . . . Still, Elijah Anderson, John Mason, and, above all, that heroic woman, Harriet Tubman. Concerning the latter, known to her people as Moses, John Brown said in his laconic way that she was "the most of a man, naturally, that I ever met with." (1989, 14)

There were no slaves living in Philadelphia by 1849 and close to twenty thousand free Blacks (Dunbar 2019). Upon arriving in Pennsylvania, Tubman said, "I had crossed the line of which I had so long been dreaming. I was free; but there was no one to welcome me to the land of freedom, I was a stranger in a strange land."

Tubman found William Still upon her arrival in Philadelphia. Still (1821–1902) was born free in New Jersey, but his parents were born enslaved. His mother and brothers lived under the radar and moved to Philadelphia in 1844 when William was twenty-three. He became a clerk at the Pennsylvania Antislavery Society, founded in 1833, and first named the General Vigilance Committee. Still was the corresponding secretary and chairman of the UGRR in Philadelphia. In 1860, he joined the Pennsylvania Abolitionist Society, following the beliefs of the Black abolitionist William Whipper.

A businessman and writer, William Still published his eight-hundred-page tome, *The Underground Railroad* in 1872 and lectured in New York and Canada. Still's monumental book focused on the Black community's efforts and on "authentic first-person accounts" (Hall 2003). Still was a meticulous notetaker and chronicler. He "was a lay historian, recording the small daily acts of bravery he witnessed in his work" (Coates quoted in Still 2019, x). "These stories with their high drama of escape, of freedom, of disguise and espionage . . . are as exciting as any Western and as suspenseful as any Mafia movie. But because these stories and their heroes cannot be made to excuse their country's crimes they have mostly existed in the collective memory and history of their descendants."

Although Still's documented eight hundred to nine hundred escapees achieved freedom in Pennsylvania, they were Canada bound. America was still fraught with possible entrapment. The Fugitive Slave Act of 1850, also known as the Bloodhound Law, as bloodhounds were deployed to capture the enslaved, was a devastating blow to abolitionist efforts. It allowed and compelled bounty hunters and masters to legally force free people back into slavery as "property" and send them back to enslavement in the South. "U.S. marshals and deputies were charged to execute that return or face a fine of $1,000. The 1850 law specified that 'all good citizens' could be 'commanded to aid and assist in the prompt and efficient execution' of the act" (Hendrick and Hendrick 2004, 9).

Still and Tubman joined forces militating against this draconian act. Still claimed about Tubman, "Yet in point of courage, shrewdness and disinterested exertions to rescue her fellow-men, by making personal visits to Maryland, she was without her equal" (Still 2019, 236). By 1860, the rewards for her capture were also without equal—some historians claim that there was a $40,000 bounty offered; in 2022 that would be the equivalent of million dollars. In any case, there was always a bounty on her head (Broyld 2014, 82).

Free Blacks intermingled with whites in Philadelphia in the 1850s and 1860s; however, when the first streetcars pulled by horses arrived in the City of Brotherly Love in 1858, they were segregated. There were for Blacks other "remaining obstacles growing out of oppression, ignorance, and poverty" (Still 2019). Still wrote an editorial to end segregation on Philadelphia's streetcars, and in 1867, he published *A Brief Narrative of the Struggle for the Rights of Colored People of Philadelphia in the City Railway Cars*. Legislation forbidding segregation was passed in 1867 because of Still's efforts.

However, the waterways were integrated and provided opportunity, protection, and liberation. Free and enslaved Black seamen, known as Black Jacks, were part of the "network of antislavery" and "links in the chain of rebellion." They communicated with enslaved men and women in the streets and markets (Bolster 1997, 193). These seafaring men, unlike white sailors who were usually single, were usually family men. They were highly skilled, and the pay and treatment by whites was better than land work. It's ironic that "[v]essels that carried Africans to New World slavery not infrequently became a pipeline to freedom for slaves on the lam" (Bolster 1997, 232).

Journeying on boats and real trains and walking for miles and miles on the UGRR, Tubman also made many visits to Saint Catharines, Canada, close to the American border. From 1851 until 1858, she helped to settle many formerly enslaved people there. She "led a transnational double life," according to Broyld. Her facile "usage of borders and transnational alertness" enabled her to help people transition with ease. The Imperial Act of 1834 abolished slavery in Canada, and Queen Victoria, whose reign started in 1837, "gave the impression of greater esteem and rights for women" and, in general, protected Black women. However, they came to realize that racism and sexism were still present in Canada. Still, American Canadian antislavery activists like Mary Ann Shadd, "at times outright overzealous in her claims about Canada, did not understand why Blacks stayed in the United States on a 'national ship' that was 'rotten' and 'sinking.' 'Why not leave it?' she strongly counseled" (Broyld 2014, 83). She connected people and "exploited the constructed international margins. In fact, Tubman was a mobile liaison between those struggling for Black liberation and equality in America as well as Canada" (Broyld 2014, 84).

Activism was thriving in America. The women's suffrage movement was catalyzed by the abolitionist movement. Tubman was one of the founders of the National Association of Colored Women (NACW) in 1896, and after attending its first convention, she went on to a women's suffrage meeting in Rochester, New York. Led onstage by Susan B. Anthony, the seventy-six-year-old Tubman famously declared to an appreciative audience how "I was the conductor on the Underground Railroad for eight years, and I can say what most conductors can't say—I never ran my train off the track and I never lost a passenger" (quoted by Larson 2003, 276).

Tubman became friendly with William Seward and his wife, Frances, in the 1850s. Seward, an antislavery activist, was U.S. secretary of state from 1861 to 1869, the twelfth governor of New York, and served as a senator. The Sewards lived in Auburn, New York, in the Finger Lakes area and sold Tubman a small farmhouse, making her one of the few women in America to own a home of her own (Wickenden 2021, 288). Tubman's parents lived with her in the house after she helped them escape slavery.

Tubman worshiped at the African Methodist Episcopal Zion Church (AME), which had a following in Auburn before she moved there.

Established in New York City in 1796 as the Freedom Church, it was a stop on the Underground Railroad, hiding many people, including Frederick Douglass. Its congregants fought against racism and slavery. In addition to Douglass, AME's members included the women's rights and abolitionist activist Sojourner Truth (1797–1883) and the actor/singer/activist Paul Robeson (1898–1976).

Tubman advocated on behalf of the elderly and worked on poverty, housing, and education. She married a younger man (by twenty-two years), a Civil War veteran named Nelson Davis, in 1869, and was married until he died from tuberculosis in 1888. The couple adopted an infant daughter named Gertie in 1874; the specifics about her birth remain vague. Tubman died on March 10, 1913, at the age of ninety-one.

Though Tubman was a captivating storyteller, according to Jean M. Humez's book *Harriet Tubman*: *The Life and the Life Stories* (University of Wisconsin Press, 2004), she never wrote her autobiography. She endeavored to but did not achieve literacy once the Civil War was over. A few letters that Tubman dictated exist, but none that she wrote herself. It has been suggested that "the blow to the head Tubman received at about thirteen may have been the root cause of her illiteracy" (Sernett 2007, 125). Humez claims that Tubman was a "performer, wherein she used narrative to reach toward a changed future and participated in creating a black feminist public sphere," noting that this aspect of Tubman's life and legacy is underestimated. Humez analyzes the "educational and rhetorical strategies Tubman used in her public speeches and storytelling, such as her rhetorical use of metaphor and parable and her performative use of emotion, dramatic climax, and song" (2004, 133–39).

One of Tubman's favorite stories to tell the children of Auburn was about "At the Slave Rescue at Troy," which happened in 1860 in Troy, New York. Tubman threw herself in the way of slave catchers to save Charles Nalle. "A police clubbed her, but she knocked him squawkin' and then attacked. The children shouted with relieved laughter as she told them that she threw him across her shoulder 'like a bag o' meal and took him away out of there" (Wickenden 2021, 157).

A friend of Harriet's, Sarah Hopkins Bradford (1818–1912), a Peter the Great biographer and children's book writer who also wrote sentimental novels, wrote the first biography of Tubman, *Scenes in the Life of Harriet Tubman*, published in 1869. In 1886, Hopkins Bradford published a chronological, edited revision titled *Tubman: The Moses of Her People*. She said Harriet was greater than Joan of Arc; Grace Darling, a Victorian lighthouse keeper's daughter who rescued a shipwreck's survivors; and the legendary nurse, hospital, and health care visionary Florence Nightingale, for "not one of these women, noble and grave as they were, showed more courage, and power of endurance, in facing danger and death than the woman known to posterity as Harriet Tubman, 'the Moses of her people'" (Bradford, quoted by Sernett 2007).

William Lloyd Garrison, the abolitionist and editor of the *Liberator*, gave Tubman the name Moses as he led the enslaved Hebrews out of Egypt. He, like Tubman, was a spiritual and political visionary who also "understood the lines between peoples and places and how to traverse them to shield himself and his followers from harsh enemy subjection and slavery. . . . [E]ach in essence transcended location and nationality to provide greater freedom and to sidestep persecution for a comparative 'Promised Land'" (Broyld 2014, 87).

Tubman met John Andrew, the former governor of Massachusetts, in 1862. An abolitionist and former lawyer who offered his legal services to John Brown following his raid on Harpers Ferry, Andrew was aware of her exploits and asked Tubman to join the Union Army after President Lincoln ended slavery with the Emancipation Proclamation in January 1863. Andrew asked her to go to Hilton Head, South Carolina—an area the Union acquired at the beginning of the war—to help fight against the Confederacy. He deduced she would make a great spy; Tubman's "intimate knowledge of the marshlands on the Eastern Shore of Maryland would come in handy for the Union officers stationed on the swampy shores of South Carolina" (Dunbar 2019, 84).

Tubman opened a "wash house" for soldiers, doing laundry while teaching women how to be laundresses and entrepreneurial. She helped nurse the sick and dying in Beaufort, South Carolina, where "more men were dying of diseases like yellow fever and cholera than bullets" (Dunbar 2019, 88). There weren't many medicinal substances available at the time, and Tubman was lauded during the Civil War for being so knowledgeable about and adept at mixing healing roots, herbs, and botanicals (Dunbar 2019, 88). She knew, for example, that the paregoric she had given to quiet babies and suppress coughing and appetites when escaping was also an antidote for dysentery.

Tubman baked pies and gingerbread and once made fifty pies in one day for soldiers and freedmen, formerly enslaved Black men now fighting for the Union. And while she fed the freedmen, they "whispered delicate information about Confederate whereabouts; she shared the info with Generals Hunter and Sherman and Colonel Montgomery, high-ranking men" (Dunbar 2019, 90). Montgomery, an ardent abolitionist and trusted lieutenant of John Brown, and his compatriots helped convince General Saxton that Tubman should establish the kind of "clandestine network" in South Carolina that she set up during her UGRR work in Maryland (Clinton 2004, 163). And so, Tubman became a spy.

Under the guidance of Edward M. Stanton, the secretary of war, Tubman hired formerly enslaved Black Union water pilots and scouts who gathered information about "large numbers" of Black men in Jacksonville, Florida, who wanted to join the Union Army. As a result, Montgomery led a successful raid in Jacksonville in March 1863 (Clinton 2004, 164).

The Combahee River is a slow-moving and short waterway that empties into Saint Helena Sound near Beaufort in the Sea Islands. Tubman worked with Colonel James Montgomery to scan the Combahee River, "knowing it was a booby trap that the Confederates had littered with naval mines. Tubman made sure that the enslaved people knew the precise locations of the naval bombs." Tubman led nearly three hundred African American soldiers of the Fifty-Fourth Massachusetts Infantry Regiment and "sailed slowly up the Combahee, intent on destroying Confederate territory," preempting supplies for the "Southern soldiers, and liberating as many enslaved people as their ship could carry" (Dunbar 2019, 91–92).

Tubman and the soldiers, on June 2, 1863, sabotaged and set fire to the Confederate soldiers' possessions, taking "pleasure in watching Southern symbols of slavery burn and fall to the ground" (Dunbar 2019, 91–92). Between 750 and 800 enslaved people grabbed their plantation belongings, including animals like pigs and chickens, jubilantly ran out of slavery, and were liberated. They climbed aboard the Union boats on their way to Beaufort. A triumphant Harriet Tubman was the first American woman to ever lead a military raid.

Earl Conrad praised Tubman on the front page of the Boston newspaper *Commonwealth* on July 10, 1863: "The whole venture owed its success to the complete preliminary survey made by Harriet Tubman's espionage troops." He goes on to put the raid in perspective: "The River Jordan has been in biblical history a reality, and in modern Negro allusion a symbol of the barrier between bondage and freedom, and it is an interesting coincidence, therefore, that the Combahee campaign should so parallel the ancient situation." A Black feminist group in 1974 took the name Combahee River Collective; its members disbanded in 1980.

Franklin Sanborn, a Boston editor and one of the Secret Six who conspired with John Brown to abolish slavery, wrote of Tubman after the Civil War: "I regard her as . . . the most extraordinary person of her race I have ever met. She is a Negro of pure or almost pure blood, can neither read nor write, and has the characteristics of her race and condition. But she has done what can scarcely be credited on the best authority, and she has accomplished her purposes with a coolness, foresight, patience, and wisdom, which in a white man would have raised him to the highest pitch of reputation" (Gilpin Faust 2004).

President Barack Obama in March 2013 created the Harriet Tubman Underground Railroad National Monument in Dorchester County to honor Tubman, placing this "true American patriot, rightfully among our nation's most beloved heroes" (Clifford Larson 2003). This honor was followed by the establishment of the Harriet Tubman National Historical Parks by Congress in December 2014. There are two sister parks, one on the Eastern

Shore of Maryland, and one in Auburn, New York, which includes her residence, Harriet Tubman Home for the Aged; her church, Thompson AME Zion Church; and her grave site.

Antithetical to her religiosity and disrespectful to her legacy, the sexually suggestive video, the "Harriet Tubman Sex Tape," created by the disgraced music producer Russell Simmons was posted in 2013, the hundredth anniversary of Tubman's passing. It sparked a controversy and his apology. Simmons, who has since been accused of sexual misconduct, showcased an outrageous representation using racist slavery tropes. The video, featuring YouTube actors DeShawn Powers, Shanna Malcolm, and Jason Horton, implied that Tubman (portrayed by Malcolm) resorted to blackmailing her "master" (played by Horton) into supporting her UGRR plans with the threat of a released "sex tape" of their sexual encounter, as anachronistically filmed by an enslaved male (played by Powers). The public discussions that erupted in response to this controversial video speak to the power of Tubman's story and iconic status, as "significant writers and public scholars came to Tubman's historical defense against present-day popular culture" (Hobson 2014). It was subsequently deleted.

Tubman in 1978 became the first Black woman to be honored on an American postage stamp; the thirteen-cent stamp kicked off the Black Heritage series (Lowery 2008). Treasury secretary Jacob Lew, appointed by President Barack Obama in 2013, proposed that her visage replace President Andrew Jackson on the twenty-dollar bill, making Tubman the first Black woman to appear on "federal sanctioned currency" paper money circulated in the United States. "Several bills printed in Confederate states during the Civil War featured sketches of enslaved people" (Berry 2016).

Tubman was voted to replace Andrew Jackson, the slaveholding seventh president (1829–37). Some, like *Guardian* columnist Stephen W. Thrasher, deemed the decision "an insult to her legacy," as currency is "the very symbol of the racialized capitalism she was fleeing"; however, others found it fitting, as Tubman was granted a monthly veteran's pension of twenty dollars in 1899, thirty-four years after her first application, in recognition of her work as a nurse during the Civil War.

The redesigned bill was scheduled for 2020; however, former president Trump's Treasury Department placed it on hold. In January 2021, Jen Psaki, President Joe Biden's press secretary, promised that the Biden administration will fast-track the redesigned bill so that it is introduced in 2024.

Tubman earned the five dollars it cost her to retain a lawyer to file a freedom suit on behalf of her mother. Loren Schweninger in his book *Appealing for Liberty: Freedom Suits in the South* (Oxford University Press, 2018) investigates primary legal documents of over two thousand cases of eighteenth and nineteenth freedom suits filed by more than four thousand enslaved people to claim their freedom by petitioning district county courts in the slave Southern states. Schweninger ran the Race and Slavery Petitions

Project (RSPP) from 1991 to 2009 at the University of North Carolina at Greensboro. In his review of the book, Bordewich provides context. He says, "Slaveowners objected to lawsuits as 'oppressive and subversive of the rights of our citizens,' as a proposed resolution in Maryland's House of Delegates put it, but the suits went forward. Maryland's Constitution of 1776 had declared that all 'inhabitants . . . are entitled to the common law of England,' creating a loophole that enabled the enslaved to petition for their freedom."

Freedom was granted in approximately half of the cases; the triumphant suits "were rooted in the claim that one of the female progenitors of an enslaved family had been white, or at least not a slave, and that her descendants had thus been held in bondage illegally" (Bordewich 2005). Schweninger examines claims regarding deeds, wills, and promises of freedom for the enslaved as well as descendants of free people of color. He discusses issues of manumission, fugitivity, and enslaved people who were able to hire themselves out. The most famous freedom suit in American history was filed by Dred Scott, born enslaved in 1799 in Southampton County, Virginia. He was taken from Missouri, a slave state, to Illinois, a free state. Driven by abolitionist fervor, Dred Scott's freedom suit went to the Supreme Court.

Even though the Missouri Compromise of 1820 granted people of color in free states the right to sue for wrongful enslavement, the Supreme Court in 1857 denied Scott his freedom. The question was "Did the enslaved have any rights at all under the Constitution? Was slavery national in scope?" (Thomas 2020, 319).

Chief justice Roger B. Taney's white-supremacist decision of *Dred Scott v. Sanford* stated that African-descended people were not equal to whites, and they weren't American citizens and therefore weren't entitled to sue in court. This vexed case was one of the catalysts for the Civil War. "Dred Scott v. Sandford is undoubtedly among the most reviled Supreme Court decisions, often invoked as a clear example of what judges should not do," claims constitutional law scholar Jeannie Suk Gersen.

Dred Scott and his family, however, were granted freedom a few months after the decision. The bust of Roger Taney was removed from public display at the Capitol on June 29, 2021, after the House of Representatives passed legislation to remove it and other Confederate statues, and on September 8, 2021, the Virginia Supreme Court ruled that the largest Confederate statue of Robert E. Lee would be removed from the capital building in Richmond, Virginia.

DEPICTION AND CULTURAL CONTEXT

Though the film conflates events and leaves out much of Tubman's later years, *Harriet* accurately presents historical dates and details of her life and accomplishments. Tubman in the film and in real life threatened her passengers with a gun if they wanted to turn back. "You'll be free or die," she said.

The fictional Black slave catchers or trackers, Bigger Long and Walter, are contrasted: Bigger Long, who is tasked to kill Marie Buchanon and does so with a vengeance, is vicious and out for blood and money, and the younger Walter, after being mistreated by Gideon, flips from being a slave tracker to aiding and abetting Tubman. Kate Clifford Larson, the historical consultant on the film, said Black slave trackers hired by enslavers to capture runaways did exist, but they were "rare." Both characters are free and own guns, and Clifford Larson says that free Black people were able to own guns (2016).

Lemmons said,

> There were many black slave trackers back then, in fact. If you had a posse of slave trackers with dogs that were running after an escaped slave, it was often led by a slave. In this case, I wanted to show that it was a very complex society where you have free people living next to enslaved people, and where people become free while the rest of their family was enslaved. You had morally ambiguous characters who worked on the side that paid them, and they would sometimes turn people in. It was a very treacherous world, and more than that, it was a corrupting system. Anybody could be corrupted. (Fagerholm 2019)

The Brodesses did have a son named Jonathan; however, not much is known about him. Gideon and his mother are portrayed as heartless enslavers only concerned with the value and not the humanity of the enslaved. Built into the arc of Gideon's relationship to and treatment of Harriet is that she stayed with him throughout his severe illness when he was a child. He is depicted saving her life when he shoots Bigger Long. He has a deeply ambivalent connection to her as well as need to belittle her and impose what he believes to be his superiority. Gideon is a ne'er-do-well; his mother alludes to him frequenting prostitutes. His character is a hackneyed and unmemorable one with no depth or substance that sets him apart.

The elegantly clothed William Still asks Tubman if she wants to change her name to mark her freedom as many ex-slaves do—in fact, she changed her name when she got married. She tells him about the overseer cracking her head open and how after that she slept for two months, an accurate rendering of the incident. Still worked for the abolitionist cause nearly his entire life, while like Tubman, working day jobs including as a custodian for the Pennsylvania Society for the Abolition of Slavery and then as a businessman. Tubman's decades of engaging in activist organizing and her alliance with the Black women's club movement and women's suffrage after the Emancipation, however, aren't mentioned.

When Tubman arrives in Saint Catharines in the movie, she's there for about thirty seconds of screen time, as if her time north of the border was a small part of her story, undermining her years as a Canadian resident and "the ways in which she perceived and employed the international lines to safeguard fugitives" (Broyld 2014, 80). Tubman was able to effectively operate in discrete spheres of influence and zones of "inbetweenness," carrying signifiers of more than one identity, while fully embodying none (Castronovo 1995, quoted by Broyld 2014, 80). Tubman possessed a transnational identity and strategically positioned herself near the border "where immigration, movement, and interaction occurred. Tubman's transnationalism was a major component of her activism" (Broyld 2014, 82).

Tubman's clothing becomes more elegant as the film story develops, and her red velvet coat and turban signify success. The enslaved for the most part wore clothing made of coarse cloth flax and hemp. Untailored jean cloth was also used in the nineteenth century. Girls upon becoming young women wore dresses. Women wore turbans, also known as head-wraps. There were laws in parts of the South that required the enslaved to wear head coverings, making it in some ways an "object of oppression from one vantage point." Enslaved men also wore head-wraps until they started wearing hats. Head coverings were a West African tradition; they are used to protect people from lice, but they also "signified communal identity," so from the "perspective of the slave community, it was a vehicle of empowerment and a memento of freedom" (https://www.thirteen.org/wnet/slavery/experience/gender/feature6.html).

Paul Tazewell, the costume designer, wanted the costumes "to feel like a tinted daguerreotype, referring to grayscale photographic images from the period that were colored by hand" (Kumar 2019). The dresses and turbans worn by the female characters are colorful and nuanced. Angie Wells, the makeup maven on the film, did not want the enslaved to appear dirty or unkempt as they often appear on screen (Mitchell 2019). Wells said most photographs showed the enslaved, "unless they were actually in the fields with their hands and arms dirty, the pictures were not of Black people covered with dirt." Research revealed that the enslaved didn't often get new clothes, so the clothes were frayed but they were clean.

Until recently, the only extant pictures of Tubman were of her as an older woman. In 2019, a previously unknown photograph of a more youthful Tubman, believed to be taken in the 1860s, was put on display at the Smithsonian's National Museum of African American History and Culture in Washington. Lonnie Bunch, founding director of the Smithsonian's National Museum of African American History and Culture, was "stunned" when he saw the picture found in a photography album belonging to abolitionist Emily Howland, as it was closer to what Tubman looked like when she was an active conductor on the UGRR. She looked strong and "there's a stylishness about her" (Keyes 2020).

The plantation scenes were shot on the Berkley Plantation in Charles City, Virginia, the birthplace of Benjamin Harrison, the twenty-third president who had served as a general during the Civil War when Berkeley was occupied by General George McClellan's Union troops.

Films about slavery have been more viable in Hollywood since in 2014 *12 Years a Slave* won three Academy Awards. Fox Searchlight's *The Birth of a Nation* (2016), Nate Parker's film about Nat Turner's insurrection, made a record-breaking $17.5 million deal at Sundance, but was ultimately mired in controversy and a box office failure. *Underground*, about the Underground Railroad, aired as a television series in 2016 and 2017 but was abruptly canceled. Barry Jenkins's ten-part Prime series *The Underground Railroad*, based on Colson Whitehead's Pulitzer Prize–winning eponymous novel, debuted to much acclaim in May 2021. It was produced by Brad Pitt, who also a producer and cast member of *12 Years a Slave*.

CONCLUSION

As Richard Brody eloquently claims, "The movie *Harriet* relates Tubman's story, and the story of her times, with the exalted power of secular scripture." The magnificent, lush shot of a joyous sunset that Lemmons and her cinematographer were lucky after a cloudy, rainy day to get when Harriet walks into freedom is a heart-stopping moment. "I looked at my hands to see if I was the same person," Tubman later told Bradford. "Now I was free. There was such a glory over everything, the sun came like gold through the trees, and over the fields, and I felt like I was in heaven" (quoted in Galli 1999).

FURTHER READING

Abdul-Jabbar, Kareem. 2019. "Are *Harriet* and Slavery Films Good for African Americans?" *Hollywood Reporter*, November 18, 2019.

Aptheker, Herbert. 1941. "The Negro in the Abolitionist Movement." *Science & Society* 5, no. 2 (Spring): 148–72.

Aptheker, Herbert. 1989. *Abolitionism: A Revolutionary Movement*. Boston: Twayne Publishers.

Berman, Judy. 2017. "Aisha Hinds on Playing Harriet Tubman in a Remarkable '*Underground*' Episode." *New York Times*, April 12, 2017.

Berry, Daina Ramey. 2016. "Harriet Tubman Isn't the First Black Woman to Appear on Currency in the U.S." Slate, April 22, 2016.

Bolster, W. Jeffrey. 1997. *Black Jacks: African American Seamen in the Age of Sail*. Cambridge: Harvard University Press.

Bordewich, Fergus M. 2005. *Bound for Canaan: The Epic Story of the Underground Railroad, America's First Civil Rights Movement*. New York: Amistad Press/Harper Collins.

Bordewich, Fergus M. 2020. "Freedom Review: Slavery on Trial." *Wall Street Journal*, November 13, 2020.

Brody, Richard. 2019. "The Stunning Achievement of Kasi Lemmons's *Harriet*." *New Yorker*, October 30, 2019.

Broyld, Dann J. 2014. "Harriet Tubman: Transnationalism in the Land of a Queen in the Late Antebellum." *Meridians*, July 1, 2014, 78–98.

Clifford Larson, Kate. 2003. *Bound for the Promised Land: Harriet Tubman, Portrait of an American Hero*. New York: One World.

Clifford Larson, Kate. 2016. "Five Myths about Harriet Tubman." *Washington Post*, April 22, 2016.

Clinton, Catherine. 2004. *Harriet Tubman: The Road to Freedom*. New York: Little, Brown.

Coyle, Jake. 2019. "*Harriet*, the First Film about Harriet Tubman Premieres in Toronto." CTV News, *Associated Press*, September 11, 2019.

Dunbar, Erica Armstrong. 2019. *She Came to Slay: The Life and Times of Harriet Tubman*. New York: 37 Ink/Simon & Schuster.

Fagerholm, Matt. 2019. "Minty, Harriet, Moses: Kasi Lemmons on Bringing Harriet Tubman's Life to the Big Screen." Rogerebert.com, October 2019.

Foner, Eric. 2015. *Gateway to Freedom: The Hidden History of the Underground Railroad*. New York: Norton.

Galli, Mark. 1999. "Harriet Tubman: Her Faith Fueled the Underground Railroad." *Today's Christian Woman*, November 1999. https://www.todayschristianwoman.com/articles/1999/november/harriet-tubman.html.

Gersen, Jeannie Suk. 2021. "The Importance of Teaching Dred Scott." *New Yorker*, June 8, 2021.

Gilpin Faust, Drew. 2004. "The General" [Book review of Harriet Tubman: The Life and the Life Stories, by Jean M. Humez]. *New York Times*, February 15, 2004.

Grady, Cynthia. 2016. *Like a Bird: The Art of the American Slave Song*. Minneapolis: Millbrook Press.

Greenidge, Kaitlyn. 2021. "Black Spirituals as Poetry and Resistance." *New York Times Style Magazine*, March 5, 2021.

Hall, Steven G. 2003. "To Render the Private Public: William Still and the Selling of 'The Underground Rail Road.'" *Pennsylvania Magazine of History and Biography* 127, no. 1 (January): 35–55.

Hampton, Rachelle. 2019. "What's Fact and What's Fiction in *Harriet*?" Slate, October 31, 2019.

Hans, Simran. 2019. "Harriet Review—Thrilling Drama about the Abolitionist Harriet Tubman." *The Guardian*, November 4, 2019.

Henderson, Taja-Nia Y. 2020. "Review" [*Appealing for Liberty: Freedom Suits in the South*]. *Journal of Southern History* 86, no. 2 (May): 464–65. https://doi.org/10.1353/soh.2020.0106.

Hendrick, George, and Willene Hendrick. 2004. *Fleeing for Freedom: Stories of the Underground Railroad as told by Levi Coffin and William Still*. Chicago: Ivan R. Dee.

Hobson, Janell. 2013. "The Rape of Harriet Tubman." *Ms. Magazine*, August 17, 2013.

Hobson, Janell. 2014. "Harriet Tubman: A Legacy of Resistance." *Meridians* 12 (2): 1–8. Duke University Press.

Hobson, Janell. 2018. "The Breathtaking Courage of Harriet Tubman." *TED-Ed animation*, July 25, 2018.

Hornaday, Ann. 2019. "No Sweet Little Old Lady, the Hero Harriet Is a Woman of Action and Moral Courage." *Washington Post*, October 30, 2019.

Howard, Gregory Allen. 2019. "Julia Roberts as Harriet Tubman? Gregory Allen Howard on *Harriet*'s Difficult Journey to the Big Screen." *LA Times*, November 19, 2019.

Humez, Jean M. 2004. *Harriet Tubman: The Life and the Life Stories*. Madison: University of Wisconsin Press.

Jabali, Malaika. 2021. "Archaeologists Discover Home Where Harriet Tubman Lived with Father." *Essence*, May 18, 2021.

Jefferson, J'na. 2022. "'Sinnerman': Nina Simone's Masterpiece Is Still Relevant Today." udiscovermusic, May 20, 2022.

Jenkins, Mark. 2019. "In Earnest, Contrived Biopic 'Harriet,' Tubman Is an Action Hero." NPR/WNYC, October 31, 2019.

Keyes, Allison. 2019. "A Previously Unknown Portrait of Harriet Tubman Goes on View." *Smithsonian*, March 26, 2019.

Keyes, Allison. 2020. "Harriet Tubman, an Unsung Naturalist, Used Owl Calls as a Signal on the Underground Railroad." *Caribmeme Magazine*, February 25, 2020.

Kumar, Naveen. 2019. "How Cynthia Erivo's Costumes, Hair, and Makeup Tell Harriet Tubman's Heroic Story." *In Style*, November 11, 2019.

King, Noel. 2019. "The Superhero Journey of Harriet Tubman, Now on Film." NPR, November 1, 2019.

Lemmons, Kasi, dir. 2019. *Harriet*. Focus Features. Performances by Cynthia Erivo, Leslie Odom Jr., and Janelle Monae.

Lowery, Beverly. 2008. *Harriet Tubman: Imagining a Life*. New York: Penguin.

Mandell, Andrea. "'*Harriet*' Fact-Check: How Accurate Is the New Movie about Harriet Tubman?" *USA Today*, October 30, 2019.

May, Vivian M. 2014. "Under-Theorized and Under-Taught: Re-examining Harriet Tubman's Place in Women's Studies." *Meridians: Feminism, Race, Transnationalism* 12 (2): 28–49. Gale Academic One File.

McClintock, Pamela. 2019. "Box Office Milestone: *Harriet* Crosses $40 Million in the U.S." *Hollywood Reporter*, December 7, 2019.

Mitchell, Amanda. 2019. "All about the Cast of *Harriet*—and How They Transformed for the Movie." *Oprah Magazine*, October 31, 2019.

Newman, Richard S. 2011. "'Lucky to Be Born in Pennsylvania': Free Soil, Fugitive Slaves and the Making of Pennsylvania's Anti-Slavery Borderland." *Slavery & Abolition* 32, no. 3 (September): 413–430.

Newman, Richard S. 2018. *Abolitionism: A Very Short Introduction*. New York: Oxford.

Obenson, Tambay. 2019. "Here's Why It Took over a Hundred Years before Harriet Tubman Got a Biopic." *IndieWire*, October 28, 2019.

Owens, Donna E. 2021. "Archaeologists Discover Home Where Harriet Tubman Lived with Father." *Essence*, May 18, 2021.

Petry, Ann. (1955) 2007. *Harriet Tubman: Conductor on the Underground Railroad*. New York: Amistad Press.

"Print the Legend: Writing the Screenplay for *Harriet*." 2019. A Q & A with Screenwriter Gregory Allen Howard. *Focus Features*. November 1, 2019.

Sernett, Milton C. 2007. *Harriet Tubman: Myth, Memory, and History*. Durham, NC: Duke University Press.

Sims, Davis. 2019. "Why *Harriet* Is Really a 'Freedom Movie.'" *The Atlantic*, October 30, 2019.

Still, William. 2019. Introduction by Ta-Nehisi Coates. In *The Underground Railroad Records*. New York: Modern Library, Random House.

Taylor, Mildred Europa. 2019. "Pastor Samuel Green, the Little-Known but Key Underground Railroad Figure Who Helped Harriet Tubman." *Face2Face Africa*, December 9, 2019.

Thomas, William G., III. 2020. *A Question of Freedom: The Families Who Challenged Slavery from the Nation's Founding to the Civil War*. New Haven: Yale University Press.

Wickenden, Dorothy. 2021. *The Agitators: Three Friends Who Fought for Abolition and Women's Rights*. New York: Scribner.

Bibliography

Alcocer, Rudyard, Kristen Block, and Dawn Duke, ed. 2018. *Celluloid Chains: Slavery in the Americas through Film*. Knoxville: University of Tennessee Press.

Bennett, Lerone, Jr. 1968. *Pioneers in Protest*. Chicago: Johnson Publishing Company.

Benshoff, Harry M., and Sean Griffin. 2009. *America on Film: Representing Race, Class, Gender, and Sexuality at the Movies*. Chichester, UK: Wiley-Blackwell.

Bogle, Donald. 2001. *Toms, Coons, Mulattoes, Mammies, and Bucks: An Interpretive History of Blacks in American Film*. 4th ed. New York: Bloomsbury Academic.

Bogle, Donald. 2009. *Bright Boulevards, Bold Dreams: The Story of Black Hollywood*. New York: One World.

Boritt, Gabor, and Scott Hancock, eds. 2007. *Slavery, Resistance, Freedom*. New York: Oxford University Press.

Campbell, Edward D. C., Jr. 1981. *The Celluloid South: Hollywood and the Southern Myth*. Knoxville: University of Tennessee Press.

Davis, David Brion. 2006. *Inhuman Bondage: The Rise and Fall of Slavery in the New World*. New York: Oxford University Press.

Erigha, Maryann. 2019. *The Hollywood Jim Crow: The Racial Politics of the Movie Industry*. New York: New York University Press.

Field, Allyson, Jan-Christopher Horak, and Jacqueline Najuma Stewart, eds. 2015. *L.A. Rebellion: Creating a New Black Cinema*. Oakland: University of California Press.

Guerrero, Ed. 1993. *Framing Blackness: The African American Image in Film (Culture and the Moving Image)*. Philadelphia: Temple University Press.

Hackett Fischer, David. 2022. *African Founders: How Enslaved People Expanded American Ideals*. New York: Simon and Schuster.

Hannah-Jones, Nikole. 2021. *The 1619 Project: A New Origin Story*. New York: One World.

Harding, Vince. 1981. *There Is a River: The Black Struggle for Freedom in America*. New York: Harcourt Brace Jovanovich.

Haygood, Wil. 2021. *Colorization: One Hundred Years of Black Films a White World*. New York: Alfred A. Knopf.
Johnson, Walter. 1999. *Soul by Soul. Life inside the Antebellum Slave Market*. Cambridge: Harvard University Press.
Kolchin, Peter. 2003. *American Slavery 1619–1877*. New York: Hill and Wang.
Patterson, Robert J., ed. 2019. *Black Cultural Production after Civil Rights*. Urbana: University of Illinois Press.
Quarles, Benjamin. 1969. Black Abolitionists. New York: Oxford University Press.
Ryan, Tim A. 2008. *Calls and Responses: The American Novel of Slavery since Gone with the Wind (Southern Literary Studies)*. Baton Rouge: LSU Press.
Van Deburg, William L. 1984. *Slavery & Race in American Popular Culture*. Madison: University of Wisconsin Press.
Watts, Jill. 2007. *Hattie McDaniel: Black Ambition, White Hollywood*. New York: Amistad.
Williams, Linda. 2001. *Playing the Race Card: Melodramas of Black and White from Uncle Tom to O.J. Simpson*. Princeton: Princeton University Press.

Index

Abolitionism, xvi, 4, 7, 91–92, 100, 129, 149; abolitionism movement, 149, 173; abolitionist cause, 90, 95–96, 99; practical abolitionism, 6
Adams, John Quincy, 90–93, 96–97, 99
African Methodist Episcopal Zion Church (AME), 175–176, 179
Allen, Debbie, 85, 100
American Colonization Society, 39, 95, 150
Amistad, 85–91; *Amistad* Africans, 93–94; *Amistad* revolt, 41, 92; historical background, 91–99; *La Amistad*, 89, 91, 97; production, 85–88
Anti-slavery patrols, 95
Aptheker, Herbert, xxii, 68, 146, 156, 173

Baldwin, James, 7, 31
Baldwin, Roger S., 90, 93, 97, 98
Birch, James H., aka Burch, 129, 131, 134
The Birth of a Nation (1915), xviii, xix, 14–15, 20, 42, 109, 143
The Birth of a Nation (2016), 143–149; historical background, 149–157; production, 143–145
Black Arts Movement, xvii, xxiii, 26

Black Jacks, 166, 175
Black Lives Matter, xviii, 81, 138, 157
Black Power Movement, 25, 31, 44, 59; Black Power, 19, 25–26, 32
Blanchard, Terence, 161–162
Bloodhounds, 2, 11–15, 79, 106, 115, 134, 165, 174
Blue-Backed Speller, 76–77
Bradford, Sarah Hopkins, 171, 176, 183
breeding wenches, 70
Brodess, Edward, 164, 168–169; daughter, Eliza Brodess, 166; son, Jonathan Brodess, 181
Brody, Richard, 51, 54, 68, 162, 183
Brown, John, xxiii, 135, 162, 172–173, 177–178
Bunch, Lonnie, 182
Burnett, Charles, xxiii, 52–53, 65, 68–69, 80–81; L.A. Rebellion, x, xvii, 52, 69; *Nat Turner: A Troublesome Property*, 68, 146
Burton, LeVar, 30
Butler, Octavia E., *Kindred*, 59

Cain, Bill, 65, 70, 78, 79, 81
Canada (via the UGRR), 1–2, 4–7, 15–16, 66, 75, 104, 167, 170, 174; British Canada, 173, 175
Chase-Riboud, Barbara, 86

Chattel slavery, xv, 3–4, 16, 32, 122, 134, 144, 149
Christianity, xvi, 16, 33, 48, 56–57, 67
Cinque, Joseph, aka Sengbe Pieh, x, 41, 85, 87–100
Civil War, xvi, xvii, xix, xxiv, 4, 6–7, 14, 39–40, 69, 72–73, 76, 85, 87, 91, 94–95, 105, 107–109, 112, 114, 133–134, 155–156, 167–168, 176–180, 182–183
Cockfighting, 35–36, 40–41
Combahee River, 168, 178; raid on, 164, 178
Confederacy, 15, 37, 40, 112, 177; Confederate army's defeat, 91; Confederate soldiers, 39–40, 108, 177; Confederate states, 179; Confederate States of America, 110; pro-Confederate organizations, 109; statues, 180
Conroy, Pat, xix
Cotton, xvi, 72, 75, 79, 94, 106, 125, 133, 151; cotton business, 3, 130, 138; cotton manufacturing, 135; cotton picking, 125, 128, 131, 135–136, 146–147; cotton plantation, 65, 122, 128; King Cotton, xvi
Covey, James, 90, 94
Creole mutiny, 99
Critical Race Theory, xxii, 156
Curtis-Hall, Vondie, 165, 167

Daly, William, 1, 3, 8
Dash, Julie, 52
Declaration of Independence, xv, 5, 97, 123, 172
DiCaprio, Leonardo, xx, 103
Dixon, Thomas, xviii, 15, 109, 143
Django Unchained, x, xx, xxiii; historical background, 107–112; production of, 103–107
Douglass, Frederick, xxiii, 11, 39–40, 56, 73, 76, 87, 93, 110, 113, 125, 129, 155, 170, 172, 176; *The Heroic Slave*, a novel, 99
Dred Scott v. John F. A. Sandford, 5, 131, 180

Drum, xvii, 24–25
Du Bois, W.E.B., 43, 77, 127, 156

Ejiofor, Chiwetel, 90, 119, 123
Emancipation, xviii, xx, 6, 31, 72, 81, 87, 137, 149–150, 172, 181; self-emancipation, 92
Emancipation, 135
Emancipation Proclamation, xvi, 3, 6, 35, 111, 177
England, xvi, xxi, 35, 39, 40, 73, 91, 113, 180
Erivo, Cynthia, 161–163

Federal Writers Project for the Works Progress Administration (WPA), 79
Fleischer, Richard, x, xx, 21, 27
Foner, Eric, x, 6–7, 68, 120, 129, 146, 156, 170, 172
Fort Pillow, 36–37, 39–40
Forten, Charlotte, 94, 121
Forten, James, 94
The Foxes of Harrow, xxiv
Foxx, Jamie, 103
Franzoni, David, 86, 100
Freedmen's Bureau, 109
Freedom papers, xxi, xxiii, 35, 71, 107, 127, 132; freedom passes, 9, 55, 71, 131, 171
Freedom's Journal, 133, 155
Freedom suits, 179–180
Fugitive Slave Law or Act, aka Bloodhound Law, 5, 110

Garrett, Thomas, 165, 170–172
Garrison, William Lloyd, 4, 57, 93, 100, 129, 154, 177. *See also The Liberator*
Garvey, Marcus, 11
Gates, Henry Louis, Jr., xv, 11, 38, 41–43, 68–69, 72, 86, 95, 112, 137, 145–146
Gay, Sydney Howard, 6, 172
Gedney, Lieutenant Thomas R., 92
Gerima, Haile, x, xvii, xxii, 47–53, 56, 58–61

Germantown Quaker Petition Against Slavery, 172
Gibbs, Josiah, 90, 94
Gone with the Wind, xviii, xix, xx, 7, 20, 27, 31, 42, 113
Goodbye Uncle Tom, xvii, 26
Goya, Francisco, 88, 122
Gray, Thomas (Ruffin), *The Confessions of Nat Turner*, 68, 145, 152–154
Great Dismal Swamp, 55, 57, 152
Green, Reverend Samuel, 164–165, 167, 169–170
Griffith, D.W., xviii, xix, 10, 15, 20, 42, 109, 143

Haley, Alex, 37, 42–44
Hammer, Armie, 146, 157
Harriet, 161–167; historical background, 168–180; production of, 161–168
Haydn, Robert, poem "Middle Passage," 38, 98
Hemings, Sally, xv, 70, 78; *Sally Hemings*, the novel, 86
Henson, Josiah, 6, 15–16
Holocaust, xxii, 21, 32, 50, 85, 105, 115, 121; African Holocaust/Maafa, 47; America's Black Holocaust Museum, 121
Hopkins, Sir Anthony, 86, 90, 96
Horton, George Moses, 39
Hounsou, Djimon, 86–87, 89, 99
Howard, Gregory Allen, 161, 163

Jackson, Andrew, 40, 130, 179
Jefferson, Thomas, xv, 70, 73, 78, 86, 91, 110, 123, 146
Jenkins, Barry, xxiii, 137, 183
Jim Crow laws, xvi, xvii, 16, 81

King, Martin Luther, Jr., 11, 30, 58
Kinte, Kunta, 32–33, 37, 44
Ku Klux Klan, xviii, 15, 17, 40, 43, 106, 108–109, 114, 143

La Amistad, 85, 89, 91
Lee, Robert E., 180

Lee, Spike, xix, 44, 104–105, 145; *Da 5 Bloods*, 51
Legree, Simon, ix, 2–3, 8, 14
Lemmons, Kasi, x, xvi, 161–162
Lewis, John, ix, 42, 68
The Liberator, 132, 154, 177
Lincoln, Abraham, xvi, 3, 7, 87
Literacy, x, xxiii, 9, 53, 67, 71–77, 79, 81, 128, 130, 146, 176; literacy laws, xxiii, 71
Lomboko Slave Fortress, 91, 94–95, 98
Los Angeles (LA) Film Rebellion, xvii, 51–52, 69
Los Angeles Race Riots, 80; the beating of Rodney King, 69, 80
Lost Cause, xix, 15, 168
Loving v. Virginia, 26
Lucas, Sam, 7

Malcolm X, 11, 26, 30, 114; *Autobiography of Malcolm X*, 30
Mandingo or Malinke, 114; Mandingo fighters, 106–107, 114
Mandingo: the film, x, xvii, xx, 19–27, 104, 113; historical background, 25–27; the novel, 113; production of, 19–24
Mandinka, 25, 36, 41, 114; Mandinkan, 30, 33–34, 43
Manumissions, 38, 71, 180
Maroons, xviii, xxii, 55–58, 60, 150
Martin Chase, Debra, 163–164
McBride, James, xxiii, 162
McConaughey, Matthew, 90
McCune Smith, James, 109–110
McQueen, Steve, x, xxi, 72, 119–122, 127–128, 136–138
Mende, 87, 90, 92–94; Mende dress, 99; Mende language, 90
Methodists, 16, 151, 169
Middle Passage, xv, xvi, 37–38, 43, 54, 60, 88, 91, 95, 98, 100, 136
Mitchell, Margaret, xx, 7, 31
Molineaux, Tom, xxi, 113

Montgomery, Colonel James, 177–178
Motion Picture Association of America (MPAA), 23

Nat Turner's Insurrection, 26, 44, 76, 183
Native Americans, xviii, 13, 51, 55, 95
New Orleans, x, xxiv, 2, 15, 22, 24, 72, 86, 99, 103, 119, 123, 134
Nightjohn, 52–53, 65–68, 77–79, 81–82; historical background, 69–77
Northup, Henry, 127, 131
Northup, Solomon, x, xxi, 72, 119–120, 123–124, 127–138
Norton, Ken, 19, 21, 24
Nyong'o, Lupita, 119, 125, 183

Obama, Barack, xxiii, 54, 178–179
Onstott, Kyle, *Falcolnhurst* series, 19, 24, 25, 113
Owens, William A., *Black Mutiny: The Revolt on the Schooner Amistad,* aka *Slave Mutiny*, 85–86

Parker, Nate, x, xvi, xxiii, 143, 146, 155, 157, 183
Parks, Gordon, xxi, 72, 120, 128
Paulsen, Gary, 65
Pennsylvania Antislavery Society, 99
Philadelphia, 4, 6, 50, 94, 98, 100, 133, 165–167, 172–174; *Philadelphia Inquirer*, 99
Phrenology, xxiii, 107, 109–110
Plantation, xx, xxi, xxii, xxiv, 2, 9, 15–16, 19–27, 30, 34–35, 48–49, 53, 55–56, 58–59, 65–67, 70–75, 77–78, 90, 103–107, 110, 115, 119, 122–124, 126–129, 131,133, 136–137, 144, 146, 149–153, 155, 157, 164, 168, 171, 178, 182
Prosser, Gabriel, 76; Gabriel's Conspiracy, 76
Purvis, Robert, 98–100

Quakers, xvi, 2, 7, 11, 35, 151, 165, 170, 172. *See also* Society of Friends
Questlove, Amir Thompson, 36

Race and Slavery Petitions Project (RSPP), 180
Reverse Underground Railroad, 134
Ridley, John, xix, 104, 119, 121, 126, 183
Roots (1977), x, xvii, xviii, xx, xxi, 33–35, 42, 44, 112, 145; historical background, 37–41; the production, 29–32
Roots (2016), 36–37

Sanborn, Franklin, 178
Sankofa, x, xvii, xxii, 47–51, 53–54, 58–61; historical background, 54–57; production of, 47–54
Seward, William (wife, Frances), 135
Sharswood, xxi
Slave catchers or slave trackers, 2, 5–6, 10–12, 14, 138, 165–167, 176, 181
Smith, Will, 135
Society of Friends, 7, 170
Solomon Northup's Odyssey, xxi, 72, 120
Southampton County, Virginia, 57, 67, 74, 143, 146, 150–151, 156, 180; the Southampton Insurrection, 145, 153 (*see also* Nat Turner's Insurrection); *Surviving Southampton: African American Women and Resistance in Nat Turner's Community*, 157
Spielberg, Steven, x, xvi, 10, 85–88, 99, 112
St. Catharines, Canada, 167, 172, 175, 181
Stanton, Edward M., 40, 69, 177
Still, William, 6, 164–167, 173–175, 181
Stono Rebellion, aka Cato's Conspiracy or Cato's Rebellion, xxix, 54–55, 73, 149

Story, Justice Joseph, 97
Stowe, Harriet Beecher, 3–5, 128

Tamango, xxiv
Taney, Roger B., xxxv, 5, 180
Tappan, Lewis, 89, 93, 98
Tarantino, Quentin, 103–105, 111–115
Tecora, 90, 92
Tom Shows, xxxiv, 3, 10, 16
Tubman, Harriet, born Araminta Ross, x, xvi, xxv, 161–183; Civil War spy, xvi, 168, 177; Harriet Tubman Underground Railroad National Monument, 178; and Quakers, 170; seizures, 164; skull injury, 168–169; transnationalism, 182; UGRR conductor, 6, 161
Tubman, John, 164, 166, 169
Turner, Nat, 8, 24, 35–36, 57, 67–68, 74, 76–77, 157, 183; the Bible, 57; *Confessions of*, 68, 145, 153–154
12 Years a Slave, x, xxi, 22; historical background, 128–137; production of, 119–123, 137–139

Uncle Tom's Cabin (novel), 1, 2, 6–12, 14–16; *Key to Uncle Tom's Cabin*, 16
Uncle Tom's Cabin (1914), other film adaptations (1903, 1927), ix, 10, 12; historical background, 4–7; production of, 1–2

Underground Railroad (UGRR), x, xvi, xviii, 1–2, 4, 6–7, 29, 66, 75, 127, 161, 168, 172–176, 182–183; Barry Jenkins's film *The Underground Railroad*, 137, 183; Reverse Underground Railroad, 133–134
Union, xvi, xxv, 4–5, 15, 36, 40, 91, 112, 155, 177–178, 182; Civil War Battle of Fort Pillow, 39–40; Union Brigadier General of volunteers soldiers, 39; Union army/soldiers, xxiv, 3, 13, 37, 40, 134, 168, 177–178, 182
Ursulines, 75

Vesey, Denmark, xxi, 8, 38, 121, 133, 150, 156; *Denmark Vesey's Rebellion*, xxi, 121; aka Telemaque, 38, 133, 150, 156
Vigilance committees, 5, 99, 133, 152; General Vigilance Committee, 174

Walker, David, 74; *The Appeal*, 154–155
Washington, Madison, 99
West Africa(n), 25, 30, 32, 52, 54, 80, 114, 182; Gambian, 37; religion, 58; spiritual beliefs, 144
Wexler, Norman, 20, 24
Wolper, David L., 30–32, 36, 42, 145
Wolper, Mark, 36

Yerby, Frank, xxiv

About the Author

CARON KNAUER has published numerous film reviews in *Educational Media Reviews Online* (EMRO) and several interviews with writers and filmmakers. She was the associate producer of the hit film *Waiting to Exhale* (1995). She received her master's degree in liberal studies from the CUNY Graduate Center and teaches English at La Guardia Community College in New York City. She is currently working on a screenplay, titled *An Embarrassment of Bitches*.

www.ingramcontent.com/pod-product-compliance
Lightning Source LLC
Chambersburg PA
CBHW050732240426
43665CB00053B/2137